Moustafa Gadalla is an Egyptian-American independent Egyptologist, who was born in Cairo, Egypt in 1944. He holds a Bachelor of Science degree in civil engineering from Cairo University.

Gadalla is the author of eleven internationally acclaimed books about the various aspects of the Ancient Egyptian history and civilization and its influences worldwide. He is the chairman of the Tehuti Research Foundation—an international, U.S.-based, non-profit organization, dedicated to Ancient Egyptian studies.

From his early childhood, Gadalla pursued his Ancient Egyptian roots with passion, through continuous study and research. Since 1990, he has dedicated and concentrated all his time to researching and writing.

Other Books By The Author
[See details on pages 316-320]

Dedicated to

the late Moustafa Kamel

who said,

"If I was not an Egyptian,

I would have wished to be an Egyptian."

Book Editing: Jason Just, New Zealand
Book Production by: Moustafa Gadalla & Faith Cross
Book Cover Artwork by: Symbolique Studios, New Zealand

The Ancient Egyptian Culture Revealed

Moustafa Gadalla
Maa Kheru (True of Voice)

Tehuti Research Foundation
International Head Office: Greensboro, NC, U.S.A.

The Ancient Egyptian Culture Revealed
by MOUSTAFA GADALLA

Published by: Tehuti Research Foundation
P.O. Box 39406
Greensboro, NC 27438-9406, U.S.A.

This book is a completely revamped edition of the originally titled book, "*Historical Deception: The Untold Story of Ancient Egypt*", copyright © 1996, 1999, and 2003, by Moustafa Gadalla (all rights reserved), which was first published in paperback in 1996 and 1999, and in eBook format in 2003. The name of this book was changed to better reflect the revamped and expanded content of this book.

Publisher's Cataloging-in-Publication Data

Gadalla, Moustafa, 1944-
    The ancient Egyptian culture revealed /
    Moustafa Gadalla.
    p. cm.
    Includes bibliographical references and index.
    Library of Congress Control Number: 2007900078
    ISBN-13: 978-1-931446-27-3 (pbk.)
    ISBN-13: 978-1-931446-28-0 (e-Book)

1. Egypt--Civilization--To 332 B.C. 2. Egypt--Antiquities. 3. Civilization, Western--Egyptian influences. 4. Egypt--Religion. 5. Cosmology--Egypt. 6. Science--Egypt--History. 7. Architecture--Egypt--Aesthetics. 8. Harmony (Aesthetics). 9. Aesthetics, Egyptian. 10. Pharaohs. I. Title.

DT61.G26 2007
932--dc22   2007900078

Manufactured in USA
Published 2007

Table of Contents

Part I. The Peoples of Egypt

Part II. The Cosmic Correlations

Part IIII. The Vibrant Economy

Appendices

Preface

Herodotus [500 BCE] gave an eyewitness account of Ancient Egypt:

Now, let me talk more of Egypt for it has a lot of admirable things and what one sees there is superior to any other country.

The Hermetic Texts (Hermatica) told us about the great status of Egypt—as the Temple of Cosmos—and how Egypt (and the world) will turn into darkness, at the beginning of our common era.

...in Egypt all the operations of the powers which rule and work in heaven have been transferred to earth below...it should rather be said that the whole cosmos dwells in [Egypt] as in its sanctuary...

There will come a time when ... the gods will return from earth to heaven; Egypt will be forsaken, and the land which was once the home of religion will be left desolate, bereft of the presence of its deities.
- Ascleptus III (25 BCE), Hermetic Texts

It is commonly acknowledged that history is "written" (more correctly dictated/colored) by the winners of the latest conflict(s). In the case of Egypt, its history is the result of Moslem/Arab invasion of Egypt in 640 CE, and later by the European history of colonization.

The major sources of presently available history books are about Europeans and their descendants in other continents. About 500 years ago, Europeans started conquering the outside world through colonization of countries. As a consequence, spreading *knowledge* (including world history) was in their total control.

The sad thing is that a large amount of our 'Egyptology' has been molded by Judeo-Christian anti-Egyptian prejudice. The Western fascination with Egypt is largely based on Biblical accounts of interaction between the Hebrews and this ancient land. And as their "view" is the Hebraic view, it is largely negative.

Academic Egyptologists make their living by degrading the Egyptians and their beliefs. The Egyptological arena is infested by those whose only intention is to destroy the credibility of ancient Egypt. Typically, they are wolves in sheep's clothing.

It is most incredible and disappointing that Western Egyptologists, who choose the subject of "Egyptology" for their careers, are the very ones who have the most disdain for Ancient Egypt and its people. Witness the British Egyptologist, Alan Gardiner, who complained about the Ancient Egyptians at the end of his book, *Egypt of the Pharaohs*, in one of his usual irate put-down litanies,

> *What is proudly advertised as Egyptian history is merely a collection of rags and tatters.*

When militaristic colonization ended in the late 20th century, many people started questioning what they had been taught for so long. Such questioning unsettled these people who want to continue feeling a sense of superiority over others. They received support from the governing class in Egypt—who impose their ironclad Islamic Arabic rule on the peaceful silent majority of Egypt.

Some people react to historical interpretations that conflict with what they've always thought and been taught, by calling the author a *revisionist*. They insist on living a lie. Refusing to hear an opposing point of

view is a sign of weakness, not strength. They are rejecting a lot of valuable information and opportunities
to grow, intellectually and spiritually, by hiding their
heads in the sand.

Because you are not an 'expert' in a particular field,
it does not mean that you have to accept or be intimidated by other so-called 'experts'. We should see the
truth—naked, as did the child in the story of *The Emperor Without Clothes*, by Hans Christian Anderson. It
was the story of two con artists, who claimed to tailor
very fine clothes which could only be seen by the honest
and the competent. The fake tailors were able to per-
suade the high officials and even the emperor to buy
invisible clothes because who among them would want
to admit dishonesty and incompetence. The emperor led
a public parade, so as to display his new "clothes". Fear
and intimidation caused the masses to ignore the truth
about their Emperor, but it was a child who refused to
be intimidated and cried out the truth, *"The emperor
has no clothes!"*

The contents of this book are sample representations of various subjects. As Egyptians would say, it is
like "a flower from each garden". To learn more about
specific subjects, consult *About TRF Books*, at the end of
this book, as well as future books on our website,
     http://www.egypt-tehuti.org/gadalla-books.html.

Moustafa Gadalla
To-Beh 16, 12955 (Ancient Egyptian Calendar)
January 24, 2007 CE

Standards and Terminology

1. As in all Semitic styles of writings, Egyptian writing was limited to the consonants of the words, because the meaning of the word was generally contained in the consonants, while the vowels were added only to indicate the grammatical forms. As such, vowel sounds were not included in the written language.

    Since we do not know the exact sounds of their words, and to simplify matters, Western academicians agreed to a certain way of pronunciation. Therefore, the vowels you see in translated Ancient Egyptian texts are an approximation, and by no means are they the true sounds.

    As a result, you may find a variety in writing the same thing such as:
    Aten/Aton
    Amen/Amon/Amun
    Mery/Mary/Merry, etc.

2. We have become accustomed to repeating wrongly interpreted words and names, from the Ancient Egyptian texts. For example, the Ancient Egyptian word **neter**, and its feminine form **netert**, have been wrongly, and possibly intentionally, translated to *god* and *goddess*, by almost all academicians. **Neteru** (plural of **neter/netert**) are the divine principles and functions of the One Supreme God.

3.   The term *Baladi* will be used throughout this book
     to denote the present silent majority of Egyptians
     that adhere to the Ancient Egyptian traditions, with
     a thin exterior layer of Islam. The Christian popu-
     lation of Egypt is an ethnic minority that came as
     refugees, from Judaea and Syria to the Ptolemaic/
     Roman-ruled Alexandria. Now, 2,000 years later,
     they are easily distinguishable in looks and man-
     nerisms from the majority of native Egyptians. [More
     details in chapter 2 of this book.]

4.   When referring to the names of cities, pharaohs,
     neteru, etc., if the "Westernized common" rendering
     is different than the true Egyptian name, we will
     show the correct Egyptian name in this font, followed
     by the "common westernized" rendering between pa-
     rentheses.

5.   When using the Latin calendar, we will use the fol-
     lowing terms:
     BCE - Before Common Era. Noted in many refer-
     ences as BC.
     CE - Common Era. Noted in many references as
     AD.

6.   Fonting of quotations varies depending on the source
     of quotation. There are generally two types of
     fonting:

     one for Ancient Egyptian records,
     and a second for historians, Egyptologists and other ref-
     erences.

Chronology of Egyptian Dynasties

Neolithic Period	before 5000 BCE
Pre-dynastic Period	c. 5000-3300 BCE
Protodynastic Period	c. 3300-3050 BCE

Dynasty   Dates

Dynasty	Dates	Period
I	3050 BCE - 2890 BCE	Early
II	2890 BCE - 2649 BCE	Dynastic
III	2649 BCE - 2575 BCE	Period
IV	2575 BCE - 2465 BCE	Old
V	2465 BCE - 2323 BCE	Kingdom
VI	2323 BCE - 2150 BCE	
VII-X - *1st Interm. Per.*	2150 BCE - 2040 BCE	
XI	2040 BCE - 1991 BCE	Middle
XII	1991 BCE - 1783 BCE	Kingdom
XIII-XVII - *2nd Inter. Per.*	1783 BCE - 1550 BCE	
XVIII	1550 BCE - 1307 BCE	New
XIX	1307 BCE - 1196 BCE	Kingdom
XX	1196 BCE - 1070 BCE	
XXI	1070 BCE - 712 BCE	3rd
XXII	945 BCE - 712 BCE	Intermed.
XXIII	878 BCE - 712 BCE	Period
XXIV	740 BCE - 712 BCE	
XXV	712 BCE - 657 BCE	
XXVI	664 BCE - 525 BCE	
XXVII *(Persian)*	525 BCE - 404 BCE	Late
XXVIII	404 BCE - 399 BCE	Kingdom
XXIX	399 BCE - 380 BCE	
XXX	380 BCE - 343 BCE	
Second Persian Period	343 BCE - 332 BCE	
Macedonian Kings	332 BCE - 304 BCE	
Ptolemaic Dynasty	323 BCE - 30 BCE	Greco-Roman
Roman Emperors	30 BCE - 323 CE	Period
Byzantine Emperors	323 CE - 642 CE	

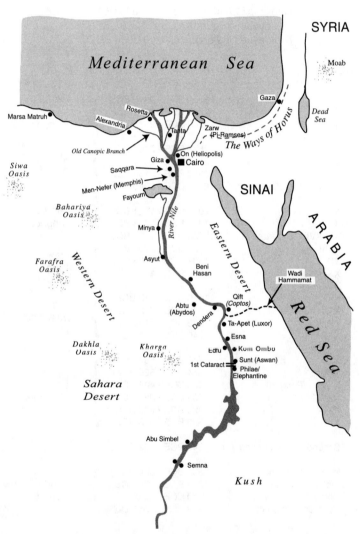

Map of Ancient Egypt

Part 1

The Peoples of Egypt

1

The Beginning

The Rising Valley

Egypt is (and was) one of the most arid areas in the world. More than 90% of Egypt consists of desert area. Only about 5% of the vast country is inhabited, along the banks of the Nile and its branches. This fertile Nile Valley is a strip, 7-9 miles [11-15 km] wide.

The Nile flows through Egypt from south to north. That's because the country slopes downhill toward the Mediterranean Sea. North of Cairo, the Nile splits into several tributaries that constitute the delta—a wide green fan of fertile countryside, some 6,000 square miles [15,500 sq km] in area.

The River Nile in Egypt received (and continues to receive) 90% of its water during a 100-day flood period every year, as noted by Herodotus, in *The Histories,* [2, 92], where he states:

> . . . . *the water begins to rise at the summer solstice, continues to do so for a hundred days, and then falls again at the end of that period, so that it remains low throughout the winter until the summer solstice comes round again in the following year.*

The floodwaters of the Nile come as a result of the rainy season in Ethiopia, which erodes the silt of the Ethiopian highlands, and carries it towards Egypt along the Blue Nile and other tributaries. No appreciable amount of water arrives to Egypt via the White Nile that starts from Central Africa. No silt is carried by the White Nile—hence the name "white" means clear.

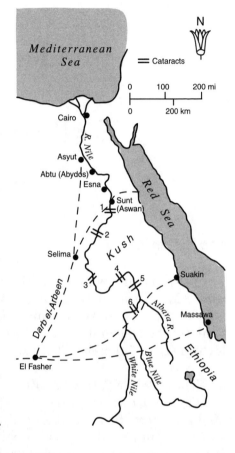

The muddy seasonal rushing water of the Blue Nile slows down, as it reaches Aswan. As a result of the slowdown, the silt in the moving water settles to the bottom. This causes the bed of the river to gradually rise from time to time; and the level of the land, which always keeps pace with that of the river, increases in varying degrees according to the distance downstream, and the variant topography of the land.

At Esna (for example), the Nile depositing its annual negligible ¼ inch of silt was able over 2 millennia to virtually bury the temple at Esna, with the modern town of Esna now sitting higher than the roof of the temple.

Another example is at Abtu (Abydos), where the very old massive structure—called the Ausarian (Oseirion)—is located, next to the New Kingdom temple of Ausar (Osiris), which was built by King Seti I (1333–1304 BCE) and his successor Ramses II. This Ausarian structure is located much below the elevation of the New Kingdom's Temple of Ausar and is partially sub-

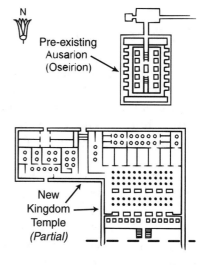

merged underneath the ground water table. The Ausarian structure's foundation is cut many feet below the present level of the water table, which has risen some 20ft (18m) since New Kingdom times.

The style of Ausarian, being massive, bare, and simple, is very different from the elegant New Kingdom temple with its acres of exquisite carvings.

It should be noted that many pharaohs have inscribed their names on buildings that they never built. Therefore, just because Seti I inscribed his name on some parts of the Ausarian building, it does not make him the builder of the Ausarian (Oseirion).

The tremendous difference in elevation between the Ausarian and Seti's Temple, as well as the dramatic difference in style between the two, suggest to many scholars that the Ausarian is a much older building.

The evidence at the Ausarian is consistent with the evidence at Giza and elsewhere regarding the greater antiquity of the Egyptian civilization.

The Point of Beginning

Herodotus reported that he was informed by Egyptian priests that the sun had twice set where it now rose, and twice risen where it now set. The statement indicates that the Ancient Egyptians counted their history for more than one zodiac cycle of 25,920 years.

The zodiac cycle of 25,920 years comes as a result of the wobbly rotation of the earth, which does not spin true upon its axis, but more like a slightly off-center spinning top. [See diagrams and explanations of the fundamentals of this phenomenon in chapter 11.] This motion is called *precession*. As a consequence of the *wobble* of the earth upon its axis, the vernal equinox each year rises against a gradually shifting background of the zodiac constellations.

The precession of the equinoxes, through the constellations, gives names to the twelve zodiac ages. It takes roughly 2,160 years for the equinox to precess through a zodiac sign. Thus it takes some 25,920 years for the spring equinox to traverse the full circuit of the constellations of the twelve zodiac signs. This complete cycle is called the Great/Full Year.

Therefore, Herodotus' statement about the sun setting/rising, where it now rises/sets, would mean that the Egyptians counted their history back for more than a complete zodiac cycle. The precessional cycles of the equinox were observed and recorded in Ancient Egypt [see *Astronomy* in chapter 11].

That the Ancient Egyptians had gone through (at least) a complete cycle is evident from the numerous Ancient Egyptian astronomical records showing observations of the perimeter stars of the various constellations. The Ancient Egyptians gave names—based on the over-

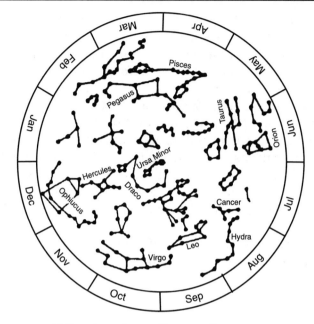

The Zodiac Constellations

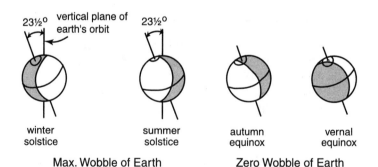

| winter solstice | summer solstice | autumn equinox | vernal equinox |

Max. Wobble of Earth   **Zero Wobble of Earth**

all outline of configurations—to these constellations, such as Taurus, Leo, etc. Since the constellations are so large, one can only see a portion of a constellation during a life-time—as the earth takes 2160 years to traverse a zodiac sign. The Ancient Egyptian texts recorded the locations of the perimeter stars of the various constellations—e.g.

the front paw of Leo the Lion, ...etc. For the Ancient Egyptians, to refer to a star of a constellation, such as the front paw of Leo, means that they knew the total shape of the constellation as a lion before the total configuration of the constellation appeared in the sky. In other words, the Ancient Egyptians [5,000 years ago] knew in advance the 12 zodiac constellations, i.e. they went through a complete zodiac cycle of 25,920 years recording the locations (and movements) of the stars, then they defined various groups of stars as the perimeters of various constellations—and gave each constellation a name to match the outline of its overall configuration.

Our present zodiac cycle (Great/Full Year) began with the Age of Leo the Lion, as follows:

Age of LEO:	10948 – 8788 BCE
Age of CANCER:	8787 – 6628 BCE
Age of TWINS:	6627 – 4468 BCE
Age of BULL:	4467 – 2308 BCE
Age of ARIES:	2307 – 148 BCE

The Ancient Egyptian history extended to a complete zodiac cycle of 25,920 years, plus a partial zodiac cycle, between 10948 BCE and the end of the Age of Aries when Ancient Egypt lost its independence. Thus, the antiquity of Ancient Egypt is [25,920 + (10,948 – 148)] = 36,720 years old.

That the Ancient Egyptian civilization is over 36,000 years old—and by extension that life on Earth is that old—goes against Christian/western establishments.

Both establishments have predetermined that life on earth is about 5,000 years old. As a result, it has been continuously repeated that the Pharaoh **Mena** (c. 31st century BCE) is reputed to have "unified Egypt" and began the Ancient Egyptian civilization.

Mena's significance in the Egyptian history is that his reign began at the end of the first third of the Taurus (the Bull) Age, i.e. 3028 BCE. It should be noted that the division of time into three cycles /segments is very common in Ancient (and present-day) Egypt—such as their division of each month into three equal segments of 10 days (like decans)—each with its own peculiar characteristics.

This repeated arbitrary and unfounded assertion about the Pharaoh **Mena** (Menes) being the beginning of the Ancient Egyptian history is contrary to the evidence. The Greek and Roman writers of antiquity, basing their accounts on information received either first or second-hand from Egyptian sources, claimed a far greater antiquity for the Egyptian civilization than what was arbitrarily established by academicians.

The chronology of the Ancient Egyptian Pharaohs, since the time of **Mena**, came basically from Manetho in the 3rd century BCE. Manetho's work has not survived— we have only the commentaries on it by Sextus Africanus [c. 221 CE] and Eusebius of Caesarea [c. 264–340 CE].

According to Eusebius, Manetho ascribed great antiquity to Pharaonic Egypt, with the age of the Ancient Egyptian antiquities of 36,000 years, which is consistent with the accounts of Herodotus. This is in a general agreement with other accounts and evidential findings, such as Diodorus of Sicily [Diodorus I, 24] and the Ancient Egyptian document known as the Turin Papyrus—an original Egyptian document dating from the 17th Dynasty [c.

1400 BCE].

The physical evidence also supports this remote antiquity of Ancient Egypt—despite the fact that so much
archeological evidence from such remote times has been
buried much below the present groundwater levels, due
to the phenomenon of the rising Nile Valley [as explained
earlier]. Evidence remains from many Ancient Egyptian
texts, temples, and tombs, which corroborates the accounts of the Greek and Roman writers. For example,
temples throughout Egypt make reference to being originally built much earlier than its "dynastic history". The
texts inscribed in the crypts of the temple of Het-Heru
(Hathor) at Dendera clearly state that the temple that
was restored during the Ptolemaic Era was based on
drawings dating back to King Pepi of the 6th Dynasty
(2400 BCE). The drawings themselves are copies of documents that are thousands of years older (time of Servants
of Heru). The text reads:

> The venerable foundation in Dendera was found in early
> writings, written on a leather roll in the time of the Ser-
> vants of Heru (= the kings preceding Mena/Menes), at
> Men-Nefer (Memphis), in a casket, at the time of the
> lord of the Two Lands... Pepi.

☞ **Due to the rising elevation of the Egyptian
land, as explained earlier, several Ancient
Egyptian temples needed to be elevated—as
confirmed by Herodotus and the physical evidence throughout Egypt. Even though a few
Ancient Egyptian temples were restored during the Greco-Roman period, they were all rebuilt according to Ancient Egyptian plans,
symbols, deities, figures, etc, that are found in
numerous temples and tombs throughout the
country—long before the Greco-Roman era.**

The Age of Leo and The Sphinx

Our present zodiac cycle began with the Age of Leo [10948–8788 BCE], and is represented by the Great Sphinx of Giza, with a human head and the body of a lion. Both the historical and the physical evidence at the Sphinx' site indicates its remote age, despite the common (but groundless) notion that the Sphinx was built somewhere between 2520–2494 BCE, during the reign of Khafra (Chephren).

Herodotus, who wrote about the pyramids of Giza and the builder Pharaohs (including Khafra) in detail, never attributed the construction of the Sphinx to Khafra. Other writers of antiquity who wrote about the Sphinx never attributed it to any particular pharaoh.

A powerful piece of physical evidence regarding the antiquity of the Great Sphinx is the Ancient Egyptian stela commonly known as the "Inventory Stela", which was found in Giza, in the 19th century. This stela describes events during the reign of Khufu [Cheops 2551–2528 BCE], Khafra's predecessor, and indicates that Khufu ordered the building of a monument alongside the Sphinx. This means that the Sphinx was already there before the time of Khufu and therefore could not have been built by his successor, Khafra [2520–2494 BCE]. Since the "Inventory Stela" contradicted the western academicians prior assertions regarding Khafra being the builder of the Sphinx, they dismissed the stela, on the basis that its *stylistic features* appeared to be from the New Kingdom [1550–1070 BCE]. This is not a sufficient cause to dismiss it, since there are numerous stelae and texts from the Old Kingdom [2575–2150 BCE] that were later copied in the New Kingdom and no one dismissed their authenticity. People everywhere copy older documents all the time so as to maintain the knowledge for future generations.

The academic attribution to Khafra as the builder of the Sphinx is based on two premises:

1. A stele that was erected by the Pharaoh Twt Homosis (Tuthomosis) IV [1413–1405 BCE] was placed between the paws of the Sphinx. The stela described Twt Homosis IV's visions as a prince and how he cleaned the sands around the Sphinx' body, ...etc. It is a long text, but the name of Khafra (Chepren) appears on it, in hieroglyphs. The text surrounding the name of Khafra was illegible. As such, no one knows why the name Khafra was mentioned on Twt Homosis IV's stela. This is the only place the name Khafra is mentioned, at the site of the Sphinx.

2. There is a causeway between the Pyramid Temple of Khafra and the Valley Temple, approximately 1650 ft [500m] long [see plan on opposite page]. Even though there are no inscriptions on the Sphinx or in this temple, western academia asserted that the presence of the causeway is sufficient evidence of some kind of a connection with Khafra. Later excavations found a number of statues in this temple, which were claimed to "resemble" the head features of the Sphinx. However, when the face profile of the statues were superimposed on the Sphinx's face profile—there was no match whatsoever.

The found statues of Khafra, the mention of his name on Twt Homosis IV's stela, and the presence of the causeway may lead us to the conclusion that Khafra was probably the last pharaoh to ***restore*** the Sphinx before Twt Homosis IV—more than 1,000 years after the time of Khafra.

The physical evidence at the site of the Sphinx supports its antiquity, of belonging to the zodiac Age of Leo.

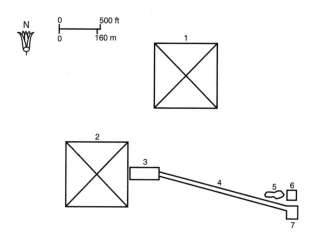

1   Great Pyramid of Khufu (Cheops).
2   Pyramid of Khafra (Chephren).
3   Pyramid Temple of Khafra.
4   Causeway to Valley Temple of Khafra.
5   Great Sphinx.
6   Temple of the Sphinx.
7   Valley Temple of Khafra.
8   Pyramid of Menkaura (Mycerinus).

The Giza Plateau (main features)

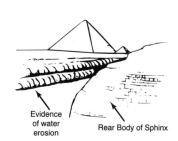

Head of the Sphinx

The original site where the Sphinx is located was a gently sloping plane with an outcrop of harder rock. The main features of the Sphinx are comprised of different geological conditions, as follows:

A.   The head of the Sphinx was carved out of this outcrop of a hard strata, which is resistant to the effects of the natural elements.
B.   The body of the Sphinx was formed by quarrying away the stone from all around the soon-to-be body. The body of the Sphinx was made of a softer limestone strata, which in turn consists of alternate harder and softer layers. These alternate layers are visible on site as weathered corrugation, which is about two feet deep into the bedrock.
C.   The base of the Sphinx, as well as the bottom of the original quarry site, are made of a harder limestone, which is resistant to the effects of the natural elements.

Since the body of the Sphinx is located in a hollow, it takes less than 20 years to fill it and cover the body totally. With the exception of the last century or so, the Sphinx has been covered by sand since the time it was created thousands of years ago. Therefore the Sphinx was protected from weathering exposure to wind and sand. However, there is a two-foot deep, smooth erosion on the wall of the excavated hollow (around the body of the Sphinx), with identical erosion patterns on the body of the Sphinx. Obviously, both the rock face and the Sphinx were carved before this severe weathering took place.

Many academicians have resigned themselves to the fact that the erosion to the body of the Sphinx was caused by water effects. The question becomes: What water caused this peculiar erosion pattern? That ground water has caused such erosion must be dismissed, since it is estimated that the ground water table was 30 ft [9m] lower in Khafra's time [2520–2494 BCE] than its present level. In other words, it is impossible for the ground water to have caused erosion of two feet deep channels into the body of the Sphinx, and the walls of the quarry pit.

As explained at the beginning of this chapter, over the course of thousands of years, the inundation of the Nile had gradually deposited additional silt on the ground of the Valley. Whenever the ground rises, so does the ground water table. It is therefore that the evidence is overwhelming against the ground water theory as the cause of erosion at the Sphinx site. There is no other rational answer except that the water erosion occurred at the end of the last Ice Age [c. 15,000–10,000 BCE]. Geologists agree that Egypt was subject to severe flooding at the end of the last Ice Age.

Another powerful piece of evidence regarding the antiquity of the Sphinx is the revelation of a recent drill hole in front of the ruined temple of the Sphinx (located in front of the Sphinx, and closed to the public), that revealed the presence of red granite at a depth of 54 ft [16.5m]. Granite is not native to northern Egypt and could have only come from Aswan—over 1,000 miles to the south. The presence of granite, at such a depth, is an additional proof of construction activities much earlier than 3,000 BCE—when the ground elevation was 54 ft [16.5m] below our present times.

In conclusion, the overwhelming physical and historical evidence, as detailed above, leads us to the rational conclusion that Khafra did not and could not have built the Sphinx—but he was one of many who restored it. Naturally, Ancient Egyptian monuments needed to be restored every few decades/centuries. The evidence at the Sphinx of Giza shows it to be the Ancient Egyptian mark of the zodiac age of Leo the Lion—c. 13,000 years ago.

The Egyptian Calendar

The Egyptians' advanced knowledge in astronomy, as reflected in their most accurate calendar, was acknowledged by the great Strabo (64 BCE–25 CE), who wrote:

*They (the Egyptian priests) revealed to the Greeks the secrets of the **full year**, whom the latter ignored as with many other things...*

Egypt's ingenious and very accurate calendar was based on the observation and the study of **Sabt's** (Sirius) movements in the sky. The Ancient Egyptian calendar is therefore called the *Sothic Calendar*, i.e. of having to do with Sirius (**Sabt**), the Dog Star.

The Ancient Egyptians knew that the *full year* was slightly over 365¼ days. The earth takes 365.25636 days to complete one revolution around the sun.

It should be noted that the chronology of 3,000 years of Ancient Egyptian history, by modern Egyptologists, was made possible only because the Ancient Egyptians followed the accurate Sothic Year of 365.25636 days. Additionally, it is the Egyptian calendar that made it possible for history students worldwide to estimate the date of events in all other countries in the world—countries that never had a (correct or any) calendar.

The practical Ancient Egyptians used a calendar consisting of 12 months, each equal to 30 days. The adjustments needed to make a complete year, i.e. the difference between 365.25636 days and the 360 (30 x 12) days, were made as follows:

1.   The difference of 5.25 days comes at the end of the

Egyptian year, by adding 5 days every year and an additional day every 4 years. The Ancient Egyptian Year currently begins (in 2007) on 11 September. The 5/6 extra days begin on 6 September.

2. The difference of 0.00636 day (365.25636 − 365¼ days) for each year requires adding another day every (1/0.00636) 157¼ years, which the Egyptians continued to do until our present times. This is accomplished by adding an extra day every 157, 314, 471, and 629 year cycles. The above adjustments by the Egyptians can clearly be seen in the last 2,000 years when comparing the Ancient Egyptian calendar with the "Latin" calendar [as explained below].

After Julius Caesar visited to Egypt in 48 BCE, he commissioned the astronomer Sosigenes (from Alexandria) to introduce a calendar into the Roman Empire. This resulted in the Julian calendar of 365 days a year and 366 days every leap year. The Roman (Julian) calendar was literally tailored to be fit for a King. The first day of the year was the coronation day for the Egyptian King at his end of the annual rejuvenation jubilee [see *Egyptian Mystics: Seekers of the Way*, by same author, for more information].

However, the Julian calendar did not take into account that the year is a bit longer than 365¼ days. The difference between 365.25 days and 365.25636 days, from the time of the adoption of the Julian calendar to our present time, is 13 days. Such a difference explains the 13 day variation in the annual observations of numerous Christian festivals—between the Orthodox and non-Orthodox churches. The reason is that one group followed the accurate Egyptian calendar, while the other group followed the inaccurate Julian calendar.

When the Julian calendar was adopted in 48 BCE,

the first day of the Egyptian calendar was 29 August. In order to find the beginning date of the Ancient Egyptian calendar—in terms of the (deficient) Latin calendar—we must account for the difference of 0.00636 day (365.25636 - 365.25 days) for each year between 29 August and 21 June (beginning of Cancer sign). We firstly find the difference between the two dates to be 69 days. By dividing the 69 days by 0.00636, the result is 10,849 years. Thus, on 29 August of the year 48 BCE, the Egyptian calendar was at least 10,897 BCE (10,849 + 48).

As stated earlier, the present zodiac cycle began in10,948 BCE. The difference between 10,897 BCE and the beginning of the Age of Leo [10,948 BCE] is 51 years. In other words, in 48 BCE, the Ancient Egyptian calendar was 1/3 through the cycle of a 157-year period.

The year 10,948 BCE, being the beginning of the Age of Leo, is consistent with the statements of all early Greek and Roman writers such as Plato, whose *Collected Dialogues* indicate that the Ancient Egyptian canon of proportion—for arts and architecture—did not change over the previous 10,000 years before Plato's time [428–347 BCE]. Plato stated,

> *That the pictures and statues made ten thousand years ago, are in no one particular better or worse than what they now make.*

Since the Islamic/Arab occupation of Egypt [641 CE], the Ancient Egyptian calendar became known as the "Coptic" calendar, even though it was developed thousands of years befor Christianity. Modern-day Egyptians still follow the Ancient Egyptian calendar, for practically all the countless annual festivals, agriculture, weather, and other matters (with just a handful of exceptions). It is by far the most practical and accurate calendar in use in the world.

2

The Egyptian Populous

The Unchanging Egyptians

The Egyptians are remarkably traditionalist to a fault. Throughout the history of Egypt, the emphasis was the adherence to traditions and Egyptians NEVER deviated from such principles. In the oldest surviving text of the world (5,000 years ago), the Egyptian scribe, Ptah Hotep, states:

> Don't modify/change anything from your father's (ancestor's) teachings/instructions—not even a single word. And let this principle be the cornerstone for teachings to future generations.

The Egyptians never deviated from this principle. Early historians have attested to this fact, such as Herodotus, in *The Histories, Book Two, [79]*:

> *The Egyptians keep to their native customs and never adopt any from abroad.*

Herodotus, in *The Histories, Book Two, [91]*:

> *The Egyptians are unwilling to adopt Greek customs, or, to speak generally, those of any other country.*

The essence of such traditionalism is in the Egyptians' total adherence to precedence established by their ancestors. Everything they did, every action, every movement, every decree had to be justified in terms of their ancestral precedence—to abide by and to explain their actions and deeds. The Ancient and *Baladi* Egyptians' entire sociology and existence, from beginning to end, is nothing but a long chain of ancestral precedents—every single link and rivet of which became a custom and a law, from their spiritual fathers unto themselves, in the flesh. Plato and other writers affirmed the complete adherence of the Egyptians to their own traditions. Nothing has changed with this attitude since then, for each traveler to Egypt since that time has confirmed the allegiances to such conservatism.

With all the false claims of how the Ancient Egyptians changed their ways, languages, religion, traditions, etc, careful study will show that such claims are mere mirages. The truth is that the ancient traditions never died, and they continue to survive within the silent majority, who are called (and they call themselves) *Baladi*, meaning *natives*. The loud minority of Egyptians (high governmental officials, academicians, journalists, and the self-proclaimed intellectuals) are described by the silent majority as *Afrangi*, meaning *foreigners*.

The *Afrangi* are the Egyptian people who compromised the Egyptian heritage to gain high positions and approval of the foreign invaders of Egypt. As a tool of foreign forces, like Arabs, the *Afrangi* rule and dominate the *Baladi*—the natives. The *Afrangi* are, like their foreign masters, arrogant, cruel, and vain. After foreign forces left Egypt, the Egyptian *Afrangi* continued their role as the righteous rulers.

The Unchanging *Baladi*—the torch-bearers of the Ancient Egyptian ancestors—were cavilerly stripped of their nationality—as explained next.

The "Racial Religions"

It is commonly acknowledged that history is "written" (more correctly dictated/colored) by the winners of the latest conflict(s). As a result, it has been written and repeated: that the Ancient Egyptians accepted the domination of the Ptolemaic and Roman rules; that they had willingly changed their religious beliefs into Christianity; and a short time later, they willingly accepted Islam as a substitute for Christianity. Accordingly, many conflicting sides (Eurocentrists, Afrocentrists, Islamists, Christians,...etc), who use Ancient Egypt to promote each's own agenda, insist that the ancient religion, language, and traditions have died. Such unfounded fallacies were reinforced by the minority *Afrangi* Egyptians— who serve the interests of the Arab conquerors ever since 640 CE—have dedicated their efforts to denouncing their ancestral heritage.

Because of the passive nature of the *Baladi* Egyptians, many people invented "theories" about the "identity" of the Egyptians that have absolutely no scientific and/or historical basis whatsoever. The premise of their baseless assertions is by division and racial identification of the people of Egypt, based on their *assumed religions*. Some claim that the Islamized population of Egypt (about 90%) are Arab settlers from the Arab Peninsula. The Christian population (about 10%) are claimed as the *true* Egyptians, referred to as *Copts*, *descendants* of the Ancient Egyptians. Others claim that the Islamized population of Egypt is of a mixed blood—of the Ancient Egyptians and of the Arabs who invaded Egypt in 640 CE. The Ancient Egyptian "blood" does not exist anymore.

In truth, the hundreds of Ancient Egyptian mummies—from all ages, together with DNA testing—as well as the numerous depicted figures in the Ancient Egyptian temples and tombs—show that present-day "Moslem" Egyptians are the same race as their Ancient Egyptian ancestors.

The Christian population of Egypt is markedly different than the "Moslem" population. Actually, the Christians in Egypt are NOT natives of Egypt, but a foreign minority that came to Egypt, from Judaea and Syria to serve the interests of the Romans—to man their military garrisons and/or to collect the various taxes imposed by the Romans. It is not a coincidence that the concentrated centers where the present Christian population of Egypt reside, are exactly the same locations where the Romans maintained their military and administrative (tax collection) centers. Now, 2,000 years later, these Syriac people are easily distinguishable in looks and mannerisms from the majority of native Egyptians. Foreign visitors, such as the British researcher, E.W. Lane, affirmed such differences in his book, *The Manners and Customs of the Modern Egyptians* [1836].

Unlike the foreigners (Syriac and otherwise) living in Egypt, the native Egyptians never converted to Christianity. It was the Syrian migration to Alexandria that constituted the bulk of the early Christians to Egypt. In 312 CE, Christianity was made the official and only religion of the Roman Empire. A short time later, the Roman Empire split. Egypt became part of the Eastern (or Byzantine) Empire in 323 CE. Constantine's declaration to make Christianity the official religion of the empire had two immediate effects on Egypt. Firstly, it allowed the Church to enhance the organization of its administrative structure and to acquire considerable wealth; and secondly, it allowed Christian fanatics to destroy the native Egyptian religious rights, properties, and temples. For example, when Theophilus was made Patriarch of Alexandria in 391 CE. A wave of destruction swept over the land of Egypt. Tombs were ravaged, walls of ancient monuments defaced, and statues toppled. The famed Library of Alexandria, which contained hundreds of thousands of documents, was destroyed. The fanatic early Christians went on appropriating Ancient Egyptian temples. In the 4th and 5th centuries, many ancient temples on the west bank of Ta-Apet (Thebes) were converted into monastic centers.

There is no archeological evidence, outside Alexandria, to substantiate the Christians' overly exaggerated popularity claims. The Ancient Egyptians did not need any new "enlightenment" from the Christian fanatics, since the very thing that is now called the Christian religion was already in existence in Ancient Egypt, long before the adoption of the New Testament. The British Egyptologist, Sir E. A. Wallis Budge, wrote in his book, *The Gods of the Egyptians* [1969],

> *The new religion (Christianity) which was preached there by St. Mark and his immediate followers, in all essentials so closely resembled that which was the outcome of the worship of Osiris, Isis, and Horus.*

The main difference between the Egyptian and the New Testament versions is that the Gospel tale is considered historical and the Egyptian Ausar/Auset/Heru story is an allegory [see Appendix, pg 277]. The British scholar A.N. Wilson pointed out in his book, *Jesus*:

> *The Jesus of History and the Christ of Faith are two separate beings, with very different stories.*

The early Christians confused fiction with fact. In their fanatic ignorance, they mistranslated the Ancient Egyptian spiritual allegorical language into alleged history. That "Christ is within you" is the Ancient Egyptian message of truth that was buried by those who want to make history out of a spiritual allegory. [For more information, see *The Ancient Egyptian Roots of Christianity*, by M. Gadalla.]

The history of the political and doctrinal struggles within the Church during and after the 4th century has largely been written in terms of the disputes over the nature of God and Christ and the relationship between them. These parties were distinguished by the familiar names *Jacobite* or *Coptic*, and *Melkite* or *Royalist*. The Jacobites were by creed Monophysites, by race mainly, though not exclusively people born in Egypt, but of foreign descent (mistakenly thought of as native Egyptians); while the Melkites were orthodox followers of Chalcedon and for the most part of Greek or European origin.

Monophysites had, from the outset, espoused a doctrine of Christ, which placed the greatest possible emphasis on his divinity, and rejected that he had a human nature. When the orthodox theologians of Rome and Constantinople agreed at the Council of Chalcedon, in 451, that Christ was to be worshipped "*in two natures inseparably united*", the Monophysite opposition contended that though Christ could be "*out of two natures*", he could not be in two natures. As a result, in 451, during the reign of the patriarch Dioscorus, the Monophysite Church in Egypt broke away from the Melkite Orthodox Church, and elected its own patriarch. Since the Council of Chalcedon in 451, each of the two Churches had its own separate patriarch and administration.

We hear a lot about the *prosecution* of the "Copts". Yet it was they who asked for it, by not accepting other religious beliefs, including their fellow Melkite Christians. Their rejection of others' religious rights was violent and destructive. Even though they were allowed to have their own patriarch, they insisted on denying Melkites and others their right to worship in their own way. The so-called persecution was blamed on Cyrus, who was sent as Imperial Patriarch to Alexandria in 631 CE. The double succession of pontiffs was maintained. Cyrus first tried a compromise between the two factions (Melkites and Monophysites). The compromise was rejected by the Monophysites—who did not recognize his authority.

Cyrus had to restore order, on behalf of his Emperor, for the Monophysites had terrorized and destroyed those who merely didn't agree with their fanatic interpretations. Did Cyrus persecute the Monophysites, or did they ask for his reaction by rejecting him and his authority? By extension, they had been prosecuting the land and people of Egypt (their host) for several centuries, and ironically, Cyrus, the Christian, gave them a taste of their own medicine.

When the Moslem Arabs, in December 639 CE, set out to conquer Egypt with a few thousand men, their task was relatively simple, aided by the active support of the non-Egyptian Christian Monophysites. After less than two years of fighting and political maneuvering between the Arab invaders and the Byzantines, Cyrus signed a treaty with the Arab Moslems on November 8, 641, which called for the total withdrawal of Roman soldiers, imposing a tribute on all able-bodied males, and a tax on all landowners. The only parties to the treaty were the Moslem Arabs and the non-Egyptian Christians, who gave away a country—(Egypt)—that was not theirs.

Because of the active cooperation of the Christians, the Moslem Arab conquerors favored the Monophysite Church, using it to assist them in collecting the poll-tax levied on the native Egyptians. In other words, the Arabs maintained the same administration of tax collection that was under the Roman/Byzantine rule. In return, the Christians were guaranteed the right to continue to practice their religion. The final defeat of Byzantine rule in Egypt came when their soldiers evacuated Alexandria, in 642 CE. From that date, Egypt became an Islamic/Arab colony—being governed by foreigners—either directly or indirectly via the *Afrangi* Egyptians.

Under Islamic rule, a person must officially announce his allegiance to one of three "approved" religions [Islam, Christianity, and Judaism], since Islamic law imposes an additional special "tax" (known as *Jizya*) on Christians and Jews. The Egyptian population, controlled or threatened by the Arab invaders (and their tax collectors—Christians), had to declare one of the three "approved" religions. Such declaration was a necessity and never a true conversion. Once a person announced his "Islamization", he could never change, since that would be considered blasphemy, which is punishable by death at the hands of any Moslem. Additionally, all the offspring of Islamized people are automatically considered Moslems—under Islamic law—and hence can never denounce Islam.

The term, *Copt*, predates Christianity and is the common word used by the Greeks for *an Egyptian*. The Arabs, after 640 CE, used this general term to label the non-Moslem Egyptians, and referred to the Islamized population as *Arabs*. In other words, the winners of the 640 CE invasion capriciously changed the race of Egyptians to Arab because of a religion that was imposed on them by the conquerors. As a result, the term *Copt* took on a different meaning by the 7th century—to mean *Christian* instead of *Egyptian*.

The Egyptians were invaded over and again, without ever putting up any real resistance. The *Baladi* Egyptians learned to maintain their ancient traditions under a thin layer of Islam. A common Egyptian proverb describes their survival mode, *"He/she plays with an egg and a stone—to protect the delicate egg from being cracked by the stone"*. [More about the "Islamization" of Egypt in other books by Gadalla, such as *Egyptian Mystics: Seekers of the Way, Egyptian Rhythm: The Heavenly Melodies,* and *Egyptian Cosmology: The Animated Universe*.]

The Mortal Mentality

The Egyptian's principal motto was/is to work for your earthly life as if you are going to live forever, but also prepare for your inevitable death as if you will die tomorrow. These dual directions made them both very religious and very happy. Because "life is short", one must live it up, but simultaneously always be on his/her best behavior—ready to meet the Creator at any time.

This Egyptian perspective was evident in an Ancient Egyptian custom where during or after their get-togethers, they would introduce a wooden image of **Ausar** (Osiris), from 1 1/2 feet (45cm) to 3 feet (90cm) in height, in the form of a human mummy, and to show it to each of the guests, reminding them of their mortality and the transitory nature of human pleasures. It was perfectly consistent with the ideas of the Egyptians to always be aware that this life is only a lodging, or "inn" along their way, and that their existence here is the preparation for a future state.

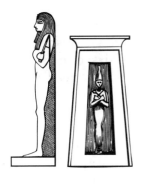

Statues of a mummy in the form of **Ausar** (Osiris).

Ausar (Osiris) represents the divine in mortal form—which is not in conflict with enjoying our earthly life journey. Such was reported by Diodorus, who wrote in his *Book I* [16, 4-5],

> *Ausar (Osiris) was laughter-loving and fond of music and the dance. . .*

The interest shown by the Egyptians in their fate

after death, arose in part from their passionate interest in life itself. This principle is shared by Montaigne, who said,

*He who would teach men to
die, would teach them to live.*

The Egyptians were therefore a gay, happy people, with a lively sense of humor. There are many humorous scenes in their paintings, including scenes of game playing, dancing, juggling, etc. Tongue-in-cheek advice is given to husbands who want to cover up their adulterous affairs: bite into an onion on the way home. The wife will be convinced that no kissing would be going on with breath like that.

The day-to-day life of the Egyptians was enlivened by a large number of festivities, most of them religious in nature. One can sense the liveliness of their participation in these activities from the depictions on the walls of the temples. Herodotus described the festive atmosphere of a religious occasion, with all the participants—men and women, poor and rich—singing, dancing, chanting, applauding, eating, drinking, ...etc.

As a consequence of their mortal mentality, they were also (and still are) fundamentally pragmatic and down to earth—the most humble. In the hundreds of discovered Ancient Egyptian texts and papyri—in various subjects (medicine, mathematics, etc)—there is never any credit in a finding/achievement attributed to any single person/persons. They consider that every achievement/talent is a gift from God, and credit can only be given to Him. It is therefore that all aspects of knowledge in Ancient Egypt are credited to the attributes/aspects/qualities of the Divine—namely the *neteru* (gods/goddesses).

The Two Lands

The Egyptian Pharaoh was always referred to as the *Lord of the Two Lands*. Western academia cavalierly stated that the *Two Lands* are literally and geographically *Upper* and *Lower Egypt*. There is not a single Ancient Egyptian reference to confirm their notion, or even to define such a frontier between *Upper* and *Lower* Egypt.

Throughout Ancient Egyptian temples, you will find numerous symbolic representations relating to the ceremony of *Uniting the Two Lands*, where two **neteru** are shown tying the papyrus and lotus plants. Neither plant is native to any specific area in Egypt. The most common representation shows the twin **neteru**, **Hapi** (a mirror-image of each other), each as a unisex with one breast.

The term, *Two Lands*, is very familiar to the *Baladi* Egyptians, who refer to it in their daily life. It is their strong belief that there are *Two Lands*—the one we all live on, and another one where our identical twins (of the opposite sex) live. The twins are subject to the same experiences from date of birth to date of death.

You and your "Siamese" twin, who "apparently" separate at birth, will re-unite again at the moment of death. The *Baladi* Egyptian enumerators describe, in their lamentations after the death of a person, how the deceased is being prepared to join his/her counterpart (of the opposite sex), AS IF it is a marriage ceremony. This is reminiscent of the many symbolic illustrations in Ancient Egypt of the tying the knot of the *Two Lands*. To be married is to tie the knot. [More about this concept is found in *Egyptian Cosmology: The Animated Universe*, by M. Gadalla.]

Housing and Gardens

In conjunction with their mortal mentality, Ancient and *Baladi* Egyptians—the most humble—have never used the "eternal stones" for their dwelling houses. Their present life was only the pilgrimage; they were taught to consider their abode here on Earth as merely an "inn" along the road.

Despite the repeated charges of vanity against the pharaohs, it is worth remembering that their abodes while on earth were never made of stone, but of mud-brick, the same material used by the humblest peasants. They all believed that the impermanent body, formed of clay, called for an equally impermanent abode on this earth. The earthly houses of the kings have long since returned to the earth from which they were raised.

Varying in form and quality, the houses were all made of sun-dried brick, sometimes made with a mixture of straw. All used this same building material, the manufacture of which occupied thousands of workers along the whole length of the Nile.

Because of the warm climate, the Egyptians lived most of their time in the open air, and the houses were constructed to be cool throughout the summer; currents of fresh air circulating freely throughout them by the practical arrangement of passages and courts. Corridors, supported on columns, gave access to different apartments through a succession of shady avenues and areas, with one side open to the air.

It is/was also common for several small Egyptian houses to share a common courtyard. The open court located in the center of the Ancient Egyptian house was planted as a garden with palms and other trees, sometimes paved with stone, with a small tank, or a fountain in its center.

Most houses had a ground-floor and one or two stories above it. In major cities, houses were as tall as five stories high. Diodorus speaks of the tall houses in Ta-Apet (Thebes) as being four and five stories high, and Ancient Egyptian paintings show some houses with four, including the basement story.

Property consisting of a house with four stories, two granaries, and an auxiliary building.

Some roofs were vaulted, especially in the warmer areas of southern Egypt, and built like the rest of the house of crude brick. The Ancient Egyptians utilized arches and vaulted roofs in their buildings, since their earliest history. The early invention of the brick, by the Ancient Egyptians, led to the invention of the arch; and we find arches in Egypt as far back as the 27th century BCE, in Saqqara. [More details in chapters 7 and 11 of this book.]

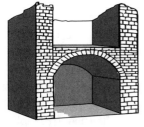

Typical Ancient Egyptian vaulted roof at Ta-Apet (Thebes).

The ceilings of the Ancient Egyptian buildings were of stucco, richly painted, tasteful both in their form and the arrangement of the colors. One of the oldest decorative trims is the guilloche, often misnamed the "Tuscan" or "Greek" border.

The Egyptians love(d) their gardens, which were always to be found in private, public, and shared spaces such as courtyards. Several papyri discovered show how the Ancient Egyptians prepared landscaping plans around all types of buildings.

As far back as Egypt's most ancient known past, there were parks and gardens. In a document from Pharaoh Snefru's time [2575–2551 BCE], we read about the design of a beautiful park and how the landscaper,

> dug a great tank and planted fig-trees and vines. . .In the middle of the garden he made a vineyard, which yielded much wine.

Landscaping public places was essential in Ancient Egypt. For example, Ramses III [1194–1163 BCE] planted trees and papyrus plants in Ta-Apet (Thebes) [as stated in the Harris Papyrus, i. 7,11], and in the new town which he founded in the Delta he made,

> great vineyards; walks shaded by all kinds of sweet fruit trees laden with their fruit; a sacred way, splendid with flowers from all countries, with lotus and papyrus, countless as the sand.

In the same above-mentioned Harris Papyrus [i.8,3-4], the text indicates that flowers and exotic plants were imported from all countries and were planted in parks for the enjoyment of gardening and growing flowers.

The Ancient Egyptians were fond of trees and flowers, and of raising numerous and rare plants. As such, according to Athenaeus,

> . . . *was the care they bestowed on their culture, that those flowers that elsewhere were only sparingly produced, even*

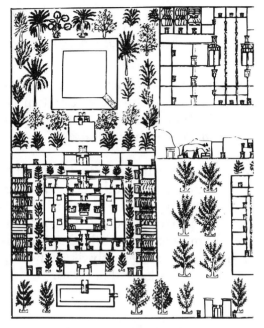

Partial plan of an Ancient Egyptian temple showing the landscaping on the temple proper [Beni Hassan]

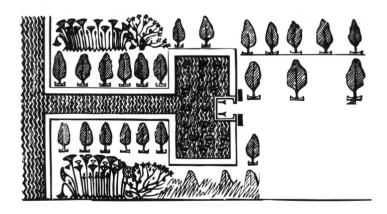

A garden in Ta-Apet (Thebes)

in their proper season, grew profusely at all times in Egypt;
so that neither roses, nor violets, nor any others, were
wanting there, even in the middle of winter.

Several remarkable pictures from Ta-Apet (Theban) tombs from the time of the New Kingdom [1550–1070 BCE] give us further details as to the arrangement of the gardens and country houses.

Large gardens were usually divided into different sections, with the main areas dedicated to the orchard (date and sycamore trees) and to the vineyard. The flower and kitchen gardens also occupied a considerable space, laid out in beds; and miniature trees, herbs, and flowers were grown in red earthen pots, exactly like our own, arranged in long rows by the walks and borders.

A typical Ancient Egyptian house (as depicted on a found papyrus) had a high castellated wall surrounding the section. The house is located at the back of the property, surrounded by a double row of palms and high trees. The vineyard is located in the center of the plan. The luxuriant vines with their large purple grapes are trained on trelliswork built up with stone; through these vine-walks the path leads straight up to the house. The plan also shows a part of the garden resembling a small park; here there is a fishpond surrounded by palms and shrubs. Two doors lead out of this garden; one into the palm garden which occupies a narrow strip on either side of the property, and the other leads to a "*cool tank*".

In all cases, whether the orchard stood apart from, or was united with, the rest of the garden, it was supplied, like the other portions of it, with an abundance of water, preserved in spacious reservoirs, on either side of which stood a row of palms, or an avenue of shady sycamores.

Egyptians: The Most Populous

Egypt was the most dominant, populous, and famed country in the ancient world, as affirmed by Diodorus, *Book I,* [31, 6-9],

> **_In density of population Egypt far surpassed of old all known regions of the inhabited world, and even in our own day is thought to be second to none_** ...
> ...*The total population, they say, was of old about seven million and the number has remained no less down to our day.*

Herodotus affirmed that 20,000 populous cities existed in Egypt during the reign of Amasis. Diodorus reported that there were 18,000 large villages and towns; and stated that, under Ptolemy Lagus, they amounted to more than 30,000. Josephus estimated the population during the reign of Vespasian, at 7.5 million in the valley of the Nile, in addition to the population of Alexandria, which was about 800,000.

Superficially, Ancient Egypt seems isolated and distinct from the rest of the world, isolated by the deserts that hem in the narrow valley of the Nile. Yet the Egyptians were in constant contact with other countries. Classical writers such as Plutarch, Herodotus, and Diodorus told how Ancient Egypt had peaceful colonies throughout the world. Diodorus of Sicily, *Book I,* [29, 5], states:

> *In general, the Egyptians say that their ancestors **sent forth numerous colonies to many parts of the inhabited world, by reason of the pre-eminence of their former kings and their excessive population**;*

Diodorus, *Book I,* [28, 1-4], tells of some Egyptian peaceful colonies that were reported to him in Asia and

Europe:

> . . . **_a great number of colonies were spread from Egypt over all the inhabited world_**. *To Babylon, for instance, colonists were led by Belus, who was held to be the son of Poseidon and Libya . . . . .*
>
> *. . . . . They say also that those who set forth with Danaus, likewise* **_from Egypt, settled what is practically the oldest city of Greece, Argos_**, *and that the nation of the Colchi in Pontus and that of the Jews, which lies between Arabia and Syria, were founded as colonies by certain emigrants from their country. . . . .*

By virtue of the eminence of the Egyptian colonists in Asia and Europe, they played a major role in the country of their new settlements. Diodorus, *Book I,* [28,6-7], discusses the significant role of the Egyptian colonists as rulers of these new colonies:

> *Moreover,* **_certain of the rulers of Athens were originally Egyptians_**, *they say. Petes,* [Called Peteus in Iliad 2. 552.] *for instance, the father of that Menestheus who took part in the expedition against Troy, having clearly been an Egyptian, later obtained citizenship at Athens and the kingship.*

Diodorus, *Book I,* [29, 1-5], also states:

> *In the same way, they continue,* **_Erechtheus also, who was by birth an Egyptian, became king of Athens_**. *. . . Erechtheus, through his racial connection with Egypt, brought from there to Athens a great supply of grain, and in return those who had enjoyed this aid made their benefactor king.* **_After he had secured the throne he instituted the initiatory rites of Demeter in Eleusis and established the mysteries, transferring their ritual from Egypt_**. *. . . .* **_And their sacrifices as well as their ancient ceremonies are observed by the Athenians in the same way as by the Egyptians_**. *. . . .*
>
> *. . . . . in charge of the more important religious ceremonies of Attica; the pastophoroi were those Egyptian priests*

who carried in processions small shrines of the gods. They are also the only Greeks who swear by Isis, and they closely resemble the Egyptians in both their appearance and manners.

Herodotus [500 BCE] stated that he came from Halicarnassus, a Dorian town. He clearly stated the connection between the Dorians and Egypt, in *The Histories, Book 6,* [Sections 53-55]:

*[53] . . . if one were to trace back, generation by generation, the lineage of Danaë the daughter of Acrisius, **the chiefs of the Dorians would turn out to be true-born Egyptians**.*

*[55] Enough has been said about all this. Others have explained how and through what achievements **they became kings over the Dorians, despite being Egyptians**, and so I will not go into that. I will record things that others have not picked up.*

Herodotus, in [55] above, stated that such a fact was common knowledge at his time [500 BCE] and needed no elaboration.

Other connections between the Dorians and Egyptians were made reference to several times by Herodotus, such as in *The Histories, Book 2,* [Section 91].

Lastly, it should be noted that Ancient Egyptian records (as well as records in other areas) have countless names of places in the world that are not recognizable in our present time. Names of places, ethnic groups, and countries keep on changing. The names of European countries just 100 years ago, for example, are unrecognizable to most present-day Europeans. Eventually, when these records disappear, a few centuries from now, the names of such countries will be totally unrecognizable.

In numerous locations in the world, there are references to tanned/brown-skinned people who provided enlightenment in regions throughout the world. They are described as:

1. of "oriental" origin and characteristics.
2. un-warlike people who settled peacefully among the local population.
3. highly advanced in metallurgy, and have manufactured large quantities of metal products.
4. highly organized and very talented in management.
5. highly advanced in dry weather farming, irrigation, etc.
6. experienced builders and artisans, and have built megalithic tombs, etc.
7. very religious people who had Animistic beliefs.

The above descriptions can only apply to one country—Egypt. By combining oral traditions, ethno-history, and archeological evidence (dating of major settlements, tombs, mining activities, ...etc.) of all the people in the Mediterranean Basin, one can see that the civilized newcomers could come only from the Nile Valley.

Immigration from Egypt occurred in several waves. It was closely related to events in Ancient Egypt. Some left in prosperous times to pursue business contacts. The majority left in stressful times.

For more information about the Egyptian immigration waves to sub-Sahara and interior Africa, read *Exiled Egyptians: The Heart of Africa*, by Moustafa Gadalla.

For more information about the Egyptian immigration waves to the Iberian Peninsula, read *Egyptian Romany: The Essence of Hispania*, by Moustafa Gadalla.

Foreign Visitors and Mercenaries

The Ancient (and *Baladi*) Egyptians were/are very friendly and hospitable. Practically all notable Greeks went to Egypt for education, as noted by Diodorus of Sicily, *Book I*, [96, 1-2]:

> But now that we have examined these matters, we must enumerate what Greeks, who have won fame for their wisdom and learning, visited Egypt in ancient times, in order to become acquainted with its customs and learning. . . .
> . . .Homer and Lycurgus of Sparta, and Plato, and that there also came Pythagoras of Samos and the mathematician Eudoxus [The famous astronomer, geographer, and mathematician of Cnidus, pupil of Plato.]. . .

Homer, more than 3,000 years ago, made references to Egypt that indicated his high esteem. In the *Odyssey*, for example, he refers to the good reputation Egypt enjoyed in the ancient world in Asia, Africa, and Europe. In other passages, Homer relates the events of the Greek King Manelaus' journey to Egypt, his arrival at Pharos Island (present-day Alexandria), and his 20-day sojourn in Egypt.

Herodotus visited Egypt during the 5th century BCE. He devoted the second volume of his *Histories* to accounts about Egypt. Herodotus spoke highly of Egypt, and stressed Greece's indebtedness to it. Herodotus stated that the Egyptians culturally and scientifically surpassed all other societies of the world. Herodotus began his account of Egypt in his *Histories*, by stating,

> Now, let me talk more of Egypt for it has a lot of admirable things and what one sees there is superior to any other country.

Crete was also indebted to the Egyptian civilization. The name Keftiu (present-day Crete) is found in Egyptian texts at least since the 12th century BCE. A passage in the *Odyssey* tells of King Odysseus' journey to Egypt from Crete. He tells how the northerly wind helped his nine boats sail easily for five days until they reached the Nile. According to Homer, the Egyptians were extremely hospitable to the king and his entourage, and he greatly enjoyed his seven year sojourn there.

Some foreigners were allowed to settle in Egypt as mercenaries and security guards. Egyptians are renowned worldwide as un-warlike—who can't (and won't) fight. The European presence in Egypt began when the Assyrians marched into Egypt and conquered the country as far as Ta-Apet (Thebes), during the 7th century BCE. In 654 BCE, the Egyptian Psammatichus, from Sais, hired Greek (Ionian and Carian) mercenaries to drive the Assyrians out of Egypt. The Egyptians allocated tracts of land as a base/garrison for the foreign troops, to use while they were fighting the enemy. Herodotus wrote about these facts in *The Histories, Book Two* [154]:

> *The docks and ruined houses of their first home, where they lived before Amasis moved them to Memphis, were still to be seen in my day.*

The temporary need for foreign mercenaries varied with the aggression of the foreigners. Therefore, when the Persians invaded Egypt, the Ancient Egyptians sought and hired mercenaries from the Greek islands to expel the Persians. Alexander the Great entered Egypt in 332 BCE, with the invitation and blessings of the Egyptians, to help them defeat and end the Persians' second period of occupation [343–332 BC] of Egypt. Western academicians declared Alexander as a "conquerer of

Egypt", even though he never claimed that or thought of himself as a ruler of Egypt.

To provide for security in Egypt, the Ancient Egyptians allowed several foreign garrisons to work to protect Egyptians. Therefore, the mercenary troops (Greeks, Macedonians, and Syrians) were giving tracts of land among the Egyptian population in towns near the capitals of the provinces. Without the western biases, one can view the "Ptolemaic" era as nothing more than the collective centers of military/security bases, consisting of foreign mercenaries that served the Ancient Egyptians and never ruled them. It was the Romans who used these foreign bases to govern the Egyptian population and to collect taxes. That led the Romans to reinforce foreign settlements, by bringing in more foreigners, mostly Jews and Syrians.

Western academia has turned these foreigners who are (uneducated) mercenaries and their settlements/garrisons into "Hellenic", enlightened centers in Egypt. Security guards, no matter what their skin color, are not intellectual geniuses.

Western academia is proud of their heritage of conquering and colonizing countries throughout the world. All conquerors picture themselves as the bringers of light and a new civilization to the people they conquer. It is therefore that western academia identifies with all other invaders as being superior to their conquered peoples. The invaders (Ptolemies, Romans, Arabs, or Europeans) actually came to profit and to dominate, not to "civilize". They are actually the uncivilized who, in course, adopted some of the civilized aspects of the Egyptians. To add insult to injury, the invaders accredited themselves with the knowledge they stole from the Egyptians. As a result, numerous civilized aspects in Egypt were arbitrarily and generously accredited to the invaders. When invaders (Byzantines, Arabs, etc) adopt/accept the cultural aspects of their conquered people (such as the Egyptians), the credit cannot be reversed to the invaders—especially that in their homeland, these foreign invaders never had such "talents".

Invaders, by their nature, are nomadic people. Ibn Khaldun—himself a proud nomad—testifies in his writings to the nature of the nomad and how it is contrary to the nature of civilization. Ibn Khaldun [1332–1406], in of his monumental *Universal History* [ch. 5, sect. 15], admits that civilized features/skills/crafts don't come out of thin air.

> *The mind does not cease transforming all kinds of (arts and crafts), including the composite ones, from potentiality into actuality through the gradual discovery of one thing after the other, until they are perfect.* **This is achieved in the course of time and of generations. Things are not transformed from potentiality into actuality in one stroke, especially technical matters**. *Consequently, a certain amount of time is unavoidable. . . .*

3

The Most Religious

Egyptian Cosmology and Allegories

As a result of the present-day assembly line "education" system, many are incapable of understanding the
Ancient Egyptian texts and thoughts. To overcome such
mental obstacles, it is therefore important to recognize
the Ancient Egyptian mode of expression in the various
subjects of their culture—such as religion.

The cosmological knowledge of Ancient Egypt was
expressed in story form, which is a superior means for
expressing both physical and metaphysical concepts. Well
crafted allegories are the only way to explain the deepest
truths about God, creation, life, the soul, our place in the
universe, and our struggle to evolve to higher levels of
insight and understanding.

Allegories are an intentionally chosen means for com-
municating knowledge. Allegories dramatize cosmic laws,
principles, processes, relationships and functions, and
express them in an easy to understand way. Once the
inner meanings of the allegories have been revealed, they
become marvels of simultaneous scientific and philosophical completeness and conciseness. The more they are studied, the richer they become. The 'inner dimension' of the

teachings embedded into each story are capable of revealing several layers of knowledge, according to the stage of development of the listener. The "secrets" are revealed as one evolves higher. The higher we get, the more we see. It is always there.

Any good writer or lecturer knows that stories are the best means for explaining the behavior of things, because the relationships of parts to each other, and to the whole, are better maintained by the mind. The Egyptian sages transformed common factual nouns and adjectives (indicators of qualities) into proper but conceptual nouns. These were, in addition, personified so that they could be woven into narratives.

The Egyptians did not believe their allegories to be historical facts. They believed *IN* them, in the sense that they believed in the truth behind the stories.

The Ancient Egyptians had numerous allegories, such as the Ausar/Auset/Heru (Osiris/Isis/Horus) allegory [see Appendix].

Monotheism & Polytheism

When we ask, *"Who is God?"*, we are really asking, *"What is God?"*. The mere *name* or noun does not tell us anything. One can only define "God" through the multitude of "His" attributes / qualities / powers / actions. To know "God" is to know the numerous qualities of "God". The more we learn of these qualities (known as neteru), the closer we are getting to our divine origin.

Far from being a primitive, polytheistic form, this is the highest expression of monotheistic mysticism.

The Egyptians regarded the universe as a conscious act of creation by the One Great God. The fundamental doctrine was the unity of the Deity. <u>This One God was never represented</u>. It is the functions and attributes of his domain that were represented. Once a reference was made to his functions/attributes, he became a distinguishable agent, reflecting this particular function/attribute, and its influence on the world. His various functions and attributes as the Creator, Healer, and the like, were called the **neteru** (singular: **neter** in the masculine form and **netert** in the feminine form). As such, an Egyptian **neter/netert** was not a *god/goddess* but the representation of a function/attribute of the One God.

The **neteru**, who were called *'gods'* by some, were endorsed and incorporated into Christianity under a new name, *'angels'*.

Ancient Egyptian depiction of *neteru* (angels)

Some examples of the Ancient Egyptian **neteru** (gods) are:

Amen/Amun/Amon – represents the hidden or occult force underlying creation. **Amen** represents the spirit that animates the universe with all its constituents.
In the three religions (Judaism, Christianity, and Islam) whenever the faithful pray, regardless of language, they always end their prayer by saying *Amen*. The "name", **Amen**, means *the Hidden One*—the invisible God of the Ancient Egyptians.

Ra (Re) – represents the primeval, cosmic, creative force. His hidden name is **Amen**, which means *secret*. All **neteru** (gods) who took part in the creation process are aspects of **Ra**. Therefore, **Ra** is often linked with other **neteru**, such as **Atum-Ra, Ra-Harakhte**, etc.

Tehuti (Thoth, Hermes, Mercury) – represents the Divine
aspects of wisdom and intellect. It was Tehuti (Thoth)
who uttered the words that created the world, as
commanded by Ra. He is represented as the messen-
ger of the neteru (gods/goddesses), of writing, language, and knowledge.

Ausar (Osiris) – represents the principle that makes life
come from apparent death. As such, Ausar symbolizes the power of renewal. Ausar represents the process, growth, and the underlying cyclical aspects of
the universe.

The Ancient Egyptians utilized pictorial symbols to
represent the divine attributes and actions. As the saying goes, *a picture is worth a thousand words.* In Egyptian symbolism, the precise role of the neteru (gods/god-
desses) are revealed in many ways: by dress, headdress,
crown, feather, animal, plant, color, position, size, ges-
ture, sacred object (e.g., flail, scepter, staff, ankh), etc. A
chosen symbol represents that function or principle, on
all levels simultaneously—from the simplest, most obvious physical manifestation of that function to the most
abstract and metaphysical. This symbolic language represents a wealth of physical, physiological, psychological
and spiritual data in the presented symbols.

A common example is how some
figures are shown with two right/left
hands. An active right hand symbolizes
giving. An active left hand signifies re-
ceiving. When the symbolic role of the
person is wholly active, he is shown
with two right hands. When his role is
wholly passive, he has two left hands.

To learn more about 88 Ancient Egyptian neteru, read *Egyptian Divinities: The All Who Are THE ONE,* by M. Gadalla.

Animal Symbolism

For the Ancient Egyptians, each animal/bird symbolizes and embodies certain divine functions and principles, in a particularly pure and striking fashion. As such, the animal or animal-headed **neteru** (gods/goddesses) are  symbolic expressions of a deep spiritual understanding. When a total animal is depicted in Ancient Egypt, it represents a particular function/attribute in its purest form. When an animal-headed figure is depicted, it conveys that particular function/attribute in the human being. The two forms of **Anbu** (Anubis), in the two illustrations shown here, clearly distinguish these two aspects.

The dog embodies the essence of spiritual guidance. The dog/jackal is known for its reliable homing instinct, day or night. The dog is very useful in searches, and is the animal of choice to guide the blind. As such, it is an excellent choice for guiding the soul of the deceased through the regions of the Duat.

The metaphysical role of **Anbu** (Anubis) the dog is reflected in his diet. The dog/jackal feasts on carrion, turning it into beneficial nourishment. In other words, **Anbu** represents the capacity to turn waste into useful food for the body (and soul)—as in the alchemical way—transforming lead into gold.

Several examples of animal symbolism can be found in *Egyptian Divinities: The All Who Are THE ONE*, by Moustafa Gadalla.

Creation of the Universe

For the deeply religious people of Egypt, the creation of the universe was not an accidental event that just happened. It was an orderly event that was pre-planned and executed according to an orderly Divine Law that governs the physical and metaphysical worlds. So, we read in the *Book of Knowing the Creations of Ra and Overcoming Apep* (Apophis), known as the *Bremner-Rhind Papyrus*:

> I conceived the Divine Plan of Law or Order (Maa) to make all forms. I was alone.

Creation is the sorting out (giving definition to / bringing order to) of all the chaos (the undifferentiated energy/matter and consciousness) of the primeval state. All of the Ancient Egyptian accounts of creation exhibited this with well-defined, clearly demarcated stages. It should be noted, that the Ancient Egyptian creation process is complete, logical, orderly, and conforms with later scientific findings in the western world.

Every Egyptian creation text begins with the same basic belief that before the beginning of things, there was a liquidy *primeval abyss*—everywhere, dark, endless, and without boundaries or directions. Egyptians called this cosmic ocean/watery chaos, Nu/Ny/Nun—the unpolarized state of matter.

The Ancient Egyptian understanding of the pre-creation state of the universe was discovered, in recent times, by western scientists. Their clue came from when they noticed that the galaxies are all moving away from us, and that a galaxy that is five times farther away than another is going five times as fast; ten times farther, ten times as fast, and so on. This led to the conclusion that there must have been a time in the past when all the matter of the universe was packed tightly together, to an infinite density. This matter is described by scientists as a very stiff *neutron soup*, where there are neither electrons nor protons, with only neutrons forming one huge extremely dense nucleus.

In addition to the chaotic pre-creation state, the spirit of God was present, independent of the chaotic pre-creation state of the universe. All Ancient Egyptian creation texts begin with the Self-Begotten and Self-Existent, who lived alone in a primeval watery mass. In the Egyptian papyrus known as the *Leiden Papyrus*, the neter (god), Amen/Amon/Amun (which means *hidden*), represents the hidden or occult force underlying creation. He is the *Breath of Life*. Even though he is indefinable himself, he is the reason why the universe can be defined.

The orderly creation process is summarized in the following principal stages:

1. The first act of creation was the Divine Utterance, as per a passage in the Egyptian *Book of the Coming Forth by Day* (incorrectly known as the *Book of the Dead*)—the oldest written text in the world,

> I am the Eternal, I am Ra (Re)... I am that which created the Word ... I am the Word ...

The Egyptian texts state that the created universe came out of the mouth (of Ra), and the mouth is the symbol of Unity—the One—in hieroglyphs. The creation process, i.e. transformation (differentiation), is achieved through sound (the Word) as the prime mover of the inert energy of the chaotic state of the pre-creation matter.

That *the word* (sound variations) *is mightier than the sword*, has been accepted by modern science, which recognizes that there are various types of sound waves. We know that infrasound waves can't be detected by our ears, but they can shake buildings and destroy body organs. Also, the ultrasound waves cannot be detected by our ears, but doctors use this power as a kind of knifeless scalpel in microsurgery. We also know that a soprano singer can shatter glass with her voice.

Egyptian creation texts repeatedly stress the belief of creation by the Word. We find that in the *Book of the Divine Cow* (found in the shrines of Twt/Tut-Ankh-Amen), Ra (Re) creates the heavens and its hosts merely by pronouncing particular words whose sound alone evokes the names of things—and these things then appear at His bidding. As its name is pronounced, so the thing comes into being. For the name is a reality, the thing itself.

The *word* (any word) is scientifically a vibrational complex element, which is a wave phenomenon, characterized by movement of variable frequency and intensity. Each soundwave frequency has its own geometrical corresponding form. Modern science has confirmed a direct relationship between wave frequency and form. Patterns and shapes of some materials occur only at specific frequencies.

The Big Bang that occurred about 15 billion years ago came as a result of the building up of the condensed energy in Nun—*the neutron soup*, until it finally exploded and expanded outward. The explosion was loud enough to be called the *Big Bang*. The Ancient Egyptian texts likewise repeatedly stressed that sound was the cause of creation.

2. The Ancient Egyptian concept of the universe is like a box. The first thing the Divine creates is a kind of bubble in what is otherwise an infinite liquidy ocean. The sky is the skin of the infinite ocean, which contains what we call the atmosphere, which was caused by two cosmic polar forces.

The world, as we know it, is held together by a law that is based on the balanced dual nature of all things. The dual principle in the creation state was expressed in the pair of Shu and Tefnut. Both Shu and Tefnut mean *atmosphere*. The pair of husband (Shu) and wife (Tefnut) is the characteristic Egyptian way of expressing duality and polarity. The two balanced complimentary forces are:

Tefnut   Shu

a.   Shu, represented by fire, air, and heat, corresponds to the quality of expansiveness, rising, centrifugal forces, positive, masculine, outgoing, etc.

b.   Tefnut, represented by moisture, corresponds to contraction, downward movement, centripetal forces, negative, feminine, receptive, inner, etc.

The above Ancient Egyptian concept concurs with modern scientists', who tell us that the galaxies are subjected now to mainly two opposing forces:

a.   The *expulsion forces*, which cause all galaxies to move away from us, resulting from the effect of the *Big Bang*; and

b.   The *gravitational/contractional forces*, which pull the galaxies together.

We are still under the effect of the Big Bang, where the expulsion forces cause the galaxies to move away from us—like an expanding bubble.

The outer limits of the expanding bubble are the firmament—the sky that is viewed poetically as a solid arch or vault—depicted in Ancient Egypt as Nut—a star-studded woman, arched over the heavens, in the act of swallowing the evening sun and giving birth to the morning sun.

3. After the creation of the atmosphere, came the creation of the biosphere, which is essential to begin life on earth. In the Ancient Egyptian orderly process, once the atmosphere was created, it was possible for Shu (heat) and Tefnut (moisture) to beget Geb (earth) and Nut (sky), who by virtue of their separation, caused the space in which life could take place on earth. The Egyptian text in the Bremner-Rhind Papyrus describes the new life on earth:

I came forth from among the roots and I created all creeping things, and all that exists among them.

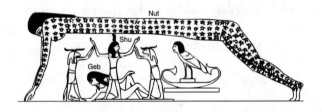

It is therefore that the commonly accepted conception of the universe is represented [shown above] as a figure of Shu, standing and supporting with his hands, the outstretched body of Nut (studded with the planets, stars, sun, moon, etc), with Geb lying at his feet. These neteru represent the characteristic elements of creation where Earth emerged out of chaos.

Once land and sustenance were created, humanity was born.

The Image of God

It is commonly recognized by all theo-
logical and philosophical schools of
thought that the human being is made in
the image of God, i.e. a miniature universe; and that to understand the universe is to understand oneself, and vice
versa.

Yet no culture has ever practiced the above principle
like the Ancient Egyptians. Central to their complete understanding of the universe was the knowledge that man
was made in the image of God, and as such, man represented the image of all creation. Accordingly, Egyptian
symbolism has always related to man. Here are two examples:

1. Man, to the Ancient Egyptians, was the embodiment
    of the laws of creation. As such, the physiological
    functions and processes of the various parts of the
    body were seen as manifestations of cosmic functions.
    The limbs and organs had a metaphysical function,
    in addition to their physical purpose. The parts of
    the body were consecrated to one of the neteru (di-
    vine principles), which appeared in the Egyptian
    records throughout its recovered history, such as from
    the *Papyrus of Ani*, [pl. 32, item 42]:

    ... there is no member of mine devoid of a neter(god)...

2. Egyptians divided the sky into 36 sectors of 10 de-
    grees each, called decans. Ausar (Osiris) likewise has
    36 forms. Like the sky, the human body, in Ancient
    Egyptian medicine, was also divided into 36 sectors,

and each came under the influence of a certain **neter/ netert** (god/goddess), each controlled by one of the 36 parts of the Egyptian zodiac. The Egyptian zodiac consists of 12 months; each month is divided into three segments of 10 days (like decans).

As such, the complicated scientific and philosophical information was reduced in Ancient Egypt to events—in human images and terms.

Thus, Egyptian symbolism and all measures were therefore simultaneously scaled to man, to the earth, to the solar system, and ultimately to the universe.

Go Your Own Way (Ma-at)

According to the Egyptian philosophy, though all creation is spiritual in origin, man is born mortal but contains within himself the seed of the divine. His purpose in this life is to nourish that seed, and his reward, if successful, is eternal life, where he will reunite with his divine origin. Nourishing plants in the soil is analogous to nourishing the spirit on earth by doing good deeds.

Man comes into the world with the higher divine faculties, which are the essence of his/her salvation, in an unawakened state. The way of the Egyptian religion is, therefore, a system of practices aimed at awakening the dormant higher faculties.

The faculty awakening emphasis of the Egyptian religion cannot be over stressed. Moral behavior, for example, does not come about from merely learning certain values, but is gained by both the mind and acquired by experience. Inner purification must be completed by practicing good social behavior daily in life. Every action impresses itself upon the heart. The inward being of a person is really the reflection of his deeds and actions. Doing good deeds thus establishes good inner qualities; the virtues impressed upon the heart in turn govern the actions of the limbs. As each act, thought, and deed makes an image on the heart, it becomes an attribute of the person. This maturation of the soul through acquired attributes leads to progressive mystical visions and the ultimate unification with the Divine.

The Ancient Egyptian wisdom has always laid great emphasis on the cultivation of ethical behavior and service to society. The Egyptian traditions and practices emphasize character building, good behavior, family values, desirability and benefits of marriage, harmonic relationships, societal duties, work ethics, accountability, etc.

The Ancient Egyptian religion is not a matter of creed and dogma, but rather of a personal charter. Each one of us is an individual. The Egyptian model recognizes the uniqueness of each individual, and as such recognizes that the Paths to God are as numerous as the number of seekers. The ways to God are like streams—they all flow to one source. All Egyptian thinking is based on this principle—*variations on a theme*. The Ancient Egyptians implemented their beliefs in the unique individuality of each person in all their texts. There were never two identical transformational (funerary) or medical (so-called "magical") texts for any two individuals.

One must live his/her own life, and each one of us must go his/her own way, guided by **Ma-at**. The concept of **Ma-at** has permeated all Egyptian writings, from the earliest times and throughout Egyptian history. It is the concept by which not only men, but also the **neteru** (gods) themselves were governed. **Ma-at** is not easily translated or defined by one word. Basically, we might say that it means *that which, of right, should be; that which is according to the proper order and harmony of the cosmos and of neteru and men, who are part of it.*

Ma-at

Ma-at, *The Way*, encompasses the virtues, goals, and duties that define the acceptable, if not ideal, social interaction and personal behavior.

A summary of the Egyptian concept of righteousness can be found in what is popularly known as the *Negative Confessions* [as discussed later in this chapter]. A more detailed picture of a righteous man and the expected conduct and the ideas of responsibility and retribution can be obtained from the walls of tomb-chapels and in several literary compositions that are usually termed as *wisdom texts* of systematic instructions, composed of maxims and precepts. Among them are the 30 chapters of the *Teaching of Amenemope* (Amenhotep III), which contain many wisdom texts that were later adopted in the Old Testament's *Book of Proverbs.*

Numerous verbal parallels occur between this Egyptian text and the Bible, such as the opening lines of the first chapter:

> Give your ears, listen to the words that are spoken, give your mind to interpreting them. It is profitable to put them in your heart.

There were additional practical wisdom texts of systematic instructions, also composed of maxims and precepts.

Some of the wisdom proverbs, as collected from survived Egyptian papyri include:

- Don't be proud of earthly goods or riches, for they come
  to you from God without your help.
- Don't repeat slanders.
- Deliver messages accurately.
- Be content.
- Be industrious, an idle man is not honorable.
- Do not enter uninvited into the house of another.
- Do not look around in the house of another. If you see
  anything, be silent about it, and don't relate it to oth-
  ers.
- Speak not too much, for men are deaf to the man of
  many words.
- Guard your speech, for "a man's ruin lies in his tongue".
- Do not overeat.
- Don't eat bread while another person is present unless
  you share the bread with him.
- He who is rich this year, may become a pauper next year.
- Be respectful, and do not sit down while another stands
  who is older than you, or who holds a higher office than
  yours.

The progression along the spiritual Path is acquired
through striving, and is a matter of conscious disciplined
action. Each new/raised consciousness is equivalent to a
new awakening. The levels of consciousness are referred
to as *death—rebirth*. Such thinking has pervaded Ancient
(and present-day) Egypt, where *birth and rebirth* are a
constant theme. The word *death* is employed in a figurative sense. The theme that man must *"die before he dies"*
or that he must be *"born again"* in his present life is taken
symbolically, or is commemorated by a ritual. In this,
the candidate has to pass through certain specific experiences (technically termed *"deaths"*). A good example is
baptism, which was the main objective at Easter, after
Lent—representing death of the old self by immersion
into water, and the rising of the new/renewed self by re-
surfacing out of the water.

Judgment Day

In a book of instructions, an Egyptian king advised his son to attain the highest qualities, because upon his death, he would see his whole lifetime in a single instant, and his performance on earth would be reviewed and evaluated by the judges. Even as far back as the period of the 6th Dynasty [2323 BCE], we find the idea that heaven was reserved for those who had performed their duty to man and to the Divine Powers while on earth. No exceptions were made—to a king or anyone else. Accordingly, in the text of King Unas we read:

> Unas hath not been spoken against on earth before men, he hath not been accused of sin in heaven before the neteru (gods).

The text tells us that the Pharaoh Unas (2323 BCE) was admitted to Heaven after his moral worthiness—both towards his fellow man and to God—was satisfied.

Ancient Egyptians expressed their metaphysical beliefs in a story form, like a sacred drama or a *mystery play*. The following are the Egyptians' symbolic representations of the process of the Judgment Day.

The soul of the deceased is led to the Hall of Judgment of the Double-Ma-at. She is "double" because the scale balances only when there is an equality of opposing forces. Ma-at's symbol is the ostrich feather, representing judgment or truth. Her feather is customarily mounted on the scales.

The seated Ausar (Osiris) presides in the Hall of Justice. The jury consists of 42 judges. Each judge has a specific jurisdiction over a specific sin or fault.

1 - Ma-at
2 - Anbu (Anubis)
3 - Amam (Ammit)
4 - Tehuti (Thoth)

5 - The deceased
6 - Heru (Horus)
7 - Heru's Disciples
8 - Ausar (Osiris)
9 - 42 Judges/Assessors

The spirit of the deceased denies committing each sin/fault before its assigned judge, by reciting the 42 Negative Confessions, in chapter CXXV of *The Book of the Coming Forth by Light/Day* (incorrectly known as *The Book of the Dead*). Here is a translation of some of them.

I have not done violence
I have not committed theft
I have not slain man or woman
I have not acted deceitfully
I have not uttered falsehood
I have not uttered evil words
I have not defiled the wife of a man
I have not been a man of anger
I have not judged hastily
I have not polluted the water

The ibis-headed Tehuti (Thoth), scribe of the neteru, records the verdict as Anbu (Anubis) weighs the heart against the feather of truth. The heart is a metaphor for conscience.

The outcome of the judgment will determine the fate of the person. The outcome is either:

a. If the pans are not balanced, the heart (symbol of conscience) will be eaten by **Amam** (Ammit)—a protean crossbreed.

    The unperfected soul will be reborn again (reincarnated) in a new physical vehicle (body), in order to provide the soul an opportunity for further development on earth. This cycle of life/death/renewal continues until the soul is perfected, by fulfilling the *42 Negative Confessions*, during his life on earth.

b. If the two pans are perfectly balanced, **Ausar** (Osiris) gives favorable judgment, and gives his final **Maa-Kheru** (*True of Voice*). The perfected soul will go through the process of transformation and the subsequent rebirth. Beings who are more spiritually aware will reside on a higher level, and less evolved souls will reside on a lower level.

Ancient Egyptian transformational (funerary) texts show that the resurrected pure soul, justified and regenerated, attains a place in the retinue of the **neteru** (gods/goddesses)—the cosmic forces—and eventually takes part in the unceasing round of activity that permits a continued existence of the universe.

The role of the successful soul is described in the Ancient Egyptian writing,
> becomes a star and joins the company of Ra, and sails with him across the sky in his boat of millions of years.

[For more detailed information about the Egyptian religions, read *Egyptian Cosmology: The Animated Universe*, *Egyptian Divinities: The All Who Are THE ONE*, and *Egyptian Mystics: Seekers of The Way*, all by Moustafa Gadalla.]

The Spread of the Egyptian Religion

The Ancient Egyptian neteru were adopted as deities throughout the Mediterranean Basin and beyond. For example, the bas-reliefs, coins, and other antiquities that have been found in Thessaly, Epirus, Megara, Corinth, Argos, Malta, and many other places, portray Ancient Egyptian neteru. Herodotus, in the *Histories, Book 2* [2-8], wrote:

> The names of nearly all the gods came to Greece from Egypt.

This makes sense once we recognize that replacing letters (sound shift) is a common phenomenon, world-wide. From the earliest days of comparative philology, it was noticed that the sounds of related languages corresponded in apparently systematic ways. As an example of the phenomenon of sound shift, a person's name can still be recognized in vastly different sounds, such as *Santiago / San Diego / San Jacob* and *Saint James. Jacob / Jack / Jaques / James*, are one and the same name, which exemplifies the phenomenon of sound shift.

It should be noted that what we commonly consider names of deities are actually the "attributes (names)" of such deities. The real names of the deities (gods, goddesses) were kept secret. The real name was/is imbued with magical powers and properties. To know and pronounce the real name of a neter/netert (god/goddess) is to exercise power over it. To guard the cosmic power of the deity, the Ancient Egyptians (and later others throughout the Mediterranean Basin and beyond) often used "*names*" with religious connotations. Baal simply means *Lord* or *ruler*, and so we hear of the Baal or the Baalat (*Lady*) of such-and-such a city. Similarly, a deity will be called Melek, meaning *King*. So too Adon, which means *Lord* or *Master*. Melqart meant *King of the City*. Other "names" meaning *favored by the gods* or *granted by the gods* were translated to Latin as *Fortunatus, Felix, Donatus, Concessus*, and so on.

To affirm Herodotus' reports of the Greek adoption of Egyptian deities, archeological evidence in the 4th century BCE shows that Athens was basically a center of the Egyptian religion, and shrines to Auset (Isis), both public and private, were erected in many parts of Greece at that period.

In Magna Graecia, the monuments found in Catania in Sicily show that this city was a center of the worship of Egyptian deities. Southern Italy contained many temples of Auset (Isis), and the remains of statues, etc, found in Reggio, Puteoli, Pompeii, and Herculaneum prove that the worship of Egyptian deities must have been common.

The Ancient Egyptian religious practices were mirrored in Greece, for example, as confirmed by the Greek father of history, Herodotus in the *Histories, Book 2,* [107]:

It was the Egyptians too who originated, and taught the Greeks to use ceremonial meetings, processions, and processional offerings*: a fact that can be inferred from the obvious antiquity of such ceremonies in Egypt, compared with Greece, where they have been only recently introduced. The Egyptians meet in solemn assembly not once a year only, but on a number of occasions.*

Affirming Herodotus' statement, Plutarch states in *Moralia, Isis and Osiris,* [378-9, 69],

Among the Greeks also many things are done which are similar to the Egyptian ceremonies in the shrines of Isis, and they do them at about the same time.

In Rome, in the 1st century BCE, Auset (Isis)was regarded as the principal **netert** (goddess) of the city. Great buildings and temples were set up in her honor, filled with Egyptian objects, obelisks, altars, statues, etc, which were brought from Egypt in order to make the shrines of **Auset** (Isis) resemble those of her native country. Priestesses, who professed to be well acquainted with the "mysteries" of **Auset**, dwelt in or near these temples, and assisted in performing services and ceremonies in which large congregations participated. From Rome, the reverence for **Auset** naturally spread to the provinces and beyond.

In the Ancient Egyptian cosmology, **Auset** represents the power responsible for the creation of all living creatures. Accordingly, Ancient Egyptians called her *Auset (Isis) with the 10,000 Names/Attributes*. Plutarch took note of that and wrote in his *Moralia Vol V*,

> *Isis is, in fact, the female principle of Nature, and is receptive of every form of generation, in accord with which she is called by Plato the gentle nurse and the all-receptive, and by most people* **has been called by countless names***, since, because of the force of Reason. she turns herself to this thing or that and is receptive of all manner of shapes and forms.*

The "many names" of **Auset** (Isis) were adopted throughout Greece and in Italy, and beyond. Thus the Greeks and Romans identified her frequently as Selene, Demeter, Ceres, and with several goddesses of crops and of the harvest in general. She was also regarded as an Earth-goddess, and as such was the mother of all fertility and abundance. Some of her attributes caused her to be identified as Aphrodite, Juno, Nemesis, Fortuna, and Panthea.

The Ancient Egyptian religious practices associated with **Auset** (Isis) and **Ausar** (Osiris) had made major strides in Italy. In Campania, an inscription, dated at 105 BCE, was found in a temple of the Ancient Egyptian

Sarapis (Sar-Apis), at Puteoli, which is evidence that the temple existed prior to that date. About 80 BCE (in the time of Sulla), a College of the Servants of Auset, or Pastophori, was founded in Rome, and a temple was built in the city. In 44 BCE, a temple was built in Rome to honor Auset (Isis) and Ausar (Osiris), and a few decades later, the festival of these Egyptian deities was recognized in the public calendar.

The main festival in Italy corresponded exactly to the Ancient Egyptian festival that commemorated the murder of Ausar (Osiris) and the finding of his body by Auset (Isis). As in Ancient Egypt, it opened in November with the singing of dirges and heartbreaking lamentations for the death of Ausar, which were, no doubt, based upon the compositions that were sung in Egypt about the same time. Then, on the second day, scenes that represented the frantic grief and anxiety of those who went about searching for the body of Ausar were enacted. On the third day Auset found the body of her husband, and there was great rejoicing in the temple. Grief gave place to gladness and tears to laughter, musicians of all kinds assembled and played their instruments, and men and women danced, and everyone celebrated.

The Ancient Egyptian religious practices, as they relate to the model story of Auset and Ausar, spread all over southern Europe, and into many parts of North Africa, and it continued to be a religious power in these regions until the close of the 4th century CE. These Ancient Egyptian ideas and beliefs survived in Christianity, whereby Mary the Virgin assumed the attributes of Auset the Everlasting Mother, and the Babe Jesus assumed those of Heru (Horus).

[For more information about the Ancient Egyptian roots of Christianity, see Appendix at end of this book and the book, *Ancient Egyptian Roots of Christianity*, by M. Gadalla.]

4

The Social/Political Order

Matrilineal/Matriarchal Society

What we consider to be a "political" structure, was for the Ancient Egyptians a natural aspect of their social structure. In order to achieve perfect universal harmony, the social structure must mirror the same orderly hierarchy of the created universe. Human survival and success require that the same orderly structure be maintained. *As above so below* is the only way to achieve order and harmony. As a result, the Ancient Egyptians (and *Baladi*) adopted the matrilineal/matriarchal system, as the social manifestation of planetary laws.

In the Ancient Egyptian model story [see Appendix], Auset (Isis) represents the sun, and her husband Ausar (Osiris) represents the moon. The light of the moon (Ausar—Pharaoh) is a reflection of the light of the sun (Auset—Queen). The Ancient Egyptian social/political system complies with the relationship between the sun (female) and the moon (male). As a result, this social/political law was reflected in the Egyptian allegory of Ausar, who became the first Pharaoh of Egypt as a result of his marrying Auset. Auset means *seat*, i.e. *authority*, and is the principle of legitimacy—the actual physical throne, as depicted in the Ancient Egyptian symbolism.

On earth, the female is the source of energy—the sun. The matrilineal/matriarchal system follows the planetary laws.

Throughout Egyptian history, it was the queen who transmitted the solar blood. The queen was the true sovereign, keeper of the royalty, and guardian of the purity of the lineage. Egyptian kings claimed a right to the throne through marriage to the eldest Egyptian princess. By marriage, she transmitted the crown to her husband, he only acted as her executive agent.

The pharaohs, as well as the leaders of smaller localities, adhered to this matriarchal system. If the pharaoh/leader had no daughters, a dynasty ended and a new dynasty began, with a new revered maiden woman as a new seed for a new dynasty.

Since women were the legal heirs to the throne, they played an important part in the affairs of state, performing as a kind of power broker. The queens of Egypt wielded exceptional influence, as advisors to the pharaohs.

Surviving records from the Middle Kingdom (2040–1783 BCE) show that the nomes (provinces) of Egypt passed from one family to another through heiresses; thus he who married the heiress would govern the province.

The matrilineal practices in Egypt also applied to the whole society, as evident from the funerary stelae of all kinds of people throughout the known recorded history of Egypt, where it is the usual custom to trace the descent of the deceased on the mother's side, and not on that of the father. The person's mother is specified, but not the father, or if he is mentioned, it is only incidentally. This tradition is still enduring secretly (because it is contrary to Islam) among the *Baladi* Egyptians.

The relationship between the husband and wife is shown symbolically in the Ancient Egyptian symbol for the wife (**Auset**) being the throne—the source of legitimacy. The husband (**Ausar**) is the overseer (the eye) that sits below the throne. It never escaped the Egyptians to notice that on the human face, the eye is located below the eyebrow. An Egyptian proverb states, *"The eye never overtops the eyebrow"*, stating the hierarchical order in the family and the society as a whole.

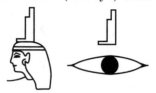

Auset (Isis)   Ausar (Osiris)
(Seat on top) (Seat & Eye)

In the **Ausar** (Osiris) allegorical folktale, **Auset** (Isis) and **Ausar**, the "sister" and "brother" were married. The relationship between **Auset** and **Ausar** was purely an allegorical fable. Some historians, such as the Sicilian Diodorus, reported that marriages between "brothers" and "sisters" were owing to and inspired by the **Auset/Ausar** allegory! This misunderstanding may have come as the result of the fact that the Ancient Egyptian word for brother and husband is the same word, *sn*, as well as the word for sister and wife, *sn.t*. These words are derivatives of the verbal stem *sni*, which has the meaning *to embrace, to kiss*. Used in context, they would represent *person whom one usually embraces*, *person whom one is familiar with*. Therefore, we must be cautious when encountering *sn* and *sn.t* in certain texts, and we should not draw too many conclusions about incest and the like.

Many "Egyptologists" (who are almost all Europeans or their descendants) don't recognize this fact, and as a result, confused the chronology and the relationships between individuals in Ancient Egypt (and the biblical characters as well). When an uninformed "scholar" gets stuck in his chronology, s/he does not hesitate to paint the Egyptian relationship as "incest".

The Matrilocal Communities

The matrilineal system was the basis of the social/political organization in Ancient Egypt. As a result, Ancient (and *Baladi*) Egyptians, married couples live with the wife's family. Consequently, there is a distinct tendency toward matrilocal residence among extended families. The very same system is to be found in the pueblo communities of Spain.

Living with the bride's parents is the preferred rule. Even when the young woman leaves the maternal hearth, she settles nearby in a pattern that might be called matrivicinal. That is, the newlyweds try to move into a house next to or nearby the mother of the bride, so the women are rarely separated. Additionally, the children of the family are brought up close to their maternal uncles. A common Egyptian proverb affirms this special relationship between the children and their maternal uncles: *"The maternal uncle is (like) a father."*

A matrilocal community generally consists of a number of extended matrilineal families who share the same female line, living in compounds clustered within a narrow area, or scattered about in groups. Each family has a specialty in which it excels, and between the neighboring family lineages, the different tasks are harmoniously divided. Each matrilocal community has its own religious center (shrine), to honor the founding ancestors of their community.

Autonomous food-producing matrilocal communities form a basic sociopolitical format varying from a few families (25-50 people), to up to several thousand. Each family has a leader, or family head, who is responsible for the material and spiritual welfare of every member. He also maintains law, order, justice, and harmony. A num-

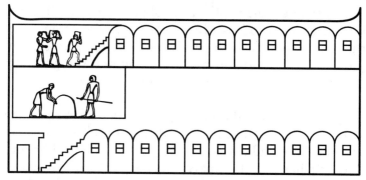

Communal grain silos, with vaulted roofs. Beni Hassan.

ber of sub-heads are also selected from each household of the community. The elders of each family lineage settle internal disputes among members of their lineages.

In some regions where people have been attacked by foreigners, which created refugees and/or forced settlements by foreigners, the village community may commonly consist of families of totally different ethnic stock. When not all members of a village share blood ties, the head of the lineage and other elders still lead the community.

The elders, representing the established lineages of the community, form a council (legislative body), which elects a headman from the founder lineage of the community. This eldership assists the headman in the governance of the community. The council of elders serves as a court, helps the headman allocate access to resources (such as land, water rights, etc), carries out rituals, organizes public works, such as co-op facilities and granaries to store products, etc.

The head of the matrilocal community (like the model Ausar) is more of an "overseer" than a ruler. His legitimacy to rule over his people, was derived from following the matrilineal principles, as explained earlier. His main function was/is to link (directly and/or with other spiritual intermediaries) the community ritually to the authority of the local spirits of the land and the ghosts of past leaders, in the context explained below.

The Ancient and *Baladi* Egyptian beliefs in Animism were also reflected in their traditional relationships between people and earth. The Egyptians believed/believe that land had no value apart from people, and, conversely, that people could not exist without land. As such, all living people must recognize, respect, and coexist with the supernatural residents of the land. The spirits of a place (trees, rocks, rivers, animals, and objects) were identified and placated by the original founders, who arrived and inhabited the land at an earlier time.

The rights of a group, defined by common genealogical descent, were linked to a particular place and the settlements within it, not through "ownership", but because of their pact with the primordial spirits of the land/ site. The spirits, both of family and place, demanded loyalty to communal virtues and to the authority of the elders in maintaining ancient beliefs and practices.

It is therefore that all living people join the pre-existing local spirit population in a new covenant between themselves and the pre-existing local spirits. This covenant legitimized their arrival. In return for regular homage to these spirits, the founders could claim perpetual access to local resources. In so doing, they became the lineage in charge of the hereditary local priesthood and village headship, and were/are recognized as "tenants of the place" by later human arrivals.

Such respect for the spirits of the land is indicative of a people who will not violate anybody or any land. Egyptians, as such, are very peaceful people.

The Grassroots Republic System

The Ancient Egyptians recognized that the needs of each matrilocal community cannot be fully satisfied with just local production. In order to protect the individuality of the polity and its sociopolitical coherence, a co-op system between several polities was needed—this would be the commonwealth-type alliance, where coalitions are formed to share specific duties and responsibilities that can benefit all of them. This was organized—as confirmed by Strabo—into basically three levels—matrilocal community, district juristiction, and province (nome). These forms of organization varied from one area to another, and from one era to another. Ancient Egyptians had traditions of these non-coercive political organizations.

Unlike the autocratic centralized-type government, the form of a commonwealth-type government recognizes the importance of the grassroots—local communities. Coalitions are formed to share specific duties and responsibilities that can benefit all of them, such as communal projects (irrigation, roadways, granaries, etc), trades, treaties of non-aggression, rights of passage, etc. Contrary to academia's autocratic thinking, the Ancient Egyptian organizational government was not formed from the top (pharaoh) to bottom (local community). It was from the bottom to the top—from local matrilocal communities to districts to regional and "national"—each under its governor. Each organizational level was the same form, only mirrored on a smaller/larger scale, i.e. representative council with administrative superintendents.

The Ancient Egyptian political system was consistent with our present-time slogans of "limited government", "government by necessity", "the best government is the least government", and "government from the people, by the people, and for the people".

Alliances can be resolved, changed or restructured, i.e. government by necessity—for specific purpose(s) and/or duration(s), and they did so throughout the Ancient Egyptian history. We should not misunderstand this to mean upheaval/chaos, but the true application of *Live and Let Live*. This is a true grassroots democracy. An example would be the state of the whole land of Egypt during this 22nd Dynasty, which may be deduced from the long inscription of King Takelot II (860-835 BCE), in the temple of Karnak. From this text, it is clear that there were several regional governments, each with their own king/leader. There were no signs of wars or strife during this time, contrary to western academia's perception.

Western academia is obsessed with a centralized-type government and anything else for them will result in chaos, strife, and civil war, ...etc. Egyptian regions consisted of a commonwealth-type government, where people ally together on matters of common interest.

The cooperative provincial polities (which were called *nomes* in Ancient Egypt) are represented by each's leader, to form a council of elders/leaders. There are several ways to run such an alliance:

1. The council elected a local leader to be recognized as a leader of a group of polities.
2. The council elected a rotating leader.
3. Commonwealth(s) found and choose a spiritual leader, like a pharaoh whose main duty was to supplicate spirits of the land to renew its fertility, and to engage the help of chiefly ancestors to foster the welfare of the land and people.

[More about the role of the pharaoh in chapter 6.]

This Egyptian system is the true form of a grassroots re-public democracy that was the source of Plato's collected dialogs on the subjects of *Laws and Republic*.

The Dual Overseeing/Administration System

On every level of government (or more correctly *public administration*)—from the smallest matrilocal community all the way to Egypt at large—there was a dual governing system. In many ways, this system of dual governing continues in our present time. In the case of Britain, there is the British monarch as the head of state, who is the head of the church of England, and who inherits the throne according to specific precedence. However, the British monarch does not run the daily affairs, which are run by a prime minister who presides/oversees the work of the various ministries/departments. The prime minister is acting on behalf of the monarch, even though the prime minister (and his political party) are elected by the people. We even find the similar dual system of governing in countries with no monarchs, such as Germany and Israel—between a president and chancelor/prime minister.

Similarly—in conceptual format—at the head of the Ancient Egyptian society was the pharaoh, who represented the cosmic link between the natural (earthly) and supernatural (divine) powers. His role was not to rule, but to perform rituals to maintain the welfare of the society. The pharaoh deputed his authority to the supreme/chief judge/governor to run the daily affairs, who was known since at least the Old Kingdom era (2575–2150 BCE) as the *Second after the King*. He was the chief of the whole administration. Each province (nome) was governed under the same dual system of spiritual and administrative leaders.

This dual system was tailored after the Ancient Egyptian cosmic allegorical prototype system of government, between **Amen-Ra** (King of the Universe) and the governor—**Tehuti** (Thoth), the **neter** (god) of wisdom—the Wise

Judge. In Ancient Egypt, Tehuti represents the Divine Tongue/Sound/Voice. Tehuti is thus the model executive and the official spokesperson.

The Ancient Egyptian governor was also known as the *chief judge*. The verb-stem of the Egyptian word for *governor—(qadi)* is *qada*, which means *to get done*, i.e. the term *qadi*—in the larger sense—means the *executive*. The chief judge and governor presided over the head (executives/judges) of the various departments called the great/public houses—such as agriculture, treasury, etc.

Likewise, on the regional and/or local levels, the office of governor was at all times of the highest importance, and to his charge were committed the management of the lands, and all matters relating to the internal administration of the district. He (and his supporting superintendents) regulated the survey of the lands, the opening of the canals, all agricultural and communal projects, commerce, and all other interests of the community/district/province/country. All causes respecting landed property and other accidental disputes were referred to the executive judge, and adjusted before his tribunal.

The "governor" was the Chief Executive Officer, who executed the policies and laws as established by the legislative branch—the Council of Elders.

The smallest matrilocal community had a leader/king who governed with a council of elders. The council of elders—as representatives of their families, were equivalent to the legislative branch. They established policies and acted as final arbitrators (judges), if need to. The leader (and council) appointed/selected an administrator (governor, judge) to run the daily affairs. He had superintendents for various communal activites. He would arbitrate in cases that couldn't be resolved at lower levels.

Lady Justice and Harmony

Ancient Egypt was a nation of laws, from its earliest times. The superiority of their legislature has always been acknowledged by the ancient Greek and other writers, as the reason for the long duration of their civilization.

The main source of their laws came from a code of laws and jurisprudence, based on precedence—which is the primary thinking in Ancient (and *Baladi*) Egypt.

The Sicilian historian, Diodorus, informed us that the Egyptian laws were neither designed to arouse men's feelings about the prospect of distant rewards or punishments, nor to threaten the possibility of divine vengeance. They were, on the contrary, immediate in their effect.

The symbol of modern-day justice is a blindfolded lady, carrying a scale. Such symbolism is derived from the Ancient Egyptian's symbol of justice—a blindfolded lady. The Egyptian lady of justice is portrayed as a woman, with her symbol, the ostrich feather mounted on her head and holding the emblem of truth, to emphasize the main concept of justice—*Search for the truth.* **Ma-at** is sometimes represented *'having her eyes closed'* to ensure equal justice for all [shown herein].

The high integrity of the Egyptian concept of justice is also represented by those statues, at **Ta-Apet** (Thebes), of judges without hands, with the chief justice having his eyes turned downwards, signifying, as Plutarch says,

> . . .that Justice ought: neither to be accessible to bribes, nor guided by favor and affection.

Statues, similar to the Ancient Egyptians', are found in the halls of justices in western countries. However, such statues are dishonestly depicted with Greek/Roman features—not Egyptian.

As depicted in the Judgment Hall scene [page 75], **Ma-at** is often shown next to the scale of justice in a double form representing the two opposing sides of a litigation, because the scale of justice cannot balance without the equality of the opposing forces.

The scene from the Ancient Egyptian Judgment Day serves as a prototype—whereby the **Ausar** (Osiris) oversees and presides over the court procedures and the jury gives their verdict—under the control of **Ma-at**—based on evidence.

There were different forms for dispute resolution—but basically they were arbitration, trial by jury, or trial by a judge (presiding over a panel of judges). There were courts (arbitration panels) to resolve disputes on several levels. Additionally, each trade/profession has its own arbitration system.

Each local district and regional jurisdiction had its own court system for the trial of minor and local offenses. An individual could pursue his case through the various levels—up to the supreme council of justice.

On the "national" level, the Egyptian high court consisted of 30 judges, who served as priests of **Ma-at**. Diodorus said that this high court served as a later model to the Areopagites of Athens, and to the senate of Lacedoemon.

The administration of justice was well organized and played an important part in the state affairs. The documents of the great lawsuit under King Ramses IX (1131-1112 BCE), against bands of thieves in Ta-Apet (Thebes), give us a distinct picture of the work of the government under the 20th Dynasty, of how crime was tracked, and how trials of suspected persons were conducted. The document shows how an inquiry panel of three distinguished independent officials was formed to collect evdence and interview witnesses. The appointed inspectors went through the desert valleys of the city, carefully examining the sites of the alleged crimes and to interview witnesses. All these activities and witnesses' testimonies were recorded in writing.

Depositions were taken before the trials. The complainant stated his case in writing. The writ included all related particulars, such as offenses, extent of injury, witnesses, points of law, and requested judgements.

The defendant then, taking up the deposition of the opposing party, wrote his response to each of the plaintiffs statements, either denying the charge, or arguing that the offense was not of a serious nature, and suggesting that the damages were incompatible with the nature of the offense/crime.

The complainant replied in writing, and the accused stated his defense, and the papers were given to the judges. The judges refer to a code, or to former precedents, or to the opinion of some learned predecessor, together with reviewing the written depositions and questioning the witnesses, and make their decision. The presiding judge then proceeded to pronounce judgment on the case.

In addition to proper restitution, punishment in Egypt was generally in the form of community service. Rehabilitation can only be possible by implanting social responsibility.

The Documentaton Order

The Ancient Egyptians were very organized, and people often communicated with one another by letter in their daily existence. All government business was put in writing. The well-known proposition that "what cannot be put into documental form does not exist" was in force in Egyptian affairs. The Egyptians kept economic and labor records on papyri. These written communications followed a particular form—models of which have survived till today.

An example of the orderly and organized Ancient Egyptian society can be recognized in a requisition, displayed in the Egyptian Museum in Cairo, which shows a wife's request to get her travel expenses paid for, so that she could visit her husband who was on an official duty. This example shows the level of a highly organized well-oiled government order.

Nothing was done under the Egyptian government without documents. Lists and protocols were indispensable even in the simplest matters of business. The pictures in the old tombs testify to this fact, for whether the corn is measured out, or the cattle are led past, the scribes are always there to record.

In the mode of executing deeds, conveyances, and other civil contracts, the Egyptians were very detailed. Marriage contracts, wills, sales of property, etc, always began with the date of the transaction, the name of the president of the court, and of the clerk by whom they were written. The body of the contract then followed. The document was witnessed by as many as 16 witnesses.

Numerous documents have come down to us, show-

Scribes of the Old Kingdom [Saqqara]

The standing figure is giving an account of the inventory to two scribes. In the middle is the box for holding writing implements.

Government bldg (partial) of the Egyptian Nome of the Gazelle.

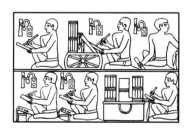

Various activities in an office building, from Ty tomb in Saqqara.

ing how the accounts were kept in the various departments. These documents show exactly how much was
received, from whom and when it came in, and the details of how it was used. This minute care is not only
taken in the case of large amounts, but even the smallest quantities of corn or dates are conscientiously entered.

To superintend and to write deeds was much the
same thing, according to Egyptian ideas, and a "scribe"
was an official. Scribes were employed in all levels of public administration and private affairs.

There were a host of scribes in each department and
in each expedition, such as the report of Wenamun on
his trip to Phoenicia and Cyprus to negotiate and pay for
the wood (and its transportation) for the Egyptian building of ships.

The various documents were orderly archived and
stored for future reference. Each document would indicate where it would go, e.g. a scribe notes: *"to be copied"*
or *"to be kept in the archives of the governor"*. The documents were then given into the care of the chief librarian
of the appropriate department, who then placed them in
large vases and cataloged them carefully.

Part II

The Cosmic Correlations

5

As Above, So Below

Cosmic Consciousness

The scenes of daily activities, found inside Egyptian tombs, show a strong perpetual correlation between the earth and heavens. The scenes provide graphical representations of all sorts of activities: hunting, fishing, agriculture, law courts, and all kinds of arts and crafts. Portraying these daily activities, in the presence of the neteru (gods) or with their assistance, signifies their cosmic correspondence—a strong perpetual correlation between the earth and heavens.

This perpetual correlation—cosmic consciousness— was echoed in *Asleptus III [25]* of the *Hermetic Texts*:

> ...in Egypt all the operations of the powers which rule and work in heaven have been transferred to earth below...it should rather be said that the whole cosmos dwells in [Egypt] as in its sanctuary...

Every action, no matter how mundane, had in some sense a cosmic corresponding act: plowing, sowing, reaping, brewing, the sizing of a beer mug, building ships, waging wars, playing games—all were viewed as earthly symbols for divine activities. In other words, for Ancient (and *Baladi*) Egyptians, every 'physical' aspect of life had a symbolic (metaphysical) meaning. But also, every symbolic act of expression had a 'material' background.

All of the Egyptian's knowledge that was based on cosmic consciousness was embedded into their daily practices, which became traditions. Such daily practices are reflective of deep understanding of themselves and the cosmos. We do many things in life, such as operating the computer, without most of us knowing how it works. This does not invalidate our computer use as being *unscientific*. Likewise, the Ancient and *Baladi* Egyptians' practices should not be dismissed because not everyone knows the scientific basis for that perpetual cosmic action. Describing these traditions as *superstitious* is reflective of ignorance of the cosmic scientific laws.

The following are a few examples of the metaphysical meanings of earthly physical activities, as portrayed in the wall scenes in Ancient Egyptian tombs:

- The typical Egyptian tomb sowing and reaping scene parallels the  biblical parable, *"Whatsoever a man soweth, that shall he also reap"*. This was intended to be a spiritual message, not agricultural advice.

- Both Heru (Horus) and Tehuti (Thoth) are shown in numerous illustrations in the Ancient Egyptian temples, performing the symbolic *Uniting of the Two Lands*.
  Heru represents conscience, mind, intellect, and is identi-

Heru   Tehuti

fied with the heart. Tehuti represents manifestation and deliverance, and is identified with the tongue. One thinks with the heart, and acts with the tongue.

- The wine-making process of growing, harvesting, pressing and fermenting is a metaphor for spiritual processes, which can be equated to the biblical wine symbolism.

The walls of the Ancient Egyptian tombs show vintners pressing new wine [as per the Ancient Egyptian tomb scene shown above], and wine-making is everywhere as a constant metaphor of spiritual processes and the themes of transformation and inner power.

The soul, or the portion of *god* within, causes the divine ferment in the body of life. It's developed there, as on the vine, by the sun of man's spiritual self. The fermented potency of wine was, at its deepest spiritual level, a symbol of the presence of the incarnated *god* within the spiritually aware person.

- A woman/man sniffing at the lotus is a recurrent theme in Egyptian tombs. The perfume of the lotus is its spiritualized essence, similar to the *"odor of sanctity"* in the Christian traditions. The depiction of the lotus is very common in Egyptian symbology. The four disciples ("sons") of Heru (Horus) are often shown coming out from a lotus flower. Also, Nefer-Tum, son of Ptah, the Creative Fire, is born from the lotus.

- People of all classes and the **neteru** (gods/goddesses) are depicted playing all types of games in Ancient Egyptian tombs and temples. Such games included board games, as well as physical activities and sporting events.

Ancient and classical writers affirmed that games owe their development, if not their very origin, to religious observances. Many accounts of games are mentioned by Homer as essential to the accompaniment of devotional ceremonies. The numerous Egyptian festivals include all types of games and activities that are an essential part of the festivities, and are as much a part of the festival as the religious processions and the visits to the holy shrines.

Numerous scenes from the Ancient Egyptian tombs portray different types of games. A few examples are shown on the opposite page.

The Ancient Egyptian game of drafts (chess) was more than just a game of fun, concentration, etc. As an example in the field of music and dancing, the select procedures of notes, modes, and movements were closely related to the Ancient Egyptian game of drafts. It is very common to find near Ancient Egyptian musical and dancing scenes a representation of a chess figure in the form of 'drafts' or 'checkers', indicative of this Ancient Egyptian branch of art of composition, which taught how to avoid and to play certain notes, how often each should be used, which one was to start, and which one to finish, etc. The Ancient Egyptian ballet, in its formations and movements, used to be ordered like a chess play, since we always find nearby a representation of a chess board.

[More info about sports and games in chapter 10, *Healthy Body*.]

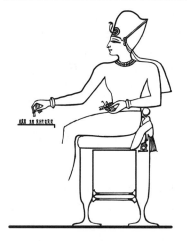

Various shapes of the game of draughts (chess). Pieces made of wood, ivory, and glazed pottery [Tomb in Ta-Apet (Thebes)].

Ramses III, playing at draughts.
His tomb in Ta-Apet (Thebes).

Egyptian dice [Berlin Museum]

Playing at mora.   Playing at odd and even.
From tombs in Ta-Apet (Thebes)

Playing at draughts.   Playing at mora.
From Beni Hassan tombs

• The bird-netting scene and the various species of birds depicted on walls have specific metaphysical significance. In general, these wild birds represent "wild" spiritual elements that must be trapped, caged, sometimes tamed, or offered to the neteru (gods/goddesses) in sacrifice. A modern similarity in symbolism is found in Mozart's Masonic opera, *The Magic Flute*, where Papageno is the free spirit whose specialty is to trap wild birds.

The birds of Egypt were very numerous, especially wild fowl. Descriptive examples of birds included geese, ducks, teal, quail, partridge, long-legged birds like cranes, waterfowl and other various avians.

The Egyptians either caught the birds in large clap-nets, or in traps—not any different than present-day practices/ tools—and they sometimes shot them with arrows, or with a throw-stick (like the present-day boomerang), as they flew in the thickets [shown herein].

The clap-net was based on the same general principle as the traps. [See example at top of opposite page.] It consisted of two sides or frames, over which the network was strained; at one end was a short rope, which they fastened to a bush, or a cluster of reeds, and at the other end was a long rope, which, as soon as the birds were seen feeding within the area within the net, a watchful man called for silence with his hand, and at the appropriate time gives the signal to the teams of fowlers (3-4 men) to pull the long rope, causing the two sides to collapse. They enticed the birds into the net, either by bait or by a decoy bird.

Fowling Scene from a tomb in Ta-Apet (Thebes)

Clap-nets depicted in
tombs at Ta-Apet
(Thebes).

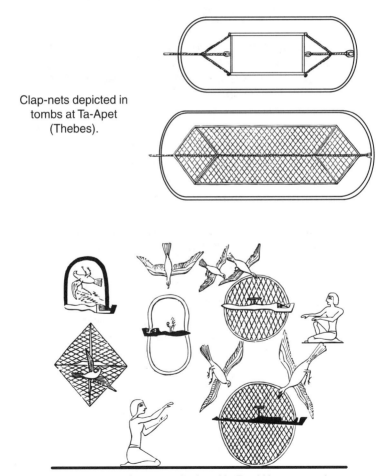

Various types of traps as depicted in Beni Hassan tombs.

• Fishing scenes are plentiful in the Egyptian temples
  and tombs. In the Egyptian texts, Heru (Horus) as-
  sumes the form of a fisherman and his four disciples
  ("sons") also fish with him. Christ used a similar symbolism by making his disciples *fishers of men.*

Plato and others noted that the Egyptians not only
caught, but tamed fish, with the same skill as they
did land animals. Texts describing fishermen's songs
were found confirming Aelian's description of how
the fish of Lake Mareotis,

> *was caught by singing to it, and by the sound of crotala
> (clappers) made of shells. . . and how dancing up, it
> leapt into the nets spread for the purpose, giving great
> and abundant sport.*

Not content with the abundance of the waters of the
river, its tributaries, the lakes, the Mediterranean
and Red Sea, the Egyptians used to build large ponds.
They stocked these with the fish they caught and
then proceeded to fatten them.

As depicted on the walls of Egyptian temples and
tombs, large-scale fishing consisted of well-coordi-
nated efforts of several people, who joined forces and
used a seine-net (a large net with cork floats along
the top edge and weights along the bottom edge).
The net was weighted down with lead [an example of
these lead weights—shown on opposite page—are presently
housed at the Berlin Museum].

Egyptian fishermen also fished with the bow-net or
the drag-net. We can see how the drag-net is set upright in the water (common nowadays), with corks
fastened on the upper edge and lead weights on the
lower edge. Seven or eight fishermen then dragged
it through the water to the land or onto boats.

Fishing scene from a tomb at Ta-Apet (Thebes). The right side shows
the fishermen trapping the fish. The left shows a boat with the fish
hanging up to dry in the sun and wind.

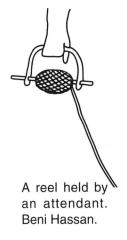

A reel held by
an attendant.
Beni Hassan.

Leads, with part of a net.
Berlin Museum.

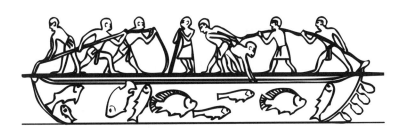

Energizing the Diationic Week

The present-day *Baladi* Egyptians follow their ancestor traditions by correlating specific activities to certain days of the week. These activities are concentrated
in two focal periods: the Eve of Monday (Sunday night)
and the Eve of Friday (Thursday night), with more focus
on the Eve of Friday [this has absolutely nothing to do
with Islam, whatsoever]. Marriage ceremonies are only
allowed on these two nights with preference to Friday
Eve. Thousands of local shrines (nothing related to Islam) are visited on both these eves, with special preference to Friday Eve. People spend the night of Friday Eve
at the tombs of their departed relatives [contrary to Is-
lam]. Intercourse between married couples is very special on Friday Eve. Courtship activities of all kinds are
more prevalent on Friday Eve. Many more similar traditions (cutting hair, butcher work, etc) are adhered to on
specific days and times.

Since Ancient Egyptian times, the week started on a
high (musical) note, namely Saturday. As such, the layout of the week, with the two active focal eves will look
as follows:

Saturday

Sunday
Monday   } Lightly Active

Tuesday

Wednesday

Thursday
Friday   } Very Active

Saturday

The concentrated activities towards both ends of the
week (with two centers of activity, one more prominent

than the other) follow the same pattern as the D [Re]-scale, which is the most popular sequence of the diatonic scale throughout the Egyptian history (ancient and present), which goes: **D—E.F—G—A—B.C—D¹**

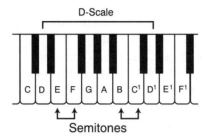

On a keyboard, the interval between any adjoined white keys that have a black key between them is therefore a whole tone, but between Me (E) and Fa (F) and Si (B) and Do (C) where the black key is missing, the interval is only that of a semitone.

Because of the presence of two semitones in the diatonic scale between E & F and B & C, the D-scale is the only symmetrical scale either ascending or descending.

By applying the sequence of the seven natural sounds of the D-scale to the days of the week, we get:

Saturday	D [Re]	
Sunday	E [Mi]	} Semitone
Monday	F [Fa]	
Tuesday	G [Sol]	
Wednesday	A [La]	
Thursday	B [Si]	} Semitone
Friday	C [Do]	
Saturday	D¹ [Re]¹	

One cannot help but notice the symmetry of the week-days with two focal points at Sunday–Monday and Thursday–Friday. This D-scale is identical to the Egyptians' traditions of weekly polar activities, as stated earlier.

The ascending D-scale is the model for one's deliberate communications with higher realms. In an ascending D-scale, the first 'interval' (semitone) comes between E (*Mi*) and F (*Fa*). Not too much energy is required at this juncture, and the octave develops smoothly to B (*Si*). However, the second semitone between B (*Si*) and C (*Do*) needs much stronger energy for its required development than between E (*Mi*) and F (*Fa*), because the vibrations of the octave at this point are of a considerably higher pitch. These are the reasons for the light Egyptian activities at Sunday–Monday and the greater activities at Thursday–Friday.

The descending D-scale represents the communications between the higher realms and our earthly realm. Taken in the downward direction, a descending octave develops much more easily than an ascending octave. Supernatural forces require less effort to communicate with us on earth. The first semitone occurs right away, between C (*Do*) and B (*Si*). Not much energy is required at this juncture, where the energy needed is often found either in the C (*Do*) itself or in the lateral vibrations evoked by C (*Do*). The octave develops smoothly to F (*Fa*). The second semitone F–E (*Fa-Mi*) requires a considerably less strong shock than the first.

The most favored scale in Egypt is called *Bayati*. It is a D-scale and thus provides the perfect harmonious communication between the above and the below—to and from.

The D-scale was known in ancient Greece as the Dorian scale/mode. Dor-ian is an Egyptian term that was and continues to be used in Egypt.

The Cyclical Renewal Festivals

The main theme of the Ancient Egyptian texts is the cyclical nature of the universe and the constant need for the renewal of such cycles, through well-designated festivals. The Egyptians viewed/view these festivals as part of human existence, which constitutes the rhythm of the life of the community and of the individual. This rhythm results from the order of cosmic life.

The renewal and rejuvenation of the life of the cosmos, of the community, and of the individual are affected by rites. These rites had/have the power to bring about the rejuvenation and rebirth of divine life. Failure to hold the festivals at the appropriate dates and times might very well produce individual or collective sentiments of culpability. As such, the Egyptian festivals came to have the function of enactments of cosmological (religious) renewals. Most of the Egyptians not only expect a blessing to follow their participation, but they also dread that some misfortune will befall them if they neglect this act.

The aim of the Egyptian festivals was (and continues to be) the rejuvenation and renewal of the cosmic energies. During the numerous Ancient Egyptian religious festivals, the participants fall back on the archetypal truth of their cosmic consciousness—*As above so below, and as below so above.* Every holy festival actualizes the archetypal holy cycle. These holy cycles have become part of the calendar. More accurately, the calendar served to indicate when the cosmological powers (**neteru/** gods) were manifested, and their renewal cycles. All early Greek and Roman writers affirmed these Ancient Egyptian cosmic correlations, such as Plutarch, in his *Moralia,* [Vol. V (377,65)]:

> *. . . They [the Egyptians] associate theological concepts*

*with the seasonal changes in the surrounding atmosphere,
or with the growth of the crops and seed-times and plowing. . .*

All the elements and rules governing the Ancient
Egyptian festivals are exactly applicable to present-day
festivals with organized and detailed schemes.

Baladi Egyptians continue to consider the festivals
and their rituals as the climax of their religious practices, which are very critical to the order and harmony of
the cosmos—and by extension the well-being of one and
all.

All present-day festivals (except for Mohammed's and
those of his immediate family) are a continuation of Ancient Egyptian festivals, camouflaged under Islamic
names.

The official annual number of festivals *(mouleds)* in
present-day Egypt, even though they are contrary to Islam, is estimated at more than 3,000. There is not a single
day in Egypt without a *mouled* somewhere, and the participation is very profound. For example, just the three
main festivals of the Sidi Ahmed el-Badawi, at the city of
Tanta, attract almost as many visitors as Mecca does
pilgrims from the whole of the Islamized world. The major Autumn *mouled* of el-Badawi is attended by more than
two million people and each of the other two *mouleds* are
attended, respectively, by more than one million visitors.
All this is indicative of the *Baladi* Egyptians' adherence
by the millions to their ancient traditions.

The procession of the sacred arks (ferry boats) is frequently depicted in sculptures throughout Egypt, such
as in the case of the **Apet** Feast [shown on opposite page],
which celebrated the one mile (2 km) journey of **Amen/
Amun/Amon** from his sanctuary at Karnak Temple to the

temple of Luxor and back again. The statue of Amen traveled partly on land, carried in a model boat on the shoulders of the priests, and partly in a real boat on the River Nile, while crowds of spectators gathered along the banks. Scenes from an **Apet** Feast, celebrated during the reign of Tutankhamen, decorate the walls of a colonnade in the Luxor temple, and give a lively impression of the occasion.

The present-day Egyptians of Luxor perform the same ancient festivities, starting at the Abu-el-Haggag mosque, located at Luxor Temple, and following the same ancient traditions camouflaged in an Islamic exterior. It is a testament to the resilience of the *Baladi* Egyptians, who maintain their ancestoral traditions forever.

In Rhythm With the Zodiac Ages

There is overwhelming and exhaustive evidence showing how Egypt responded to the different zodiac ages. There was a shift of symbolism, from Leo (the lion), Gemini (the twins), to Taurus (the bull), to Aries (the ram). These shifts coincided with the dates of the astronomical precession. Egyptians applied different means and modes of expression for each zodiac age, which were based upon the inherent specific nature of each age.

The last zodiac age in the Ancient Egyptian history was the Age of Aries (the Ram) [2307–148 BCE]. When the Age of Aries (the Ram) arrived, the Egyptian records revealed this

new Age—Amen rose to eminence with his ram-headed symbol. Ram-headed figures dominated the Egyptian buildings. Ram-headed sphinxes were aligned at the entrance of the Karnak Temple, dedicated to Amen [see illustration above]. The pharaohs incorporate Amen in the names they assumed: Amenhotep, TutankhAmen, etc.

Additional confirmation of the ram-headed Amen and its symbolism during the Age of Aries, is found in the Triple Shrine of Amen/Mut/ Khonsu, at the

Karnak Temple. On the left wall, Amen/Amon/Amun is pictured as a ram, traveling across the heavens on his barge [shown herein]. This representation, together with the references in many texts to Amen as a ram in the sky, support the astronomical/astrological significance.

War-minded academicians invented, without any evidence whatsoever, that the changes during the new Age were due to a priestly power struggle, and the result was the "victory" of Amen's priests. There is absolutely no evidence of priestly warfare during the history of Ancient Egypt, except with the 'apparent' case of Akhenaton. [His story is told in *The Ancient Egyptian Roots of Christianity*, by M. Gadalla.]

6

The Pharaoh,
The Cosmic Link

The Master Servant

Contrary to the Bible and Hollywood's distorted image of the pharaoh as a harsh tyrant, living a luxurious useless and easy life, the pharaoh had no political power, lived in a mud-brick dwelling, and spent his time performing his duty to act as intermediary between the natural and supernatural worlds, by conducting rites and sacrifices. The Egyptian pharaohs were not expected to be leaders of victorious armies, but were expected to secure a regular succession of rich harvests. They were identified with the crops, and were addressed as: *Our Crop* and *Our Harvest*.

In the first place, the pharaoh's main function was fundamentally religious. He was a representative of the people to the powers of the universe/*neteru*/energies. He must be elevated to them. He was the conduit, the go-between. He was the source of prosperity and well-being of the state, to his people. He was their servant, not their tyrant. He laid the seeds at the beginning of the season and collected the "fruit" at harvest time. He spent his time serving the interests of his people, by performing

the necessary rituals, from one temple to another throughout the whole country.

Based on his extensive training with the powers of
the supernatural, the pharaoh's body was believed to be
charged with a divine dynamism that communicated itself to everything he touched.

The authority of a leader/king, and his legitimacy to
rule over his people, were derived from his acceptance by
his subjects as the descendant of the founding ancestor
of the people. He was, in essence, the cosmic link between
the present and the past.

The right to rule was considered to be a continuous
chain of legitimacy, which was based on the matriarchal
principles, where the line of royal descent in Egypt was
through the eldest daughter. Whoever she married, became the pharaoh. If the pharaoh did not beget a daughter, a new "dynasty" was formed. There was no "royal
blood" in Ancient Egypt. [as explained earlier in chapter 4].

"Woman Pharaohs"

Throughout Egyptian history, it was the queen who
transmitted the solar blood. The queen was the true sovereign. Egyptian kings claimed a right to the throne
through marriage with the eldest Egyptian princess.

Western academia incorrectly "installed" women as
pharaohs into the Ancient Egyptian chronology—such as
Queen Hatshepsut. She was never a pharaoh, because
the Ancient Egyptian system is based on harmony and
balance between the wife and her husband.

It is most unfortunate that many people like to view the story of Hatshepsut/Twt Homosis III as an ancient contest between a man and a woman. The Ancient Egyptian society was based on the matriarchal/matrilineal principles, practices, and traditions—not gender conflict.

Twt Homosis III's father, namely Twt Homosis II [c. 1510–1490 BCE] married Hatshepsut, and had a daughter, Neferure from Hatshepsut. Twt Homosis II also had a son, Twt Homosis III, by a concubine named Isis. Twt Homosis II died shortly after the birth of his son.

The line of the throne inheritance, in Ancient Egypt, went through the eldest daughter—whoever married her became the next pharaoh. But Neferure did not get married, so there was no husband to become the pharaoh.

Faced with the absence of an active and legitimate pharaoh, the priesthood in Ta-Apet (Thebes)—based on divination—selected and declared Twt Homosis III as their Highest Priest—namely the pharaoh. Because of his young age, Queen Hatshepsut appointed herself as his guardian. A guardian is not recognized as a king. Therefore in the chronology of the kings, Twt Homosis III is shown to begin his reign at 1490 BCE. Two years later, Hatshepsut, dressed as a man, began sharing kingship with Twt Homosis III, while Twt Homosis III was kept powerless until Year 16 of the co-regency, when Neferure, the legal heiress died.

After Neferure's death, Twt Homosis III gained increasing importance. When Hatshepsut died, after 22 years of the co-regency, Twt Homosis III became the sole ruler of Egypt in 1468 BCE.

[For more info about Twt Homosis III, Amenhotep III, Akhenaton, and TwtAnkhAmen, read *The Ancient Egyptian Roots of Christianity*, by M. Gadalla.

For more info about the pharaohs of the Pyramid Age, read *Pyramid Handbook*, by M. Gadalla.]

The Divine (Virgin) Birth

Because of his special training, the Egyptian king was considered to be the spiritual son of God. In Ancient Egypt, the divine birth of the king was looked upon as a symbol of spiritual purity. Although the child was regarded spiritually as the son of the deity, this did not exclude the human father or the sexual relationship between the parents. In symbolic terms, the spirit of the deity (the Holy Spirit) used the physical body of the queen to produce the child.

The immaculate conception of the king is documented in scenes as well as texts found in many places, such as on the north wall of the central colonnade of the temple at Deir el Bahari, as well as at the Luxor Temple. In the Luxor Temple, at the Birth Chamber, as called by classical Egyptologists, we find the scene of the spiritual conception and birth of the king [shown herein]. It shows the divine conception of Amenhotep III by Amen-Ra and Queen Mutemwiya, supported by the netert Selket (left) and Net (right).

The reliefs on the west wall depict a scene with many similarities to the familiar Christian's Immaculate Conception. However, in Christianity, no human father is involved: the mother is a virgin, and the child is conceived by the Holy Spirit without any sexual relationship.

The People Rule

The Pharaoh's conduct and mode of life were regulated by prescribed rules, since his main function was to ensure the prosperity and well-being of his subjects. Laws were laid down in the sacred books, for the order and nature of his occupations. Diodorus reported that the pharaoh typically led a restricted life. Not even the most intimate of his courtiers might see him eat or drink. When the king ate, he did so in private. The food was offered to him with the same ritual as was used by priests in offering sacrifice to the neteru (gods).

He was forbidden to commit excesses; even the kind and quality of his food were prescribed with precision.

Even if the king had the means of defying prescribed rules, the voice of the people could punish him at his death, by the disgrace of excluding his body from burial in his own tomb. When the body of the deceased king was placed in state near the entrance of his tomb, the assembled people were asked if anyone objected to the king's entombment because he did not perform his duties. If the public showed their dissent by loud murmurs, he was deprived of the honor of the customary public funeral and burial in his tomb.

The body of an unaccomplished Egyptian pharaoh, though excluded from the burial at the necropolis, was not refused his right to be buried somewhere else. A case in point is the communal gravesite that was found in 1876, in the immediate vicinity of the Hatshepsut Commemorative (wrongly known as "Mortuary") Temple on the West Bank of the River Nile at Ta-Apet (Luxor). It contained the mummies of 40 pharaohs, queens, and nobles, whose performances were unsatisfactory to the common populace. Such rejected pharaohs included the mummies of well recognized and influencial names, such as: Amenhotep I, Tut Homosis II and III, Seti I, Ramses I and III.

As shown on page 74 of this book, the Egyptian king can only have his place in Heaven if he:

> hath not been spoken against on earth before men, he hath not been accused of sin in heaven before the neteru.

The Heb-Sed Festival (Time of Renewal)

The fertility of the soil, the abundant harvests, the health of people and cattle, the normal flow of events and all phenomena of life, were intimately linked to the potential of the ruler's vital force. It is therefore that the Egyptian king was not supposed (or even able) to reign unless he was in good health and spirit. Accordingly, he was obliged to rejuvenate his vital force, by regularly attending physical and metaphysical practices, which are known as the Heb-Sed rituals.

The purpose of the Ancient Egyptian annual Heb-Sed festival (which was regularly held towards the end of December), was to renew the pharaoh's power in a series of rituals including ritual sacrifice. The renewal rituals aimed at bringing a new life force to the king, i.e. a (figurative) death and a (figurative) rebirth of the reigning king. One of the Heb-Sed rituals was to induce a near death experience, so that the king could travel to the higher realms, to rejuvenate his cosmic powers. When he returned back, he would be a "new" king.

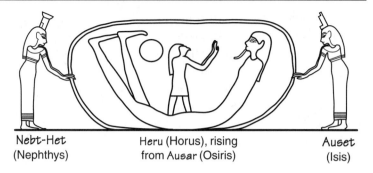

| Nebt-Het (Nephthys) | Heru (Horus), rising from Ausar (Osiris) | Auset (Isis) |

All Egyptian pharaohs identified themselves with Heru (Horus)—as a living king, and with the soul of Ausar—as a dead king. This is eloquently illustrated in the Ausar Temple at Abtu (Abydos) [shown above], whereby Heru is being born out of Ausar, after his death.

The Victorious King

It is widely recognized that the Egyptians (ancient and present) are an un-warlike people. It is therefore that Egypt was not interested in an empire, and certainly not in military occupation. Egypt was only interested in neutralizing the hostile elements that threatened to disrupt her own security. Egypt had to rely almost exclusively on foreign mercenaries for such a task. The pharaohs of the New Kingdom utilized diplomacy and marriage to foreign princesses to avoid conflict, with force only being used when all else failed.

War, for the Ancient Egyptians, followed rules as strict as a chess game and had specific rituals. They were truly the civilized people. A war had a profound religious significance. It symbolized the forces of order controlling chaos and the light triumphing over darkness.

In Ancient Egyptian temples, tombs, and texts, human vices are depicted as foreigners (the sick body is sick because it is/was invaded by foreign germs). Foreigners are depicted as subdued—arms tightened/tied behind their backs—to portray inner self-control. The most vivid example of self control is the common depiction of the Pharaoh (*The Perfected Man*), on the outer walls of Ancient Egyptian temples, subduing/controlling foreign enemies—the enemies (impurities) within.

The same "war" scene is repeated at temples throughout the country, which signifies its symbolism and not necessarily a representation of actual historical events. The "war" scenes symbolize the never-ending battle between Good and Evil. In many cases there is no historical basis for such war scenes even though a precise date is given. Such is the case for the war scenes on the Temple Pylon of the Temple of Ramses III, at Medinat Habu.

Western academicians are incapable of understanding metaphysical realities, and hence "make" historical events out of metaphysical concepts. The famed "Battle of Kadesh" is really the personal drama of the individual royal man (the king in each of us) single-handedly subduing the inner forces of chaos and darkness. Kadesh means holy/sacred. Therefore, the Battle of Kadesh signifies the inner struggle—a holy war within each individual.

7

Egyptian Temples

The Function/Objective of The Temple

It is the common tendency to ignore the religious function of the Ancient Egyptian temples. Instead, they are viewed as merely an art gallery and/or an interplay of forms against a vague historical presentation.

In reality, the Egyptian temple was the link, the proportional mean, between the macrocosmos (world) and microcosmos (man). It was a stage on which meetings were enacted between the *neteru* (gods/goddesses) and the king, as a representative of the people. We must try to see it as the relationship between form and function.

The Egyptian temple was a machine for generating and maintaining divine energy for the benefit of one and all. It was the place in which the cosmic energy of the *neteru* (gods/goddesses) came to dwell and radiate their energies to the land and people.

As described in various Ancient Egyptian texts, the temple or pylon is:

> ...as the pillars of heaven, [a temple] like the heavens, abiding upon their four pillars ... shining like the horizon of heaven ... a place of residence for the lord of neteru...

The harmonious power of the temple plans, the images engraved on the walls, and the forms of worship—all led to the same goal; a goal that was spiritual, as it involved setting superhuman forces in motion, and practical, in that the final awaited result was the maintenance of the country's prosperity.

It is therefore that the Egyptian temple was not a place of public worship—in our "modern" understanding. These truly divine places were accessible only to the priesthood, who could enter the inner sanctuaries, where the sacred rites and ceremonies were performed. In some instances, only the King himself or his authorized substitute had permission to enter.

The general public participated in the many great festivals and celebrations held outside the temples in honor of the various deities. The public participation was a duty by everyone and an essential aspect in the "worship" process—to maintain the universal harmony. [For more info, see *Egyptian Mystics: Seekers of the Way*, by M. Gadalla.]

In general, the Egyptian temple was surrounded by a massive wall of mud-brick. This wall isolated the temple from its surroundings which, symbolically, represented the forces of chaos. Metaphorically, the mud resulted from the union of heaven and earth. The brick wall was therefore typically set in wavy courses to symbolize the primeval waters, representing the first stage of creation.

The exterior walls of the temple resembled a fortress, so as to defend it against all forms of evil. The temple was entered through two pylons, beyond which lay an open court. This court sometimes had colonnades along the sides and an altar in the middle. Next, along the temple axis, came the hypostyle, a pillared hall often surrounded by small rooms that were used for the storage of temple equipment and for other secondary functions. Finally, there was the sanctuary, which was a dark room containing the shrine, where the figure of the **neter** was placed. The sanctuary's doors were shut and sealed all year long, and were open only for the great festivals. The sanctuary was called the *Great Seat*. Outside the walls of the temple were the residences of the priestly staff, the workshops, storerooms, and other ancillary structures.

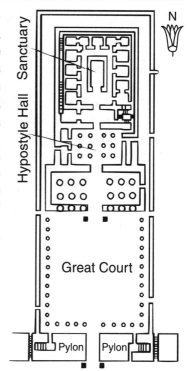

The Building Code

All Egyptian art and architecture, including representations of the human figure, followed a precise canon of proportion. Such a canon was also applied to Egyptian sculptures, friezes, and paintings, and they were carefully planned according to harmonic, geometric, and proportional laws. Plato attested to the remote age of the Ancient Egyptian canon of proportion, and how the executed works of the Ancient Egyptians never changed in character or design over the previous 10,000 years, before his time (428-347 BCE).

That the pictures and statues made ten thousand years ago, are in no one particular better or worse than what they now make.

The choice of location and design peculiarities of a temple were not based on economical considerations, but rather on a deeper knowledge of the macrocosmos.

The Egyptian temples were not built quickly, or by one king alone. Such temples were built over the centuries, by successive kings. A good example is the huge complex of the great Karnak Temple, which was built over a span of more than 1,500 years. The Karnak Temple features six pylons, and is an imposing and homogeneous achievement that produced a harmonious plan of buildings covering about 7,550 ft [2,300m] in perimeter. It is obvious that the overall plan pre-existed and that it was known to those who made the additions over a span of more than 1,500 years.

The Ancient Egyptian knowledge that manifested itself in their monuments was prescribed into technical specifications that were kept in archives throughout the country. These earliest Egyptian records indicate that the forms of the statues of *neteru* (gods/goddesses), as well as other artistic and architectural features, had the following characteristics:

- They were well defined.
- The definitions were transmitted by means of written specifications.
- The specifications were kept in archives.
- The archives existed in all official institutions, such as law courts, public works, as well as in temples.
- High officials, as well as kings, had access to archives.
- The high officials were required to study and implement the specifications.

The types of stone used in the pyramids and temples of Egypt were chosen with care. The choice of stone type was neither necessitated by economics, nor by practical structural consideration. It is believed that each stone type represents specific aspects of the cosmic process.

Here are the cosmic representations of some stones:

Alabaster	=	Air
Sandstone	=	Earth
Limestone	=	Water
Granite	=	Fire

A very common proof of such a choice is that the lioness netert (goddess) Sekhmet statues are made of granite—representing fire.

The basic features of architects' plans in Ancient Egypt were drawn on papyri. Only a few examples have survived. There are a number of architectural sketches that were executed on limestone fragments.

Ancient Egyptian records found from after the 5th Dynasty were set out upon a grid of squares (equivalent to our graph paper) that made it easier to determine the precise proportions. As such, the vertical (or horizontal) proportions can be read in terms of the number of squares (or fraction thereof) in the grid.

About 100 such grids are preserved, some dating from the Old Kingdom [2575–2150 BCE].

Found written Ancient Egyptian documents attest to their adherence to the (cosmic) building code. An example is a writing by Queen Hatshepsut [1490–1468 BCE], regarding the building of her "new" temple on Ta-Apet's (Thebes/Luxor) West Bank,

. . . It was according to the ancient plan

Senmut, Hatshepsut's architect, wrote:

I had access to all the writings of the nobles; there was nothing that I did not know of that which had happened since the beginning.

The Ancient Egyptians manifested their knowledge in harmonic proportion, long before its pre-dynastic era (more than 5,000 years ago), and continuing throughout its history.

The Harmonic Design Parameters

Harmonic design in Ancient Egyptian architecture was achieved through a unification of two systems:

1. arithmetic (significant numbers along a centerline axis)

2. graphic (square, rectangles, and a few triangles).

The union of the two systems reflects the relationship of the parts to the whole, which is the essence of harmonic design.

This union of arithmetic and graphic design follows the elements described below.

The Arithmetic System Consisted of:

a. Active Axes

An axis is an imaginary and ideal line about which a moving body revolves. In geometry, an axis is equally imaginary—a line without thickness.

The Egyptian temple was regarded as an organic, living unity. It is in constant motion; its intricate alignments, and its multiple asymmetries, make it oscillate about its axes.

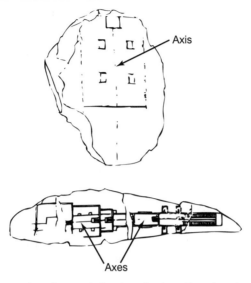

Two examples of axes defined on Ancient Egyptian drawings.

The axis line can be found in a few recovered architectural drawings or sketches on papyri and tablets from various periods. The axis line is drawn in the same conventional way as in modern drawings.

In the buildings themselves, the axis is marked by an engraved line on the stones of the upper course of a foundation slab, such as the case at Luxor Temple.

b. Significant Points (Along the Axis)

Significant points were determined along the design axis. These points mark the intersection with transverse axes, the alignment of a central doorway, the position of an altar, the center of a sanctuary, etc. These significant points follow a precise arithmetic progression. In many of the best plans, these significant points are at harmonic distances from one another, and their distances from one end to the other express the figures of the Summation (so-called *Fibonacci*) Series, 2, 3, 5, 8, 13, 21, 34, 55, 89, 144, 233, 377, 610, . . . The harmonic analysis shows a series of significant points readable from both ends, i.e. if inverted, a system of significant points would also correspond to the Series with the reference point starting at the opposite end of the plan.

The Summation Series was utilized in the Egyptian monuments ever since the Old Kingdom. The design of the pyramid temple of Khafra (Chephren)at Giza reaches the figure of 233 cubits in its total length, as measured from the pyramid, with a complete series of TEN significant points [see illustration on page 191]. The Karnak Temple follows the Summation Series' figures up to 610 cubits, i.e. TWELVE significant points. [See diagrams of several Ancient Egyptian temples in *Egyptian Harmony: The Visual Music* or *Egyptian Architecture*, both by same author.]

The Graphic System Consisted of:

a. The Telescopic Triangles

The design of the temple usually started from the sanctuary, which is the focal point. The typical Egyptian temple plan increases in width and height from the sanctuary towards the front. This over-all delimitation was based upon a "telescopic system" of design since the Old Kingdom [2575–2150 BCE]. The increase in width was accomplished by the use of consecutive 1:2, 1:4, and 1:8 triangles from one or more significant point(s), as shown in the diagram of the Karnak Temple [(partial) on the opposite page.]

The same telescopic configuration applied to the vertical plan, whereby the floor of the temple descended and the roofs ascended, outwardly towards the temple's pylons.

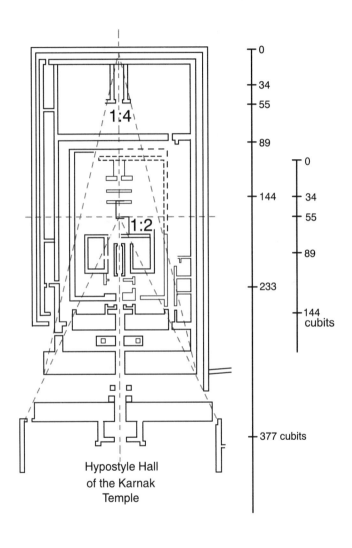

0
34
55

1:4

89

0

144
34
55

1:2
89

233

144
cubits

377 cubits

Hypostyle Hall
of the Karnak
Temple

Typical Telescopic Triangles in Ancient
Egyptian Design

b. The Rectangular Perimeters

The general horizontal and vertical outlines are basically rectangular in shape, for the overall plan as well as its constituent parts. The most common configurations that were used are:

* A simple square, such as utilized in the Pyramid Temple of Khafra (Chephren) in Giza. [See diagrom on page 191.]

* A double square or 1:2 rectangle, such as the Zoser Complex at Saqqara, the inner enclosure at Karnak, and the festival hall of Twt Homosis III. [Also see overall configuration of an Egyptian doorway on page 200.]

* Root Rectangles—numerous examples [shown below].

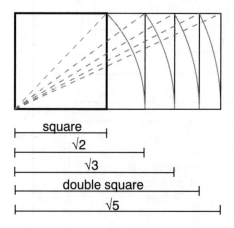

* The Neb (Golden) Rectangle, where the "numerical value" of the ratio between the two sides equals 1.618—numerous examples such as in the Pyramid Temple of Khafra in Giza [see diagram on page 191].

c. The Vertical Plane

The Ancient Egyptians were the masters of the vertical principle as well as the horizontal line. Vertical heights followed the same proportional increase as horizontal widths, as additions were made to the front of monuments—an aspect characteristic of the Egyptian temples.

Harmonic proportion was applied by the Ancient Egyptians in all three dimensions, such as:

• The pyramids (square bases and triangle volumes).

• The striking case of the King's Room in Khufu (Cheops) Pyramid, which affords exact relations for the great diagonal in space with respect to the dimension of the side. [See diagram in books: *Pyramid Handbook*, *Egyptian Harmony: The Visual Music*, or *Egyptian Architecture*, by same author.]

• Pylons. [See diagrams in books: *Egyptian Harmony: The Visual Music*, or *Egyptian Architecture*, by same author.]

• Doorways/portals/gates, as per diagram on page 200.

• Their mastery of the vertical principle was manifested, among other things, in the long lines of their lofty pyramidal towers, their obelisks and the lengthy columns that extended up the whole front of their buildings.

This vertical principle was adopted afterwards by the Greeks and the Romans, as evident in their arches and columns.

For example, the wrongly-called Greek Doric columns were actually fashioned in Egypt, at least two thousand years before they were copied by the Greeks—as evident in the Zoser Complex in Saqqara.

- The arch was employed in Egypt at a very early period. Underneath Sekhemket's [2611–2603 BCE] Pyramid in Saqqara, there is a door framed by an arch [depicted herein]. This 3rd Dynasty arch is the oldest known arch in the history of the world.

Stone arches were also found from the time of Psammitichus [c. 700 BCE]. Other stone arches, of the same time period, were found at Giza.

Crude brick arches were commonly used in roofing tombs, at least as far back as 1600 BCE, in Ta-Apet (Thebes).

All shapes, types, and material (brick, stone, etc) of arches can be found in Ancient Egypt—centuries and even millennia before Greek and Roman times.

[For more information about design and sacred geometry, read *Egyptian Harmony: The Visual Music* or *Egyptian Architecture*, by Moustafa Gadalla.]

[For more information about festivals, read *Egyptian Mystics: Seekers of The Way*, by Moustafa Gadalla.]

[For more information about temple rituals, read *Egyptian Architecture*, by Moustafa Gadalla.]

[For more information about layouts and details of various temples, read *Egyptian Harmony: The Visual Music, Egypt: A Practical Guide,* all by Moustafa Gadalla.]

Part III

The Learned Egyptians

8

The Divine Language

The Divine Mother Language

The more one studies the various languages (and dialects) in the world, it becomes clearer and clearer that there was originally one language that split into various tongues. The Bible and ancient writers affirm such an original language. Because of false pride and prejudices of western academia and religious (Judaism, Christianity, and Islam) zealots, the origin of this universal mother language has been ignored. Evidence ratifies that Ancient Egypt is the single source of the universal language. On this subject matter, Plato admits the role of Egypt from his *Collected Dialogues* [*Philebus* 18-b,c,d]:

> SOCRATES: The unlimited variety of sound was once discerned by some god, or perhaps some godlike man; you know the story that there was some <u>such person in Egypt called Theuth</u>. He it was who originally discerned the existence, in that unlimited variety, of the vowels—not 'vowel' in the singular but 'vowels' in the plural—and then of other things which, though they could not be called articulate sounds, yet were noises of a kind. There were a number of them too, not just one, and as a third class he discriminated what we now call the mutes. Having done that, he divided up the noiseless ones or mutes until he got each one by itself, and did the same thing with the vowels and

*the intermediate sounds; in the end he found a number of the things, and affixed to the whole collection, as to each single member of it, the name 'letter.' It was because he realized that none of us could ever get to know one of the collection all by itself, in isolation from all the rest, that he conceived of 'letter' as a kind of bond of unity, **uniting as it were all these sounds into one, and so he gave utterance to the expression 'art of letters,' implying that there was one art that dealt with the sounds**.*

The reference to *Theuth* above is the same *Theuth* mentioned in the *Phaedrus*, where we are explicitly told that he was an Ancient Egyptian **neter** (god), *'the one whose sacred bird is called the Ibis'*, so as to exclude all doubt about his identity. It is obvious that his account is based on a genuine Egyptian tradition, because the ibis-headed Tehuti (Thoth) is an Egyptian **neter** (god).

The Ibis-headed
Tehuti (Theuth)

Plato, in *Philebus* [18-b,c,d], tells us (in his obscure way) that:

1.   The Egyptian Tehuti was the first to observe the *'infinity of sound'* that was divided into three distinct categories: *regular vibrations (pitch)*, *random vibrations (noise)*, and *muting (absence of sound)*.

2.   Tehuti isolated the individual elements of sound in each of these categories *'until he knew the number of them'*.

3.   Tehuti is the discoverer of the concept of letters. Each individual letter is a picture of its own sound (visual music), indicative of the unity of speech and script, i.e. sound and form.

4.   Each "letter" is an original unity that consists of its unique vibrational patterns.

The Alphabetical Form of Writing

It is very clear that Plato (in *Philebus* [18-b,c,d]) did not refer to pictorial forms of expression (hieroglyphs), but rather to expression by individual and diverse letters, each with its particular sound value. Other classical writers also stated that Egypt was the original source of alphabets. Contrary to facts, the Phoenicians were given the credit of inventing alphabets. The following quotation from Isaac Taylor's book, *The History of the Alphabets*, Vol. I [pg 83], separates the facts from fiction:

> The tradition of the ancient world, which assigned to Phoenicia the glory of the invention of letters, declared also, though in more doubtful tones, that it was from Egypt that the Phoenicians originally derived the knowledge of the art of writing, which they afterwards carried into Greece. Eusebius has preserved a passage from the alleged writings of the so-called Tyrian historian Sanchuniathon, from which we gather that the **Phoenicians did not claim to be themselves the inventors of the art of writing, but admitted that it was obtained by them from Egypt. Plato, Diodorus Siculus, Plutarch, Aulus Gellius, and Tacitus, all repeat the same statement**, thereby proving how widely current throughout the ancient world was the opinion that the ultimate origin of letters must be sought in Egypt. It may suffice to quote the words of Tacitus, who says, "Primi per figures animalium Aegyptii sensus mentis effingebant; (ea antiquissima monimenta memoriae humanae inpressa saxis cernuntur) et litterarum semet inventores perhibent. Inde Phoenicas, quia mari praepollebant, intulisse Graeciae, glorimque adeptos, tanquam reperirint quae acceperant." Tacitus, Ann., xi. 14.

Most modern western scholars affirm explicitly and implicitly that the Ancient Egyptian alphabet (and language) are the oldest source in the world. In his book,

The Literature of the Ancient Egyptians [page xxxiv-v], the German Egyptologist Adolf Erman admits,

> *The Egyptians alone were destined to adopt a remarkable method, following which they attained to the highest form of writing, the alphabet. . .*

The British Egyptologist, W.M. Flinders Petrie, in his book, *The Formation of the Alphabets* [page 3], concluded,

> *From the beginning of the prehistoric ages, a cursive system consisting of linear signs, full of variety and distinction was certainly used in Egypt.*

Petrie has collected and tabulated alphabetical signs from very different ages; the earliest belong to the early prehistoric age of Egypt, probably before 7000 BCE, extending to the Greek and Roman Eras. Petrie also compiled (from several independent scholars), similar looking alphabetical signs from 25 locations in Asia Minor, Greece, Italy, Spain, and other locations throughout Europe—all are much younger than the Ancient Egyptian alphabetical signs

Petrie's tabulation of these alphabetical signs shows that:
1.   All alphabetical signs were present in Ancient Egypt since early predynastic eras (over 7,000 years ago), prior to any place else in the world.
2.   All the Egyptian alphabetical signs are clearly distinguishable in the oldest recovered so-called Egyptian "hieratic writing", more than 5,000 years ago.
3.   The same exact Ancient Egyptian signs were later adopted and spread by other people throughout the world.

A small sample of the first 4 letters of alphabets, as they spread from Egypt to Asia Minor and Europe, is shown on the opposite page.

The oldest Ancient Egyptian Script (approx. 7,000 years ago)	Moabite Script	East Greek	West Greek	Etruscan	Archaic Latin	Classic Latin	
𐤄	𐤀	Δ Δ	ΛΛ	Λ	ΔΛ	Λ	a
𐤁	𐤁	Β Β	Β Β		Β Β	Β	b
𐤂	𐤂	Γ Λ	Γ⟨⟨	) [k]	) [k,g]	⟨ [k]	g
◁ △	◁	Δ D	ΔD		◁	D	d

The Imagery and Alphabetical Writing Modes

It must be emphasized that neither Plato (in *Philebus* [18-b,c,d]), nor any other classical writers—including Clement of Alexandria (in *Stromata Book V* [chapter IV]), ever indicated that the Egyptian alphabetical form of writing was a "cursive" or "degenerated" form of the Ancient Egyptian pictorial hieroglyphics. Yet shamelessly, some "scholars" invoked the writing of Clement of Alexandria to insist that out of hieroglyphs sprang a more cursive writing known to us as hieratic, and out of hieratic there again emerged a very rapid script sometimes called enchorial or demotic.

Many rational scholars, however, recognized that the pictorial writings are a series of images conveying conceptual meanings and not individual sound values, such as the British Egyptologist, W.M. Flinders Petrie, who wrote in his book, *The Formation of the Alphabets* [pg. 6],

The question as to whether the [alphabetical] signs were derived from the more pictorial hieroglyphs, or were an independent system, has been so little observed by writers on the subject, that the matter has been decided more than once without any consideration of the various details involved.

Hieratic script shows clearly identifiable alphabetical and syllabic signs. Surviving hieratic texts generally show careful calligraphy for literary or religious texts and lesser quality for business and personal documents.

Enchorial/Demotic script was the script for everyday use for the ancient Egyptians. It was kind of a very cursive shorthand for rapid writing. It contained conventional modifications of the carefully executed hieratic characters. It was also used for religious texts as well as business documents.

There were various styles of writing (formal, cursive, semi-formal, or semi-cursive). Some were extremely stylized/ornate/ornamented, others were simple and plain. The orientation of the writing varied in direction from horizontal (right to left) to vertical (top to bottom), or vice-versa. In some cases, they used a combination of horizontal and vertical for the same word, and/or for the same sentence. The purpose of each document determines the style of writing used. These ways of writing produced different forms of the letters at various times. Varying styles appear to the foreign, untrained eyes as different alphabets, but for people of the same culture, they read these different handwritings as of one language.

By sheer repetition (and contrary to facts), it has been stated that a "Coptic" form of writing was developed, which consisted of the letters of the *Greek alphabet*, with an additional six characters (derived from the Ancient Egyptian demotic script) to express sounds that were peculiar to the Egyptian language. The so-called "Coptic"/ "Greek" script is in fact an Ancient Egyptian cursive form of writing. It was one of several recognized regional forms of scripts known at that time. **It was the Greeks who adopted them from the Egyptians**, when they came to Egypt as mercenaries or to study, and not the reverse.

In the 17th century, Father Athanasius Kircher has acknowledged, in his extensive analytical works, that the "Greek" script is Ancient Egyptian in origin. And for that, he was ridiculed badly by his fellow Europeans.

The Pictorial Metaphysical Symbols/Script

The Ancient Egyptians' pictorial system is commonly called *hieroglyphs*, which comprises a large number of pictorial symbols. The word, *hieroglyph*, means *holy script* (*hieros* = holy, *glyphein* = impress). Hieroglyphic writing was in use in Egyptian temples until about 400 CE.

All the signs of hieroglyphs are images from the Egyptian natural world, and therefore it was of an Egyptian origin—not imported or influenced by other cultures.

Each pictorial symbol is worth a thousand words—representing that function or principle, on all levels simultaneously—from the simplest, most obvious physical manifestation of that function to the most abstract and metaphysical. This symbolic language represents a wealth of physical, physiological, psychological and spiritual data in the presented symbols—such as the dog symbolism analysis, discussed on page 63 of this book.

The metaphorical and symbolic concept of the hieroglyphs was unanimously acknowledged by all early writers on the subject, such as Plutarch, Diodorus, Clement, etc.

The best description came from Plotinus, who wrote in The *Enneads* [Vol. V-6],

> *The wise men of Egypt, either by scientific or innate knowledge, and* **when they wished to signify something wisely, did not use the forms of letters which follow the order of words and propositions and imitate sounds and the enunciations of philosophical statements, but by drawing images and inscribing in their temples one particular image of each particular thing,** *they manifested the non-discursiveness of the intelligible world, that is, that* **every image is a kind of knowledge and wisdom and is a subject of statements,** *all together in one, and not discourse or deliberation. But [only] afterwards [others] discovered, starting from it in its concentrated unity, a representation in something else, already unfolded and speaking it discursively and giving the reasons why things are like this, so that, because what has come into existence is so beautifully disposed, if anyone knows how to admire it he expresses his admiration of how this wisdom, which does not itself possess the reasons why substance is as it is, gives them to the things which are made according to it.*

In the 12th Dynasty (2000-1780 BCE), about 700 signs were in more or less constantly used. There are practically unlimited numbers of these natural symbols.

Since deciphering the metaphysical Ancient Egyptian hieroglyphs is beyond western academia's capabilities, they have dubbed it as a *primitive* form of writing. Academic Egyptologists cavalierly chose 24 symbols out of hundreds of hieroglyphs, and called them an *alphabet*. Then they gave various "functions" to the other hundreds of symbols, calling them "syllabic", "determinative", etc. They made up the rules as they went along, and the end result was chaos. One can easily see the struggle of academia to understand the Ancient Egyptian hieroglyphic (metaphysical) texts.

The Cultured Language

The Ancient Egyptian texts reflect the high culture of the Egyptian language and people.The German Egyptologist, Adolf Erman, in his book, *The Literature of the Ancient Egyptians* [page xxiv], wrote,

> As far back as we can trace it, the Egyptian language displays signs of being carefully fostered. **It is rich in metaphors and figures of speech, a "cultured language", which "composes and thinks" for the person who writes**.

The British Egyptologist, Alan Gardiner, in his book, *Egyptian Grammar* [page 4], wrote,

> No less salient a characteristic of the language is its concision; the phrases and sentences are brief and to the point. Involved constructions and lengthy periods are rare, though such are found in some legal documents. The vocabulary was very rich. The clarity of Egyptian is much aided by a strict word-order. . .

The variety of subjects found in Ancient Egyptian writings is wide, including:

1 - Religious and funerary texts
2 - Business and legal records
3 - Scientific literature/documents (such as mathematical papyri)
4 - Astronomical observations
5 - Medical works
6 - Wisdom literature
7 - Meditations
8 - Letters
9 - Poetry, lyrics, and hymns
10 - Magic
11 - Egyptian stories
12 - Travel

Because there is no distinction between sacred and mundane for the Ancient Egyptians, interpretations of Egyptian texts are, to a very considerable extent, determined by the attitudes of academia involved in the work. Uninformed western academia will (and has) come up with one kind of useless interpretation, while those, who are truly studious, will make of the same text a totally different interpretation, showing the knowledge and enlightenment of the Egyptians.

Egyptians were able to utilize writings in all aspects of their lives, by inventing excellent writing materials and books. They used writing materials of leather, stone, wood, and papyrus, as opposed to the Minoan-Mycenean, Babylonians, and others, who had to imprint their signs on clay, a procedure that has produced the unpleasant crude shapes of cuneiform.

The Ancient Egyptians manufactured books by gumming separate sheets of papyrus together; and there are magnificent manuscripts measuring 65 and 130 ft [20 and 40 m]. The Egyptians utilized pens and ink of indestructible permanence, which they ground on wooden palettes. These writing surfaces and tools were plentiful, allowing the scribes to write manuscripts drawn in clear, elegant, round, firm signs. Using a pen (instead of a pointed tool) results in more round-shaped letters.

For more information about the subject of Egyptian modes of writing, see our publications by Moustafa Gadalla coming out in 2008 and beyond.

9

The Egyptian Musical Heritage

The Egyptian Harmonic Musical Laws

Music and dance, nowadays, are considered to be types of "art". The term, "art", has made it possible for anyone to qualify any absurdity and label it as a "work of art".

For the Ancient and *Baladi* (the present silent majority) Egyptians, music and dance are not just a way of life, they are life itself. They are as natural, critical, and vital as breathing. It is therefore that they considered music a mandatory subject for the education of all youth; for to teach music, you teach everything.

Since all aspects of the universe are harmoniously interrelated, Egyptians can never separate music and dance from astronomy, geometry, mathematics, physics, theology, medicine, traditions, ...etc. The Egyptian musical system is a beautiful blend of all aspects of nature.

Ancient Egypt was Plato's only source for his Ideal Laws, and the plan that he laid down for the education of youth follows precisely the plan that was developed long ago by the Egyptians.

ATHENIAN: *Every means, then, shall **we say, must be employed to keep our children from the desire to reproduce different models in dance or song**, . . **can any of us find a better device for this purpose than that employed in Egypt? . . . [where] . . . the plan is to consecrate all our dances and all our tunes**.*

Plato [Laws VII, 798e–799b]

Plato admitted that musical "theory" did exist in Ancient Egypt, and was detailed by appropriate rules and laws.

*Long ago the Egyptians determined on the rule ... that the youth of a State should practice in their rehearsals postures and tunes that are harmonically pleasing. These they prescribed in detail and posted up in the temples ... As regards music, it has proved possible for **the tunes, which possess a natural correctness to be enacted by law and permanently consecrated**.*

Plato [Laws, 656-7]

Clement Alexandrinus (200 CE) mentions 42 volumes accredited to the Egyptian Tehuti (Thoth) on various subjects. **Two books were on music**, four others on astronomy, one containing a list of the fixed stars, another on the phenomena of the sun and moon, two others on the rising of the stars. Another contained a cosmography and geography, **the course of the sun, moon, and the five planets**.

The heavenly music of the seven (wandering) planets (Sun, Moon, Mercury, Venus, Mars, Jupiter, and Saturn) provided the archetype for both the harmonic natural sounds of the diatonic scale and the seven days of the week—as stated by Dio Cassius in his volumes, *Roman History* [Book XXXVII],

The custom of referring the days to the seven stars called planets was instituted by the Egyptians. . .
    . . .and to them already an ancestral tradition. . .

*you will find **all the days to be in a kind of musical connection with the arrangement of the heavens**.*

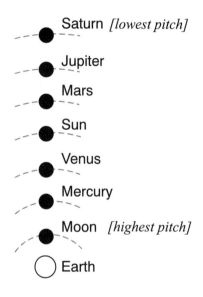

Saturn *[lowest pitch]*

Jupiter

Mars

Sun

Venus

Mercury

Moon *[highest pitch]*

Earth

    All swiftly vibrating, whirling (dancing) bodies produce sounds—like a vibrating string that produces sound when it is struck. The sound produced from the string depends—among other things—on its thickness/weight, the speed of its movement, and its distance from the human ear. Likewise, the sounds (relative pitches) produced from the whirling planets are a function of the weights of the bodies, their particular speeds, and their relative position. As such, the harmony of the spheres is not a romantic notion but the essence of music.

The Musical Heritage

The archeological and traditional Egyptian history of music is much more abundant than in any other country. The wall reliefs of the Ancient Egyptian temples and tombs depict numerous types and forms of musical instruments, the technique in which these instruments were to be played and tuned, the ensemble playing, and much, much more.

These musical scenes visibly show the hands of the harp player striking certain strings, and the wind instrument players playing certain chords together.

The distances of the lute frets clearly show that the corresponding intervals and scales can be measured and calculated. The positions of the harpists' hands on the strings clearly indicate ratios such as the Fourth, the Fifth, and the Octave—revealing an unquestionable knowledge of the laws governing musical harmony. The playing of musical instruments is also depicted as being controlled by the conductors' hand movements, which also help us identify certain tones, intervals and functions of sound.

The intervals of Fourth, Fifth, and Octave were the most common in Ancient Egyptian representations. Curt Sachs [in his book, *History of Musical Instruments*] found that out of 17 harpists represented on Egyptian art works (with sufficient realism and distinctness to be reliable records), seven are striking a Fourth chord, five a Fifth chord, and five an Octave chord.

The most frequently depicted harps were found to have seven strings, and according to Curt Sachs' study of the Egyptian instruments, the Egyptians tuned their harps in the same diatonic series of intervals.

One of the two harps found depicted in Ramses III's tomb [shown herein] has 13 strings, where if the longest string represented *pros-lambanomenos,* or *D,* the remaining 12 strings would more than supply all the tones, semitones, and quarter-tones, of the diatonic, chromatic, and enharmonic genera, within the compass of an octave.

In addition to the numerous representations of musical scenes pictured in temples and tombs from all periods throughout Egypt's dynastic history, we also have access to hundreds of various Ancient Egyptian musical instruments that have been recovered from their tombs. These Egyptian instruments are now spread in museums and private collections throughout the world.

The depicted musical scenes in Ancient Egyptian tombs, as well as instruments found from the Old and Middle Kingdoms, indicate ratios between the open strings of the harp, the densely ordered frets on the long necks of string instruments, as well as the measurements between the fingerholes in wind instruments that reveal/confirm that:

a. several types of musical scales were known/used.
b. narrow-stepped scales were common from the earliest known Egyptian history (more than 5,000 years ago.
c. playing and tuning techniques of string instruments provided solo and chordal playing of instruments.
d. playing techniques of wind instruments provided small increments and the organ effect.
e. both the cyclic (up-and-down) method and the divisive method of tuning were in use.

The Ancient Egyptians were/are famed worldwide for their mastery of the playing techniques of their musical instruments. The skill of the Egyptians, in the use of these instruments, was affirmed by Athenaeus, who stated (in his texts [iv, 25]) that *both the Greeks and "barbarians" were taught music by Egyptian natives.*

All these findings, together with the early historian writings of Egyptian musical heritage, as well as the traditions of modern Nile inhabitants, corroborate to provide the most authentic case of the musical history of Ancient Egypt.

The Musical Orchestras

Musical bands varied in Ancient Egypt. Smaller and larger ensembles were employed for various purposes, as evident from depicted musical scenes in the Ancient Egyptian buildings. It is sufficiently evident from the bas-reliefs by the Ancient Egyptians, that their musicians were acquainted with the triple symphony—the harmony of instruments, voices, and voices with instruments. The playing of musical instruments was controlled by the conductors' movements of hands (chironomids). Their hand signs show a variety of playing: unison, chord, polyphony, ...etc.

The Egyptian orchestra/ensemble consisted generally of the four instrument groups:

1. String instruments with open strings, like trigonon, lyre, harp, ...etc.

Many Egyptian lyres were of considerable power,

having 5, 7, 10, and 18 strings. They were usually supported between the elbow and the side, and played with the hand and/or with the plectrum. The plectrum was made of tortoise-shell, bone, ivory, or wood, and was often attached to the lyre by a string.

Ancient Egyptian harps varied in form, size, and the number of their strings. They are represented in the ancient paintings with 4, 6, 7, 8, 9, 10, 11, 12, 14, 17, 20, 21, and 22 strings.

2.   String instruments with stopped strings on a neck, like the tanboura, guitar, oud/lute, violin, etc.

The Ancient Egyptians utilized tanboura-type string instruments in an unlimited variety, providing variation in sound and design, such as: different body shapes with short necks like a lute, and long necks like a guitar.

Strings were made of catgut, silk or horsetail threads, and were produced in different thicknesses. When all the strings of an instrument were of the same thickness, a tuning peg was needed for each string. When the thicknesses of the strings were varied proportionally, so as to provide the different musical ratios between the strings, fewer tuning pegs were required. As such, a tuning peg may control several strings (of variable thicknesses) that can be tuned in unison. The tanboura-type instrument was played with a plectrum or bow.

3.   Wind instruments like the flute, pipe, double pipe, trumpet, etc.

The Ancient Egyptian wind instruments can generally be classified into:

a. Instruments in which the wind vibrates in a hollow tube, like the flute, the single pipe, ordinary pipes of the organ, etc.

b. Instruments in which a single reed causes vibration, like the clarinet, bass clarinet, reed pipes of organ, etc.

c. Instruments in which a double reed causes vibration, like the oboe and the double pipe.

d. Instruments in which elastic membranes set in vibration a column of air (lips in a mouthpiece), like the trumpet, trombone, and tuba.

Most pipes have equidistant fingerholes. The various musical scales and notes are produced by the size of the holes, the breath, the fingering, or some special device, as well as various playing techniques.

4. Percussion instruments like drums, clappers, bells, ...etc.

Percussion instruments can be categorized under membrano- and non-membrano-phone instruments, i.e. whether or not a skin or parchment-type sheet is used. The membrano-phone instruments include drums of different shapes, sizes, and functions—cylindrical, small hand drums, and single skin drums, tambourines, etc. Non-membrano-phone instruments include percussion sticks, clappers, sistrums/sistra, cymbals, castanets, bells, xylophones, etc.

[For more info about descriptions of the major Ancient Egyptian musical instruments, etc, see Egyptian Rhythm: The Heavenly Melodies, by M. Gadalla.]

The Vocal Music (Singing & Poetry)

The Egyptians perceived language and music as two sides of the same coin. Spoken, written, and musical composition follow the same exact patterns. Both poetry and singing followed similar rules for musical composition. Poetry is written not only with a rhyme scheme, but also with a recurring pattern of accented and unaccented syllables. Each syllable alternates between accented and unaccented, making a double/quadruple meter and several other varieties. Patterns of set rhythms or lengths of phrases of Ancient Egyptian poems, praises, hymns, and songs of all kinds, which are known to have been chanted or performed with some musical accompaniment, were rhythmic with uniform meters and a structured rhyme.

Ancient Egyptian texts show that Egyptians spoke and sang in musical patterns on all occasions and for all purposes—from the most sacred to the most mundane. Present-day Egyptians are like their ancestors—they love to sing about anything and everything.

The Ancient (and present-day *Baladi*) Egyptian poetry follows the same exact structural form and artistic features. The most common form is an octosyllabic quartet with loose alternate rhyme. Many are composed of three, five, and six lines of varying syllabic length. The normal vocal musical sentence is that of eight measures, frequently (but not necessarily) divided into two half sentences of four measures each. That is, after four or eight bars of the music you will instinctively expect and will usually get a rhythmic cadence.

Just like musical compositions, there are sentences or phrases that are shorter or longer than four or eight phrases; these are brought about by omissions, overlappings, extensions, repetitions, or expansions.

The singer often repeats and lengthens lines, depending on the traditional vocal ornaments of a given style.

Artistic rhythms, naturalness, brilliance, and charm of Egyptian poetry strive on wordplay, alliterations, tropes, and puns.

The following is a summary of the various forms/ styles of poetry that are found in Ancient (and present-day *Baladi*) Egypt:

1. Parallelism of the phrases—where two short sentences follow each other and correspond in arrangement and tenor/sense.

2. The parallel phrases may group themselves in strophes, as is shown in numerous poems. These parallel phrases are, moreover, frequently arranged in different order.

3. The antithetical style of poetry.

4. Alliterative style was used as a definite poetic form.

5. Poetry of metrical nature—poetry divided into short lines, which were distinguished in the manuscripts by red dots. These little verses are punctuated, not merely so as to denote the sense, but also the divisions that are to be observed in recitation. Each verse contains a certain number of primary accents—usually two. The peculiar law of accentuation in the Egyptian language—that several words closely allied in syntax should be invested with one primary accent—lies at the root of this verse construction.

Dancing & Ballet

The significant role and impact of dance (as well as music) in Ancient Egypt was clearly acknowledged and appreciated by Plato, in *Laws VII* [798e–799b]. Here are the sentences related to dance only:

> *The plan is to consecrate all our dances. . . .*
> *. . . Certain authorities must determine what hymn is to be sung on the feast of each divinity, and by what dances the ceremony of the day is to be graced.*

Dancing is movement of various degrees (slow to fast). Movements cause vibrations that in turn produce sounds. We don't hear all soundwaves (resulting from these vibrations), but we are affected by them, nevertheless. The vibrating (dancing) body produces sound—kinetic intermittence at regular intervals—just like the musical tones produced by a vibrating string of an instrument.

Dancing is much more than sensation and pleasure. It is life and unity with nature. The proper rhythm of the dance elevates the dancer to a higher realm. His/her body becomes a medium which, through connecting to the ancestors, becomes the bearer of all the forces of nature. The dancer, possessed by his deified ancestor, is being transformed into this spirit, and is drawn into the circle of those supernatural forces in charge of the operation of fertility, victory, and the course of the stars.

The Ancient Egyptian temples maintained dancers of both sexes as a special class. We find them over and over again, either in the quiet dance, with gentle steps and with arms outstretched in rhomboid form, or in the most daring acrobatic positions.

The walls of the Ancient Egyptian tombs and temples depict a wide variety of dancing styles, forms, and purposes—each for a certain time and place.

The energy level for the different types varied from the slow/gesture dance, to acrobatic, to dances out of harmony with the body—either as pure or weakened convulsive dances, to the most frenzied exhausting dances. Except for the latter, they were all choreographed.

One could dance either individually or in groups, with the sexes either together or apart. They danced with immense vigor, accompanying their motions with rhythmic jumps.

In the Tomb of Kagemni, at Saqqara, in the three-pillared room, five dancers are shown performing an acrobatic ballet. Ballet performances can also be seen on the western wall of the Luxor Temple.

On these wall scenes dating around 1800 BCE, the women performed pirouettes forward and backward, cartwheels, splits, and backward flips. Sometimes they performed these exercises in pairs, one of the female dancers standing up and the other on her back. They would do pirouettes in that position, head up and head down alternately. These were difficult exercises that could only be done with extensive training and practice.

Many of their postures do not differ from our modern ballet, and the pirouette delighted Egyptian parties, 4,000 years ago.

[Read more about the theory and practice of music and dance, as well as detailed descriptions of the major Egyptian instruments, playing techniques, functions, etc, in Ancient Egypt in *Egyptian Rhythm: The Heavenly Melodies*, by Moustafa Gadalla.]

10

Health and Medicine

General

We continuously hear of *'western medicine'*, *'modern medicine'*, *'scientific medicine'*, ... etc. All these terms infer that medicine from other regions and other ages do not count. Seeking the definitions of the words *health* and *medicine* in the Webster dictionary, we find:

health: *"Physical and mental well-being; freedom from disease, pain or defect; normality of physical and mental functions, soundness."*

medicine: *"The science and art of diagnosing, treating, curing and preventing disease, relieving pain, and improving and preserving health."*

According to the above definitions, the practice of health and medicine in Ancient Egypt is closer to true health and medicine than *'modern medicine'*.

For Egyptians, good health meant wholeness, integration and preservation. Healing, for them, was the search for wholeness, not just for our bodies, but for our souls, our minds, our spirits, our relationships, and for the environment around us.

International Reputations

Today's familiar sign for prescription, **Rx**, originated in Ancient Egypt. In the 2nd century, Galen used mystic symbols to impress his patients. Accordingly, he borrowed  the eye of Heru (Horus) from the Egyptian allegory. The story tells how Heru attacked his uncle Set (Seth) to avenge his father's murder. In the fight, Heru's eye was torn into fragments, whereupon Tehuti (Thoth) restored it for Heru.

The eye symbol has gradually evolved into today's familiar sign for *prescription*, **Rx**, which is used throughout the world no matter which language is used.

Many of the Egyptian remedies and prescriptions have been passed on to Europe via the writings of Pliny, Dioscorides, Galen and other Greek writers.

Warren R. Dawson, in *The Legacy of Egypt*, writes:

The works of the classical writers are...often merely the stepping-stones by which much of the ancient medical lore reached Europe, apart from direct borrowings...From Egypt we have the earliest medical books, the first observations in anatomy, the first experiments in surgery and pharmacy, the first use of splints, bandages, compresses and other appliances, and the first anatomical and medical vocabulary...

It is evident that the medical science of the Egyptians was sought and appreciated in foreign countries. Herodotus told us that Cyrus and Darius both sent to Egypt for medical men. In later times too, they continued to be celebrated for their skill: Ammianus says it was enough for a doctor to say he had studied in Egypt, to recommend him. Pliny also mentioned medical men going from Egypt to Rome.

The care which the Egyptians took of their health was a source of astonishment for foreign observers, particularly Greeks and Romans. Pliny thought that the large number of doctors meant that the population of Egypt suffered from a great number of diseases—a paradoxical piece of logic. Herodotus, on the other hand, reported that there were no healthier people than the Egyptians.

The Harmonic Sound Man

Ancient sources refer to the Egyptians, as the healthiest race of the ancient world. Herodotus wrote, in the 5th century BCE:

Of all the nations of the world, Egyptians are the happiest, healthiest and most religious.

The excellent condition of the Egyptians was attributed to their application of metaphysical realities, in their daily lives. The Egyptian medicine understood man as a whole, in tune with the cosmos. The body is an immensely complex vibratory system. Everything is in a constant dynamic state of movements that are intimately connected to the rhythms, harmonies and pulsation of the universe. Accumulating evidence proves the existence of cycles in the incidence of diseases, and in their intensities, which are indicative of cosmic resonance. If a person's orderly rhythmic patterns were disturbed, this was an indication of trouble ahead. When out of tune, the body was seen as unhealthy or diseased.

To heal a person, is to bring that person back into tune, by the deliberate summoning-up of the specific harmonic phenomena pertinent to the case. Magic for Ancient Egyptians was the profound understanding of cosmic resonance, as opposed to the current shallow notion, that magic is a synonym for superstition.

It is known that musical vibrations induce organic and inorganic substances into patterns and forms, such as plants responding to sound. We also know of the ability of infrasound waves to shake buildings or destroy organs, and how the ultrasound waves are used in microsurgery as a knifeless scalpel. It follows logically, that specific human organs and glands can respond to specific sounds. It is therefore that the Egyptians used controlled soundwaves for treatment of certain ailments. This was done in the form of incantation and chanting.

Incantation and poetic chanting are scientifically controlled soundwaves that generate sonar fields, establishing an immediate vibratory identity with the essential principle that underlies any object or form. By pronouncing certain words or names of powers, in the proper manner and in the proper tone of voice, a priest/doctor could heal the sick.

Healthy Body

In our present times, we say, *"Cleanliness is next to Godliness,"* and *"Your body is a temple."* The Egyptians applied such premises to their daily life. A healthy and clean body is a prerequisite to all daily activities, in the Egyptian model. Good preventative measures are essential in maintaining good health and to avoid getting sick. Preventative measures primarily consist of:

1. outer body cleanliness
2. inner body cleanliness [see pages 70-73]
3. physical activities on a regular basis
4. keeping a healthy active mind
5. being at peace with inner and outer harmonic balance(s).

To have a healthy mind and spirit, one must have a healthy body and surroundings. In their conceptions of moral purity, the Ancient Egyptians always emphasized sanitary observances of the human body and surroundings. The most sacred of Ancient Egyptian texts, such as the *Book of Coming Forth by Light* (incorrectly known as the *Book of the Dead*), emphasize:

• Maintaining a clean body, such as: frequent bathing, mouth washing, clipping and cleaning fingernails and toenails, shaving (including body hair), washing hands and feet, etc.

• Purity of the food. Herodotus (500 BCE) describes the measures taken by the Egyptians to ensure the ceremonial purity of sacrificial animals.

The ancient traditions emphasize maintaining good eating habits, with an attitude of *eat to live*—not *live to eat*. They also recommend going through cyclical internal cleansing by fasting (abstention from eating fish, meat, and dairy products for a cycle of 40 days), and other means, such as a safe managed colon-cleansing to empty the bowel from potential disease causes.

The Ancient Egyptians were reputed to be the cleanest people in the ancient world. The squalid appearance and unrefined habits of Asiatic Greeks and Romans, with their long beards, were often the subject of ridicule to the Egyptians. Their abhorrence of the bearded and long-haired Greeks was so great, that, according to Herodotus,

> *. . .no Egyptian of either sex would on any account kiss the lips of a Greek, make use of his knife, his spit and cauldron, or taste the meat of an animal which has been slaughtered by his hand.*

The same habits of cleanliness are also indicated by the *"changes of raiment"* given by Joseph to his brethren when they set out to bring their father to Egypt.

The Romans never shaved until 454 years after the foundation of Rome, when Ticinus had barbers brought from Sicily and established the custom of shaving. Pliny tells us that Scipio the African was the first Roman to adopt the habit of daily shaving.

Warm as well as cold baths were used by the Egyptians. Egyptians felt obliged to wash their hands several times a day, but most importantly before and after each meal. It is common knowledge now that hand washing is an essential preventative measure. Even the most modest of Ancient Egyptian dwellings had a bathroom of sorts; these could vary from a very simple installation all the way to the extreme refinements of the richest villas.

The Egyptian priests took several complete baths every day. They also shaved their whole body, including eyelashes and eyebrows. It was the same concern for purity that inspired them to observe chastity. A healthy soul could hardly develop in a body that was not clean.

Circumcision of male children originated in Ancient Egypt, prior to any other country. The procedure signifies cleanliness as being holiness. This Ancient Egyptian practice was adopted later by other "religions" and races.

Sports and Rhythmic Movements—Maintaining a healthy athletic body was/is essential in the Egyptian model. Long ago, before the Greeks and Romans, games were (and continue to be) performed in honor of certain *neteru* (gods). Such games included (but were not limited to) wrestling, lifting weights, running, ball games, and other gymnastic exercises.

Such perfect conditioning is attributed to Tehuti (Thoth). Diodorus, in *Book I* [16], wrote:

> It was by Tehuti (Hermes), for instance, according to the Egyptians, that . . . . he was the first . . . . **to establish a wrestling school, and to give thought to the rhythmical movement of the human body and its proper development**. . . . .

Rhythmic movements/ exercises/games that are practiced by the Egyptians include, but are not limited to: yoga, martial arts, wrestling, etc. A unique Egyptian rhythmic ritual/game is the

performing of routines with wooden swords [as shown herein]. This is a very ritualistic and graceful game that requires immense concentration, agility, strength, and talent and can still be seen in Egypt to this day.

Wrestling games constitute a perfect combination of ritual and sportsmanship. Wrestling is mentioned in the holiest of Ancient Egyptian texts, and was considered an important element of the most religious activities of the

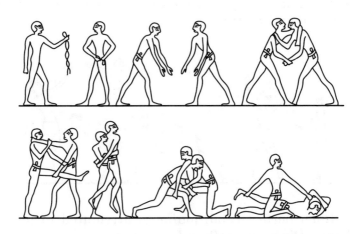

Ancient Egyptian festival (*mouled*) [as shown above, from a Beni Hassan tomb], and is one of the many sports that is practiced in the numerous Egyptian festivals.

Other sports that are practiced by the Egyptians (Ancient and *Baladi*) include: horsemanship, running, etc. Exercises and staying in shape were/are essential for the Ancient and *Baladi* Egyptians. The Ancient Egyptian king was not supposed (or even able) to reign unless he was in good health and spirit. The pharaoh, as the Perfected Man, was required to maintain perfect physical condition and he was required to go through annual endurance exercises such as running. He was required to run a 5-mile [8 km] course in the annual Heb-Sed rituals.

Medical Profession

The Physicians

The names and titles of more than a hundred doctors were determined from archeological findings, with sufficient detail to uncover an overall picture of the medical practice. The name of Imhotep [3rd Dynasty] has become forever linked with Egyptian medicine, who was later deified and identified with Asklepios, the Greek god of healing.

As far back as the Old Kingdom, the medical profession was highly organized, with doctors holding a variety of ranks and specialties. The ordinary doctor was outranked by the *Overseer of doctors*, the *Chief of doctors*, the *Eldest of doctors* and the *Inspector of doctors*. A distinction was made between physicians and surgeons.

Each physician was well trained, and practiced only in his area of specialization. Egyptian doctors were highly specialized. Herodotus points out that,
they could practice no branch other than their own.

There were eye doctors, bowel specialists *(Guardians of the Anus)*, physicians who specialized in internal diseases *who know the secret and specialize in the body fluids*, nose doctors, *sickness of the upper air passages*, doctor of the abdomen, and dentists.

Childbirth was basically the province of the midwives. Herodotus saw in that a sign of scientific advancement, and the result of truly profound knowledge.

Ta-urt is the Egyptian patroness of women in pregnancy, childbirth, and after birth. She represents much more than our common understanding of a midwife.

Midwives, among the Ancient and *Baladi* Egyptians, possess the physical and metaphysical knowledge of bringing a new baby into the world—body and soul, and the impact on the mother throughout the entire process.

The Conduct & Practice

Some surgical tools and instruments are depicted in tombs and temples, such as:

* The Tomb of Ankh-mahor at Saqqara, which contains several unique medical and surgical reliefs. Among them was a flint knife which some considered as evidence of its remote origin. The most recent surgical research is vindicating the flint instruments of antiquity. It has been found that for certain neurological and optical operations, obsidian possesses qualities that cannot be matched by the finest steel, and an updated version of the old flint knife is coming back into use.

* On the outer corridor wall of the temple at Kom Ombo, a box of surgical instruments is carved in relief. The box includes metal shears, surgical knives, saws, probes, spatulas, small hooks and forceps.

Surgical operations were performed by the Ancient Egyptians, even in pre-dynastic times. Mummies were found, having very neatly cut parts of their skulls, indicating a highly advanced level of brain surgery. A number of skulls have been found indicating the nature of the operations; and sometimes the severed section of the skull had knit to the parent bone, proving that the patient had survived the operation.

Although no surgical scars have been reported in mummies (apart from embalmers' incisions), there are thirteen references in the Smith Papyrus to 'stitching'.

The Papyrus also mentions wounds being brought together with adhesive tape which was made of linen. Linen was also available for bandages, ligatures and sutures. Needles were probably of copper.

Egyptian doctors distinguished between sterile (clean) wounds and infected (purulent) wounds. The former were written using the determinative for *'blood'* or *'phlegm'* and the latter, using the determinative for *'stinking outflow'* or *'feces'*. A mixture of ibex fat, fir oil and crushed peas were ingredients used as an ointment to clean an infected wound.

Each temple had a full-scale laboratory, where medications were made and stocked.

When the first Egyptian medical papyri were deciphered by German scholars, they were shocked. They called Egyptian medicine *"sewage pharmacology"* because Egyptians treated various inflammations, infections and wounds by applying dung and similar substances.

The later invention of penicillin and antibiotics in recent decades, has made us realize that the Ancient Egyptians were applying rudimental and organic versions of these remedies. What the Germans described as "sewage pharmacology" was recently ratified as "modern medicine". Moreover, Egyptians knew of the different types of antibiotics. Their prescriptions called for specific types of antibiotics to correspond to specific maladies.

Academia studying the Ancient Egyptian techniques of furnishing statues with inlaid eyes, concluded that the Egyptians must have understood not only the anatomy of the eye but also its refractive properties. The Egyptians approximated those properties by using combinations of stones and crystals (up to four different kinds, in a single eye). When photographs are taken of these Egyptian statues, the eyes actually look real.

The Medical Library

According to Clemens Alexandrinus, living in Alexandria in about 200 CE, the priests of Early Dynastic Egypt had written the sum total of their knowledge in 42 sacred books, which were kept in the temples and were carried in religious processions. Six of these books were concerned totally with medicine, and dealt with anatomy, diseases in general, surgery, remedies, diseases of the eye and diseases of women.

The 42 Ancient Egyptian sacred books, including the six about medicine, were brought—among hundreds of thousands of Egyptian texts—to the Library of Alexandria. This beacon of knowledge was destroyed by the early Christians, zealots of Alexandria.

Several medical papyri have survived the ages. They contain prescriptions for treating diseases of the lungs, liver, stomach, bladder and for various afflictions of the head and scalp (including recipes for preventing the hair falling out or turning gray). They also contain prescriptions for rheumatic and arthritic complaints and for woman's diseases.

Several other Egyptian papyri that deal with non-physical ailments are dubbed as "magical papyri" by western academia. The following is a summary of the major medical papyri:

Edwin Smith Papyrus
The Edwin Smith Papyrus has been dated to about 1600 BCE. The presence of Old Kingdom words in the text, suggest that the Papyrus was copied from earlier work around 2500 BCE when the pyramids were built.

This is the earliest book of surgery in the world. It contains a total of 48 surgical cases, of a traumatic nature, methodically arranged from the head and generally going down the body to the lower limbs.

Each case is preceded by a brief caption expressing a summary diagnosis, followed by another detailed diagnosis, a brief but clearly formulated prognosis and sometimes the therapy.

The diagnosis was established after extraordinarily precise observations had been made. In its conclusion it proposed three possibilities: a doctor could act with full success, he could try with some chances of success, or he stood no chance at all, in which case he should do nothing.

The techniques were numerous and varied. Fractures were properly set, splints were applied, and wounds were sutured. There was a sort of adhesive plaster that worked wonders with broken bones. Perfectly healed fractures can be seen in numerous mummies.

The most exciting sentences are to be found right at the beginning of this papyrus:

> The counting of anything with the fingers [is done] to recognize the way the heart goes. There are vessels in it leading to every part of the body ... When a Sekhmet priest, any doctor ... puts his fingers to the head ... to the two hands, to the place of the heart ... it speaks ... in every vessel, every part of the body.

The medical papyrus proves that the Egyptians understood the relationship of the heart to the circulation of the blood, and that they believed the heart to be the source of life within the body, and they felt the pulse and measured it, by comparison with their own pulses.

The Egyptians also believed that all the 'inner juices of the body' flowed through vessels radiating from the heart and collected at the anus, whence they could again be redistributed to various parts of the body. Air, blood, urine, mucus, semen and feces flowed around the system, usually in harmony, but occasionally getting out of hand and thence causing an illness.

The Smith Papyrus contains what is probably the first documented description of the human brain:

> When you examine a man with a ... wound on his head, which goes to the bone; his skull is broken; broken open is the brain of his skull ... these windings which arise in poured metal. Something is there ... that quivers (and) flutters under your fingers like the weak spot in the head of a child which has not yet grown hard ... Blood flows from his two nostrils.

Advances in modern neurology prove that the Egyptians understood, in detail, the workings of the nervous system, and the relationship between the areas of the brain and the manner in which these areas controlled the bodily functions.

Ebers Medical Papyrus

The date of its origin of the Ebers Medical Papyrus is about 1555 BCE. It is considered to be a manual for the teaching of anatomy and pharmacy.

It contains 876 remedies and mentions 500 different substances used in medical treatments.

The Ebers Papyrus describes treatment of and prescriptions for stomach complaints, coughs, colds, bites, head ailments and diseases, liver complaints, burns and other kinds of wounds, itching, boils, cysts and the like, complaints in fingers and toes, salves for wounds and pains in the veins, muscles and nerves, diseases of the tongue, toothache, ear pains, women's diseases, beauty preparations, household remedies against vermin, two books about the heart and veins, and diagnoses for tumors.

Berlin Papyrus

The Berlin Papyrus has been dated between 1350 and 1200 BCE.

It deals with childbirth and infants.

It <u>contains a test for pregnancy</u>, which recognized that urine carried the pregnancy factor. It calls for steeping some wheat and some barley in her urine. If the wheat sprouts, it will be a boy, if the barley sprouts, it will be a girl.

In 1963 Ghalioungui found that, whilst urine from non-pregnant women prevented the growth of (modern) barley and wheat, it proved impossible to detect the sex of an unborn child from the rate of growth of either grain, possibly because the grains and the soils were both different in Ancient Egypt. Nevertheless, the fact that <u>the Egyptians recognized that urine carried the pregnancy factor</u> was remarkable. The standardization of reliable urine tests for pregnancy did not occur until 1929.

It is astounding to know that this Egyptian recipe found its way to Europe, for in an ingenious book of the 17th century, Peter Boyer wrote:

> *Make two holes in the ground, throw barley into the one*
> *and wheat into the other, then pour into both the water of*

*the pregnant woman, and cover them up again with earth.
If the wheat shoots up before the barley, it will be a boy, but
if the barley comes up first, thou must expect a daughter.*

There is also a little English book, called *The Experienced Midwife*, in which this recipe appears, in a somewhat modified form.

The Hearst Papyrus

It has been dated to about 1550 BCE and it appears to be the guideline for a practicing physician.

It contains over 250 prescriptions and spells, and has a section on bones and bites, afflictions of fingers, tumors, burns, diseases of women, ears, eyes and teeth.

Cures & Prescriptions

The Ancient Egyptians had full knowledge of the uses of herbs and natural therapies, to the extent that they perfected the procedure of embalming the corpses of their dead, a feat which modern man is yet unable to conquer.

The various prescriptions in the Ebers and Hearst papyri, as well as other medical papyri, are quite rational and present natural applications for the alleviation of symptoms. These prescriptions are the product of knowledge of general physiological properties and actions of plants, animals and minerals as well as the human body.

The Ebers Papyrus, alone, contains 876 remedies and mentions 500 substances used in medical treatment. It gives recipes for many remedies, such as plasters, balms and ointments—consisting of vegetable, mineral, and also animal origin.

The ingredients were sometimes crushed, and sometimes boiled or blended. Some were sifted through a piece of fabric or diluted with clear water, beer, wine, oil, or milk.

From the Ebers Papyrus we learn that a single prescription may include as many as 35 substances.

Prescriptions were given in different forms, either as a drink or in the form of pills or as a rubbing oil or fomentation. Some prescriptions were inhaled.

They weighed and measured their prescriptions very carefully.

Dosages of medicine varied according to the age, weight and sex of the patient.

Incantations (magical spells) were spoken over various remedies in order to endow them with the right power, as explained earlier in this chapter.

Medical plants were well known. Medical plants not native to Egypt were imported from outside Egypt. Fir came from Syria and Asia Minor, its pungent resin, invaluable as an antiseptic and an embalming material. Oil of fir was used as an anthelmintic, and to clean infected wounds. From eastern Africa came aloe, used to 'expel catarrh from the nose', and cinnamon, an essential ingredient in an unguent for ulcerated gums and in incense.

An important constituent in most remedies was honey. Honey is highly resistant to bacterial growth. It also has an antibiotic action due to the presence of a bactericidal enzyme called inhibine. In modern studies honey has proven to be effective against staphylococcus, salmonella and candida bacteria. It is also used to treat surgical wounds, burns and ulcers, having more rapid healing qualities than conventional treatment.

Another bee product called propolis (bee glue) is a hard, resinous material derived by bees from plant juices, and is used by bees to seal cracks in their hives. Propolis also has antibiotic as well as preservative properties. A small mouse, which crept into an Ancient Egyptian hive 3,000 years ago, was found perfectly preserved, covered with propolis, and with no sign of decomposition.

Beer is also mentioned as an agent by which many drugs were administered, and beer was a popular and healthy drink.

They knew and used the benefits of yeast, applying it raw to boils and ulcers, and swallowing it to clear digestive disorders. Yeast contains vitamin B as well as antibiotic agents.

Earlier we mentioned the use of antibiotics in Ancient Egypt, to treat wounds or open sores.

In summary, Ancient Egypt was highly advanced and appreciated for its medical products, which Pliny frequently made references to in his writings.

Homer, in the *Odyssey*, describes the many valuable medicines given by Polydamna, the wife of Thonis, to Helen while in Egypt,

> *a country whose fertile soil produces an infinity of drugs, some salutary and some pernicious; where each physician possesses knowledge above all other men.*

11

Total Science

Scattered vs. Total Science

It is the common belief of the modern world that our society is the most advanced that has ever existed, and that all science prior to our era was undeveloped. Yet when we check the meaning of the word, *"science"*, we will find that it was the Ancient Egyptians who followed the essence and meaning of the term.

Science, as defined in Webster's dictionary, is:

Systemized knowledge derived from observation carried on in order to determine the nature of what is being studied.

The Ancient Egyptians have achieved such a definition and more. The vast majority of scientific findings attributed to westerners have basically came out of thin air—and not by a true scientific process—as defined above. From Leonardo DaVinci to Kepler and many other western "notables" in between, we are informed of their "ingenious" findings. Yet, we are not presented by their actual scientific observations and analyses that led to their "ingenious" findings.

The totality of the Egyptian civilization was built

upon a complete and precise understanding of universal laws. This profound understanding manifested itself in a consistent, coherent and interrelated system, where art, science, philosophy and religion was intertwined, and employed simultaneously in a single organic Unity. Science in Ancient Egypt intertwines with other aspects of life and cannot be easily carved out as a separate subject. It is this fusion that left the world with unmatched accomplishments.

The comprehensive knowledge of Ancient Egypt was expressed in story form, which is a superior means for expressing both physical and metaphysical concepts. Any good writer or lecturer knows that stories are superior to exposition for explaining the behavior of things, because the relationships of parts to each other, and to the whole, are better maintained by the mind.

The Ancient Egyptians had a "scientific and organic system" of observing reality. Modern-day science is based on observing everything as dead (inanimate). Modern physical formulas in scientific studies almost always exclude the vital phenomena throughout statistical analyses. Our modern science remains piecemeal and unable to handle the non-quantifying factors of life. This is "incomplete science".

The modern frontier sciences of high energy physics and molecular biology and genetics can now be related to the Ancient Egyptian creation allegories. The Big Bang theory, which was described in the Ancient Egyptian allegorical stories, is now recognized by almost all scientists. Scholars can now recognize a coherent and consistent system behind the Ancient Egyptian cosmology and cosmogony.

In this chapter, we will overview a sample of scientific subjects in Ancient Egypt.

Astronomy

A few decades ago, those who suggested that astronomy had reached an advanced state, long before the invention of the telescope, were generally ridiculed or ignored. "Modern" astronomy is attributed to the works of Johannes Kepler [1571–1630 CE], and he is credited with having "discovered" the three planetary laws, without the "benefit of a telescope". Planetary laws that show the relationships between planets, distances, variations in speed, orbit configurations, etc. can never be determined without regular observations, measurements, recording, and analysis—yet none of these western academicians tell us how Kepler arrived (out of thin air) at these planetary laws. In truth, Kepler himself boasted in print, at the end of *Book V* of his series, *Harmony of the World*, that he rediscovered the lost laws of Egypt, as stated below:

> *Now, eighteen months after the first light, three months after the true day, but a very few days after the pure Sun of that most wonderful study began to shine, nothing restrains me; it is my pleasure to yield to the inspired frenzy, it is my pleasure to taunt mortal men with the candid acknowledgment that I am stealing the golden vessels of the Egyptians to build a tabernacle to my God from them, far, far away from the boundaries of Egypt.*

The jubilant Kepler did not state that he himself discovered anything. Rather, it was all Ancient Egyptian.

Clement Alexandrinus (200 CE) reported about the advanced knowledge of astronomy in Ancient Egypt. He referred to five interrelated volumes in Ancient Egypt on astronomy—one containing a list of the fixed stars, another on the phenomena of the sun and moon, two others on the rising of the stars, another contained a cosmography and geography, the course of the sun, moon, and the five planets. These references indicate a complete under-standing of astronomy—unmatched even in our present times.

Astronomers studying Egypt have long argued that Egyptian astronomy was highly advanced, that the pre-cession of the equinoxes was known to them, as was the heliocentric system, and many other phenomena suppos-edly only recently discovered.

The main theme in all Ancient Egyptian texts is the cyclical nature of everything in the universe. The Egyp-tians were very much aware of their dependence on the cycles of earth and sky. Therefore, temple priests were assigned the task of observing the movements of these heavenly bodies. They were also responsible for noting other celestial events and interpreting them.

Numerous monuments can be found throughout An-cient Egyptian sites attesting to their full awareness and knowledge of cosmology and astronomy. A systematic kind of astronomical observation began in Ancient Egypt at a very early time. The Ancient Egyptians compiled information, making charts of the constellations, based on observations and recordings.

The most ancient astronomical texts, presently known, are found on the lids of wooden coffins dating from the 9th Dynasty [c. 2150 BCE]. These texts are called *diagonal calendars* or *diagonal star clocks*, which signi-fies the objectives and contents of these texts—to observe and document the relationship between the stars' move-ment and time. The word *diagonal* signifies measure-ment of angles, i.e. the arc distance of movement during a specific time period. These Ancient Egyptian texts give the names of the decans (stars that rise at ten-day inter-vals at the same time as the sun), of which there are 36. More elaborate star charts and tables were found on the ceilings of numerous tombs from the New Kingdom [1550–1070 BCE], such as on the ceiling of the tomb of Senenmut, Queen Hatshepsut's architect, and on the ceiling at the temple of Abtu (Abydos). In the tombs of Ramses IV, VII, and IX, inscriptions that relate to the first and the 16th day of each Egyptian sothic month, give the position occupied by a star at each of the 12 hours of the night.

The Ancient Egyptian knowledge of timekeeping is reflected in their division of the day into 12 hours of day and 12 hours of night. The length of the hour was not *fixed*, but varied with the seasons. Long days in the summer meant longer hours of the day, and the opposite in the winter months. March 21 and September 23, when the sun crosses the equator and day and night are everywhere of equal length, are known as *equinoxes* (equal nights). The variable length of the hour signifies their understanding of the equinox—as well as their full understanding of accurate time measurement, as explained below.

Because the earth revolves around the sun in the plane of its orbit once each year, the reference line to the sun is changing constantly, and the length of one solar day is not the true time of one rotation of the earth. It is therefore that our "modern" astronomy recognizes that the true time of one rotation of the earth, which is known as the sidereal day, is based on one rotation with respect to the vernal equinox—when the length of day and night are exactly the same.

The Ancient Egyptians knew the secrets of time, because they observed and studied the apparent motion of the stars, the moon and the sun. Because all celestial bodies are in constant apparent motion with respect to the observer, it is extremely important to know the precise time of an observation of a celestial body—which the Ancient Egyptians mastered a long time ago.

Observations, for Ancient Egyptians, were made with the help of very basic sighting instruments. They avoided optical equipment—physicists recognize the various types of distortions caused by their use. It is widely accepted that the Ancient Egyptians used a sighting instrument they called *maskhet*, which was a wooden staff with a slit at one end, the latter used as a collimator to aim at stars. They also used a simple plumb-line to measure the vertical. With such sighting rods and plumb-lines, the altitude of a star at the meridian, or its azimuth at rising, can be measured with a very good degree of accuracy. The motion of each celestial body was measured in angular change as a combination of declination and right ascension, these being the given coordinates of the stars on a sky map.

The observations were recorded and plotted on a grid, by superimposing—under the center of the sky—a human figure sitting upright, and that the top of his head was placed below the zenith. The grid was typically 8 horizontal segments and 12 vertical segments—representing the 12 hours of the night. The stars which were approaching the zenith were referenced over a portion of this figure, and their position was indicated in the lists of stars: over the left ear, over the right ear, etc.

The Ancient Egyptian astronomical texts give the position of the stars during the 12 hours of the night—at intervals of 15 days—and from this information, the change in location of a particular point in the sky can be measured. These frequent, regular measurements and recordings led them to correlate the rate of speed of the heavenly bodies, and as such, the Ancient Egyptians were able to record major and minor irregularities in the perceived motion of these celestial bodies.

In the case of Ramses IX's (1131-1112 BCE) tomb, the ceiling shows the positions of the various stars over

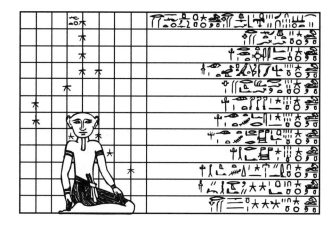

List of stars on the 16th of Babeh (Paophi)—27 October—from Ramses IX's tomb in Ta-Apet (Thebes).

12 consecutive 15-day periods. From these star charts, the Ancient Egyptians determined the positions and changes of location and/or time of stars. As such, the Ancient Egyptians were aware of the fact that the stars shifted slowly and that this was easily measurable at meridian transit, and thus the Ancient Egyptians knew and worked out the rate of precessional change.

The Ancient Egyptians made reference to the stars that define the perimeter of the various constellations, such as:

leg of the giant
claw of the goose
head of the goose
hinderpart of the goose
star of thousands
star S'ar
fingerpoint of the constellation S'ah (Orion)
the stars of S'ah(Orion)
star that follows Sabt (Sirius/Sothis)

fingerpoint of twin-stars
stars of the water
point of finger of the S'ah
head of the lion
tail of the lion

The Ancient Egyptian descriptions of the constellations as animal shapes are the source of the Greek origin of the English word, *zodiac*. The "Greek" word, *zodiakos* (kyklos), means (literally), *circle of animals.*

The star chart of the north pole of the sky, from the tomb of Seti I [1333–1304 BCE] [shown above], reinforces the Ancient Egyptian meaning of the word *zodiac*—as a circle of animals.

The main reason for our awareness—on earth—of the zodiac is the complex interactions between the earth, sun, and moon. Among the several volumes of the Ancient Egyptian knowledge, acknowledged by Clement Alexandrinus, was a whole volume on the phenomena of the sun and the moon. The significance of the sun and moon in the cosmic rhythms is ascribed allegorically to

Auset (Isis) and Ausar (Osiris), which was best described
by Diodorus of Sicily, *Book I, 11. 5-6,*

> *These two neteru (gods), they hold, regulate the entire*
> *universe, ...*

The twin actions of the sun and moon—on earth—is
the cause of precession. The moon and the sun both tug,
gravitationally, on the equatorial bulge of our earth. The
moon tries to pull the bulge into the plane of its orbit
around the earth, and the sun tries to pull this bulge into
the plane of the earth's orbit around the sun. As a result,
the earth does not spin true upon its axis, but more like
a slightly off-center spinning top. The combined result of
these two tendencies causes the axis of the earth to make
a double cone in space, centered on the center of earth, a
sort of wobble. This motion is called *precession.*

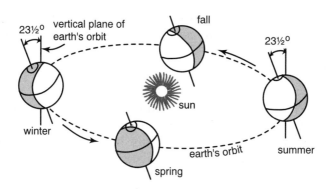

The earth rotates from west to east on its polar axis
and revolves about the sun in an elliptical orbit with the
sun at one focus of the ellipse. It completes one revolution in a period of 365.2564 days. The inclination of the
earth (23½ degrees with the perpendicular to the orbital
plane), combined with its revolution around the sun,
causes the lengths of day and night to change and also
causes the different seasons [shown above].

There are several components of this wobbly motion of the earth—the main component is on such a large scale that it dwarfs the remaining terms—the biggest of which is *nutation*. They are simply different frequency components of the same physical effects—the tug of war between the three bodies.

If the sky is regarded as a constellated backdrop, then because of the *wobble* of the earth upon its axis, the vernal equinox each year rises against a gradually shifting background of constellations. The effect is not real but apparent, and only involves the stars. The stars do not actually move but appear to move because of the earth's precessional wobble. Astronomers call this the *precession of the equinoxes*.

The continuous shifting of the stars' position acts as a sort of star-clock for our planet. For the Ancient Egyptians, by knowing the exact rate of precessional change and the coordinate of a star, they were able to determine its altitude at the meridian for any given time or its rising point on the eastern horizon.

The precession of the equinoxes, through the constellations, gives names to the twelve zodiac ages. It takes roughly 2,160 years for the equinox to precess through a zodiac sign. Thus it takes some 25,920 years for the spring equinox to traverse the full circuit of the constellations of the twelve zodiac signs. This complete cycle is called the Great/Full Year.

The signs of the zodiac are represented in two locations at the Het-Heru (Hathor) Temple at Dendera. It is clearly Ancient Egyptian, with its figures, symbols, etc. The same exact symbolism of depicted zodiac ages, deities, figures, etc, are found in numerous Ancient Egyptian temples and tombs throughout the country, long before the Greco-Roman era.

The circular zodiac [shown above] is depicted on the ceiling of the upper level of the temple, where the signs are arranged in a spiral form.

Western academia disregarded the overwhelming physical evidence, as well as the affirmation of Ancient Egyptian sources, that the precession of the equinoxes was known in Egypt since time immemorial. Academia handed the credit to the "Greek" Hipparchus of Alexandria [c.160–125 BCE]. This is yet another pathetic attempt to credit a European with a major achievement. Yet in this case, Hipparchus (who never claimed himself as the source) could never have single-handedly done something that requires astronomical observations, measurements, and recordings for centuries and millenia.

While Western academia attributes the knowledge of astronomy to the Greeks, the Greeks themselves attributed their astronomical knowledge to the Egyptian priests. The Great Strabo [64 BCE–25 CE] admitted in c. 20 BCE (about 100 years after Hipparchus) that,

> *The Egyptian priests are supreme in the science of the sky...[the Egyptians]...impart some of their precepts; although they conceal the greater part. [The Egyptians] revealed to the Greeks the secrets of the **full year**, whom the latter ignored as with many other things...*

Geodesy

In a country that relies on agriculture, *geodesy* (the science of earth measurement) was developed, long before the time of **Mena** (Menes). Measurement of the superficial area as well as the various elevations of the country were very important in the design, construction, and operation of canals and dikes, in order to distribute the water to the farmlands. It is therefore that the Ancient Egyptians studied, compiled, and utilized immense geographical data about the surface of the earth (including water surfaces) with actual measurements.

The pavilion of **Senwasert** (Sesostris) I [1971–1926 BCE], at Karnak Temple, incorporates geodesic knowledge in its design, and it also provides a wealth of geodesic information. It shows (among many things) a list of all the provinces of Egypt with their respective land surface areas, proving that actual surveys were made. Major towns are listed, the total length of Egypt is given, and the normal height of the Nile flood noted at three principal points along the length of the river. A lot of other useful information is also provided.

Little, if any, credit is given to Ancient Egypt as the source of the detailed descriptions and measurements that are found in Strabo's volumes, *Geography*. Strabo obtained the detailed descriptions of the world geography (that took centuries to compile by the Egyptian geographers) from Egypt—where he studied for several years.

Sacred Geometry and Natural Science

Geometry for the Ancient Egyptians was much more than a study of points, lines, surfaces, and solids, and their properties and measurement. The harmony inheret in geometry was recognized in Ancient Egypt as the most cogent expression of a divine plan that underlies the world—a metaphysical plan that determines the physical. For the Ancient Egyptians, geometry was the means by which humanity could understand the mysteries of the divine order. Geometry exists everywhere in nature: its order underlies the structure of all things, from molecules to galaxies. The nature of the geometric form allows its functioning. The design using the principles of sacred geometry must achieve the same goal, i.e. form to serve/represent a function.

Sacred geometry deals not only with the proportions of the geometrical figures, but also of the harmonic relations of the parts to the whole, such as the parts of the human being with one another, the structure of plants and animals, the forms of crystals and natural objects— all of which are manifestations of the universal continuum.

The key to divine harmonic proportion (sacred geometry) is the relationship between progression of growth and proportion. Harmonic proportion and progression are the essence of the created universe. It is consistent with nature around us. Nature around us follows this harmonious relationship. The natural progression follows a series that is popularized in the West as the *"Fibonacci Series"*.

Since this Series was in existence before Fibonacci (born in 1179 CE), it should not bear his name. Fibonacci himself and his western commentators, did not even claim that it was his "creation". Let us call it as it is—a *Summation Series*. It is a progressive series, where you start with the first two numbers in the Ancient Egyptian system, i.e. 2 and 3. Then you add their total to the preceding number, and on and on; any figure is the sum of the two preceding ones. The series would therefore be: 2, 3, 5, 8, 13, 21, 34, 55, 89, 144, 233, 377, 610, . . .

This series is reflected throughout nature. The number of seeds in a sunflower, the petals of any flower, the arrangement of pine cones, the growth of a nautilus shell, etc...all follow the same pattern of these series.

The overwhelming evidence indicates that the Summation Series was known to the Ancient Egyptians. Many Ancient Egyptian plans of temples and tombs, throughout the history of Ancient Egypt, show that the major elements of the temples are positioned along their longitudinal axes following the consecutive numbers of the Summation Series 2, 3, 5, 8, 13, 21, 34, 55, 89, 144, 233, 377, 610, . . . [as shown on page 131 of this book].

Once the dimensions of the Ancient Egyptian monuments are shown in the Ancient Egyptian units of the cubit (1.72 ft/0.528 m), it will become crystal clear that the Summation Series is the brainchild of the Ancient Egyptians. The Summation Series conforms perfectly with, and can be regarded as an expression of, Egyptian mathematics, which has been defined by everyone as an essentially additive procedure.

There is evidence about the knowledge of the Summation Series, ever since the Pyramid (erroneously known as mortuary) Temple of Khafra (Chephren), at Giza, built in 2500 BCE, i.e. about 3700 years before Fibonacci.

The essential points of the temple [shown herein] comply with the Summation Series, which reaches the figure of 233 cubits in its total length, as measured from the pyramid, with TEN consecutive numbers of the series.

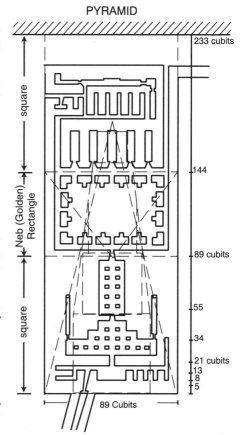

PYRAMID

Regarding the present-day narrow application of the term *geometry*, all aspects of our modern *geometry* were perfected in Ancient Egypt, a long time ago. Their advanced knowledge is clearly evident in a few recovered papyri, which are commonly known as the Ancient Egyptian "mathematical" papyri. More details regarding these papyri will be shown in the next few pages.

As is the norm with western academia, they handed the knowledge of geometry to—the Greeks. Fortunately, there are honest people, such as the famed Egyptologist, Sir J. Gardiner Wilkinson, who wrote in his book, *The Ancient Egyptians, Their Life and Customs*,

> ... Herodotus, and others, ascribe the origin of geometry to the Egyptians; but the period when it commenced is uncertain. Anticlides pretends that Moaris was the first to lay down the elements of that science, which he says was perfected by Pythagoras; but the latter observation is merely the result of the vanity of the Greeks, which claimed for their countrymen (as in the case of Thales, and other instances) the credit of enlightening a people on the very subjects which they had visited Egypt for the purpose of studying.

Mathematics and Numerology

For the Ancient Egyptians, the two primary numbers in the universe are 2 and 3. All phenomena without exception are polar in nature, treble in principle. As such, the numbers 2 and 3 are the only primary numbers, from which other numbers are derived.

Two symbolizes the power of multiplicity—the female, mutable receptacle, while Three symbolizes the male. This was the *music of the spheres*—the universal harmonies played out between these two primal male and female universal symbols of **Ausar** and **Auset**, whose heavenly marriage produced the child, **Heru**. Plutarch confirmed this Egyptian knowledge in *Moralia Vol V*:

> *Three (Osiris) is the first perfect odd number: four is a square whose side is the even number two (Isis); but five (Horus) is in some ways like to its father, and in some ways like to its mother, being made up of three and two...*

The significance of the two primary numbers 2 and 3 (as represented by **Auset** (Isis) and **Ausar** (Osiris) was made very clear by Diodorus of Sicily [*Book I*, 11. 5],

> *These two neteru (gods), they hold, regulate the entire universe, giving both nourishment and increase to all things...*

In the animated world of Ancient Egypt, numbers did not simply designate quantities but instead were considered to be concrete definitions of energetic formative principles of nature. The Egyptians called these energetic principles **neteru**.

For Egyptians, numbers were not just odd and even. These animated numbers in Ancient Egypt were referred to by Plutarch, in *Moralia Vol V*, when he described the Egyptian 3-4-5 triangle:

> *The upright, therefore, may be likened to the male, the base to the female, and the hypotenuse to the child of both, and so Ausar [Osiris] may be regarded as the origin, Auset [Isis] as the recipient, and Heru [Horus] as perfected result.*

The vitality and the interactions between these numbers shows how they are male and female, active and passive, vertical and horizontal, ...etc.

The divine significance of numbers is personified in Ancient Egyptian traditions by Seshat, *The Enumerator*. The netert (goddess) Seshat is also described as: *Lady of Writing(s)*, Scribe, *Head of the House of the Divine Books (Archives)*, the *Lady of Builders*.

Seshat

Seshat is closely associated with Tehuti (Thoth), and is considered to be his female counterpart.

The Egyptian concept of number symbolism was subsequently popularized in the West by and through Pythagoras [ca. 580–500 BCE]. It is a known fact that Pythagoras studied for about 20 years in Egypt, in the 6th century BCE.

Pythagoras and his immediate followers left nothing of their own writing. Yet, western academia attributed to him and the so-called *Pythagoreans*, an open-ended list of major achievements. They were issued a blank check by western academia.

Pythagoras and his followers are said to view numbers as divine concepts, ideas of the God who created a universe of infinite variety, and satisfying order, to a numerical pattern. The same principles were stated more than 13 centuries before Pythagorus' birth, in the heading of the Egyptian's Papyrus, known as the *Rhind Mathematical Papyrus* [1848–1801 BCE], which promises,

Rules for enquiring into nature and for knowing all that exists, every mystery, every secret.

The intent is very clear that Ancient Egyptians believed and set the rules for numbers and their interactions (so-called mathematics) as the basis for *"all that exists"*.

All the design elements in Egyptian art and buildings (dimensions, proportions, numbers, ...etc.) were based on the Egyptian number symbolism, such as the Ancient Egyptian name for the largest temple in Egypt, namely the Karnak Temple Complex, which is **Apet-sut**, meaning *Enumerator of the Places*. The temple's name speaks for itself. This temple started in the Middle Kingdom in ca. 1971 BCE, and was added to continuously for the next 1,500 years. [Evidence of this knowledge is also shown in ch. 7, *Egyptian Temples*]

[For more information about numbers and their significance, see *Egyptian Cosmology: The Animated Universe* and *Egyptian Harmony: The Visual Music, Egyptian Architecture*, all by M. Gadalla.]

Regarding the present-day narrow application of the subject of "mathematics", the perfection of the Ancient Egyptian monuments attest to their superior knowledge. For a starter, the Egyptians had a system of decimal numbering, with a sign for 1, another for 10, 100, 1000 and so on. The evidence at the beginning of the 1st Dynasty (2575 BCE) shows that the system of notation was known up to the sign for 1,000,000. Addition and subtraction were used by them. Multiplication, except for the most simple cases in which a number had either to be doubled or to be multiplied by ten, involved a process of doubling and adding, which is, by the way, how the computer process works. Our multiplication tables rely totally on memorization and nothing more, and can by no means be considered a human achievement. The computer process is easier, more accurate and faster, as we all know.

Academicians ignore the knowledge imbedded in the numerous Ancient Egyptian works. They want to refer only to a few recovered Ancient Egyptian papyri that come from a Middle Kingdom papyrus and a few fragments of other texts of a similar nature. The study of mathematics began long before the found "mathematical" papyri were written. These found papyri do not represent a mathematical treatise in the modern sense, that is to say they do not contain a series of rules for dealing with problems of different kinds, but merely present a series of tables and examples worked out with the aid of the tables. The four most referred to papyri are:

1. The Rhind "Mathematical" Papyrus (now in the British Museum) is a copy of an older document during King Nemara (1849–1801 BCE), 12th Dynasty. It contains a number of examples to which academic Egyptologists have given the serial numbers 1-84.

2. The Moscow "Mathematical" Papyrus (in the Museum of Fine Arts of Moscow) also dates from the 12th Dynasty. It contains a number of examples to which academic Egyptologists have given the serial numbers 1-19. Four examples are geometrical ones.

3. The Kahun fragments.

4. The Berlin Papyrus 6619, which consists of four fragments reproduced under the numbers 1-4.

Below, is a synopsis of the contents of the Rhind "Mathematical" Papyrus:

• Arithmetic
  - Division of various numbers.
  - Multiplication of fractions.
  - Solutions of equations of the first degree.
  - Division of items in unequal proportions.

• Measurement
  - Volumes and cubic content of cylindrical containers and rectangular parallelopi pectal

- Areas of:
  rectangle
  circle [also see page 189, andGadalla's books: *Egyptian Cosmology, Egyptian Harmony*, and *Egyptian Architecture*, regarding the subject of squaring the circle.]
  triangle
  truncated triangle
  trapezoid
- Batter or angle of a slope of a pyramid and of a cone.
- Miscellaneous problems:
  - Divisions into shares in arithmetical progression.
  - Geometrical progression.

Other Mathematical Processes known from other Papyri include:

- Square and square root of quantities involving simple fractions [Berlin 6619].
- Solution of equations of the second degree [Berlin Papyrus 6619].

☞ **It must be noted that the Rhind Papyrus shows that the calculation of the slope of the pyramid** [Rhind Nos. 56-60] **employs the principles of a quadrangle triangle, which is called the *Pythagoras Theorem*. This Egyptian Papyrus is dated thousands of years before Pythagoras ever walked this earth.**

This theorem states that the square of the hypotenuse of a right triangle is equal to the sum of the squares of the other two sides. Plutarch explained the relationship between the three sides of the right angle triangle 3:4:5, which he (like all the people of his time) called the "Osiris" Triangle. [Read the complete text of Plutarch on page 285 of this book.]

The Sacred "Ratios"

The Ancient Egyptians knew the transcendental numbers *pi* and *phi*. They manifested their knowledge in their harmonic proportioning of their buildings and art-work.

1. The Golden Proportion (which numerically = 1.618), to which western academia has recently assigned an arbitrary symbol—the Greek alphabet letter ϕ (*phi*)—was known and used long before the Greeks. And what is worse is that there is no factual evidence that the Greeks knew it at all!

Integrity and honesty demand that an Ancient Egyptian term be used for this proportion, i.e. **Neb** (Golden) Proportion. **Neb** means *gold, divine*. This proportion is also known in Western texts as *Golden* and *Divine*—since the 19th century.

The **Neb** (Golden) Proportion can be derived mathematically from the Summation Series, which the Ancient Egyptians manifested its knowledge of at least 4,500 years ago. As the Summation Series progresses (2, 3, 5, 8, 13, 21, 34, 55, 89, 144, . . .), the ratio between successive numbers tends towards the **Neb** (Golden) Proportion. The ratios 55:34, 89:55, 144:89, . . .etc, are all of the same "value" of 1.618. As shown earlier, Ancient Egyptian temples and shrines were segmented along the progressive numbers of the Summation Series—the significant points along the axis of the building plan [see pgs 128-131].

The **Neb** (Golden) Proportion can also be derived graphically, in several ways, which were all common in the Egyptian buildings throughout its dynastic history. [See details of the various ways in *Egyptian Harmony* or *Egyptian*

Architecture, by M. Gadalla.]   Below is one of these ways, which is obtained by inscribing a square within a semi-circle.

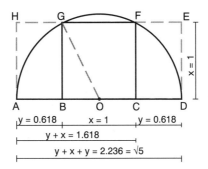

2. The Circle Index is the functional representation of the circle. It is the ratio between the circumference of the circle to its diameter. It is popularized by western academia by the Greek letter *pi* and given a value of 3.1415927.

The Egyptians manifested their knowledge of the circle properties and other curves, as early as their surviving records. A 3rd Dynasty [~2630 BCE] record shows the definition of the curve of a roof, in Saqqara, by a system of coordinates [shown above].

This shows that their knowledge of the circle enabled them to calculate the coordinates along this vertical curve. Accordingly, the construction workers followed precise dimensions in their executed circular curves.

The Egyptians built their capitals with nine elements and occasionally with seven, in addition to 6, 8, 11, and 13-sided polygons, because they knew the properties of the circle and its relationship to perpendicular coordinates and other geometric figures.

Such application was evident in Egypt at least 2,000 years before Archimedes walked this earth.

The typical Ancient Egyptian doorway layout incorporated both sacred ratios (*pi* and *phi*), as shown and explained herein.

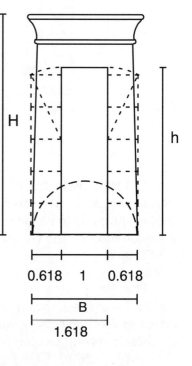

1. The overall outline in the vertical plane is the double-square, 1:2 ratio. [H = 2B]

2. The opening width is based on a square inscribed within a semi-circle, the typical Ancient Egyptian way of proportioning a root-five rectangle.

Thus, the thickness of the doorjamb is 0.618 the width of the opening. [Also see diagram on page 199.]

3. The height of the aperture (h) = 3.1415 = *pi*

Part IIIII

The Vibrant Economy

12

The Cultivating Culture

Dry-Weather Farming

Egypt is (and was) one of the most arid areas in the world. The River Nile in Egypt received 90% of its water during a 100-day flood period every year, as noted by Herodotus, in *The Histories,* [2, 92], where he states:

> . . . . the water begins to rise at the summer solstice, continues to do so for a hundred days, and then falls again at the end of that period, so that it remains low throughout the winter until the summer solstice comes round again in the following year.

The floodwaters of the Nile come as a result of the rainy season in Ethiopia, which erodes the silt of the Ethiopian highlands, and carries it towards Egypt along the Blue Nile and other tributaries. No appreciable amount of water comes to Egypt via the White Nile, which starts from Central Africa.

The Ancient Egyptians managed their limited water resources efficiently, and became the best dry-weather agrarians in the world. Ancient Egypt was renowned worldwide for its dry-weather irrigation and farming techniques. Diodorus spoke of the efficient Egyptian farming system,

> *. . .being from their infancy brought up to agricultural pursuits, they far excelled the husband-men of other countries, and had become acquainted with the capabilities of the land, the mode of irrigation, the exact season for sowing and reaping, as well as all the most useful secrets connected with the harvest, which they had derived from their ancestors, and had improved by their own experience.*

Several entities were formed along the Nile Valley to manage the gushing floodwaters by observing, recording, and regulating the water flow to the whole Nile Valley. As a consequence, a highly organized communal irrigation system was developed and used since time immemorial.

The limited available water resources in Ancient Egypt were managed most efficiently by utilizing organized methods of water conservation and diversion. According to Strabo, the Egyptian communal irrigation system was so admirably managed,

> *. . .that art contrived sometimes to supply what nature denied, and, by means of canals and embankments, there was little difference in the quantity of land irrigated, whether the flood was deficient or abundant.*

The Ancient Egyptians made precise observations of the increase of the Nile elevation during the inundation season. Nilometers, devices used for measuring the gradual rise and fall of the Nile, were constructed in various parts of Egypt, and water surface fluctuations were recorded and reported. The elevations at the Nilometers throughout Egypt were all tied to a single common datum. Regulating the flow amounts and duration was controlled by knowledgeable officials, using sluice gate(s) to control the flow of water to a determined height and duration. Diodorus, in *I.* [19. 5-6], affirms:

> . . .at flood-time it might not form stagnant pools over the land to its detriment, but that the **flood-water might be let upon the countryside**, in a gentle flow as it might be needed, **through gates which they [Egyptians] had built**.

The water of the inundation was managed differently in various districts. This depended on many factors, such as the relative heights/elevations of the adjoining lands, and what the crops they happened to be cultivating at the time, etc.

The Ancient Egyptians understood the different types of soil—to provide a variety of agricultural products. They even took advantage of the edge of the desert, where the soils are a mixture of clay and sand, for growing the vine and some other plants, which are suited for these soils.

Besides the admixture of nitrous earth which was nourished with silt from Ethiopian hills, the Egyptians made use of additional soil nourishment, such as natural fertilizers—manure from different animals and birds—for different purposes. In addition, the Ancient Egyptians also used "chemical" fertilizers, which were spread over the surfaces. These were used for certain crops, particularly those grown late in the year.

Not only did the Ancient Egyptians provide water to the lowlands, but they were able to irrigate the lands that were too far from the river to be directly flooded by it. To reach all the way to the sands of the desert, they utilized a system of canals and water elevating devices. Water was elevated to higher canals in Ancient Egypt by using:

1. The *shadoof*—the common mode of raising water from the Nile or feeding channels for a small quantity of water. It consists basically of a pole and a bucket.

2. The foot machine (pump) mentioned by Philo, which is echoed in Deuteronomy [xi. 40],
   Egypt where thou sowedst thy seed, and wateredst it with thy foot as a garden of herbs.

3. The hydraulic screw—Egyptian water pumps were famed worldwide, and were used in the mining activities in Iberia, as per the following testimony of Strabo, *Geography,* [3.2.9]:

   So Poseidonius implies that the energy and industry of the Turdetanian [southern Spain] miners is similar, since they cut their shafts aslant and deep, and, as regards __the streams that meet them in the shafts, oftentimes draw them off with the Egyptian screw__.

   The "Egyptian screw" was designed and manufactured on the same principle as our modern-day pumps, which consist of a spiral tube coiled around a shaft, or a large screw in a cylinder, revolved by hand or mechanical means. The hand-driven type is commonly known in Egypt now, as the *tanbour*.

4. The waterwheel, with its scoops for taking up water from the rivers and feeding it into irrigation canals. They are efficient in providing water to higher levels and therefore can be found in places like the Fayoum Oasis, south of Cairo.

   The Ancient Egyptian waterworks and land reclamation projects were huge—even by our present-day standards of projects that use heavy equipment. Here are a few examples:

1. A major waterway diversion project was carried out— over 4,000 years ago. The project began at present- day Asyut, where a large quantity of the Nile waters used to go to the region of present-day Fayoum— located about 65 mi [100 km] southwest of Cairo. The Fayoum Oasis lies below sea level, and contains Lake Qarun. The lake was originally used as a catchment basin for the Nile overflow, and once filled the en- tire region. This water carried with it, and depos- ited, the fertile Nile silt on the bottom of the lakebed. This ancient major project caused the diversion of millions of gallons that was wasted at the deserts around the Fayoum region. The flow of water into the lake was reduced. As a result, about 80% of the original lake area was reclaimed and the rich soil was cultivated. A series of waterwheels were used to raise water to the banks along this branch of the Nile. Additionally, more water was available along the Nile Valley north of Asyut—increasing arable lands.

2. There is archeological evidence of major public projects in Kush, which were built in order to estab- lish a permanent presence in the area during the Middle Kingdom. King Senwasret III [1878–1844 BCE] established (modern-day) Semna [location map on page 255]. The area above the Third Cataract was fertile and supported a large population. During the Middle Kingdom, an artificial dam blocked the chan- nel. A portion of this dam is still visible, to this date, at Semna East. The dam construction raised the level of the Nile for hundreds of miles to the south, en- abling trading expeditions to navigate far into the interior of Africa. There are about 25 inscriptions on the rocks below the channel fortresses of Semna East and Semna West. They represent Nile flood levels recorded during the Middle Kingdom, and all of them show a level about 25 ft [8m] higher than the maxi- mum water levels of today.

Division of Labor

The arid weather of Egypt, and the limited duration of the flood period of the River Nile, led to a highly organized communal irrigation system based on organized methods of water conservation and diversions. Farmers needed superintendents for soil, water flow regulators, fisheries, etc. Local superintendents coordinated with regional superintendents, and those in turn coordinated their activities with national superintendents.

In Ancient Egypt, the social consequences of successful and efficient dry-farming practices were far reaching, since the more efficient farming is, the more dependent the society becomes on leaders or superintendents. A ranked society was developed, the leaders of which coordinated the various activities of the society. This prompted a more efficient distribution of the workforce, with various interactive specialized groups.

Ancient Egypt did not have castes, in the strictest sense of the word. But there was a general division of labor into four main groups:

1. The farming community, consisting of nobles, farmers (who made up the bulk of the population), stock breeders, gardeners, superintendents of waterway activities and duties such as irrigation, water and fishing rights, etc., huntsmen, boatmen of the Nile, traders, shopkeepers, and servile bondsmen.

    A closely related group of people in the farming community are the servile bondsmen, who were generally in the form of servitude, and it was relatively benign—an extension of lineage and kinship systems. It was a case of adoption—they were always well treated and could rise to respected positions in households and communities with the same equal rights as biological siblings.

2. Specialized professionals (artisans), such as: the smiths, leatherworkers, carpenters/woodworkers, boat builders, public weighers and notaries, paper makes, scribes, weavers, musicians, and bards (storytellers/wordsmiths), as well as masons/builders, and probably potters.

3. Intermediaries, consisting of the clergy (temples and shrines), judges, and doctors.

4. This last group consisted mainly of people working just outside populated areas, such as the herdsmen groups, pastors, oxherds, shepherds, goatherds, swineherds, poulterers, and fowlers.

These four main groups were usually subdivided again, according to their peculiar trade or occupation.

There is mobility not only between the different occupations but also within any particular occupation. Individuals are not necessarily confined to this occupation for life. They have the option of seeking out other occupations but can only perform the less complicated tasks, as they wouldn't have had the lifelong training.

More details of the four major groups are scattered throughout this book, to fit with the various subjects.

Ancient and *Baladi* Egyptians are identified by their work. The person's *family* name was/is the family's profession/trade (Carpenter, Smith, Farmer, Taylor, ...etc.).

All the most essential parts of life—marriage, housing, occupation and status—revolve around profession. It is clear that one's profession defines one's existence.

Inborn Destiny (Genetic History)

The division of labor in the Ancient (and *Baladi*) Egyptian societies were/are, to some extent, hereditary, i.e., an individual's labor group was/is determined by birth.

Heredity is important in determining most people's destinies. A common expression, "nature vs. nurture", raises the eternal question—how much is inborn, and how much is a result of our upbringing/environment.

People are born with certain skills, i.e. there is a hereditary factor(s) in our making. In the United States, people refer to the reason for someone's genius, by saying, *"It's in her/his genes"*, i.e. the reason is genetic— implying hereditary.

It would take several generations to acquire the knack or the special skills peculiar to a given type of job. Relying on habit, the sense of custom, and tradition, Egyptians generally preferred not to run risks, and therefore chose to stay within the confines of the profession in which they had been raised—the ancestral profession—for their own personal good and for that of society as a whole. Such logical reasoning was noted in Diodorus' writings about the labor system in Ancient Egypt.

All the professions were clearly demarcated, and highly efficient and specialized. Encroachment on the preserves of others was not desired or encouraged.

This "genetic" system allowed the building up of work experience at an early age. The inborn skills, together with such acquisition of experience, were much more efficient and productive than our common education system nowadays.

In our post-Industrial Revolution societies, we waste time and energy in schooling. Most people don't become effective in their trade/profession until they are about 30 years old. To be born into a trade/profession, one would be able to contribute at a much earlier age.

There is a common misconception that a "caste" is a ranked endogamous division of society in which membership is hereditary and permanent. The emphasis on hierarchy inhibits our understanding. A more accurate analysis would be to distinguish castes by culturally defined sources of capacity or power.

Castes are not some type of hereditary succession. Although a son usually followed the profession of his father, owing to habit, thoughts, education, or patronage and connection, he could still enter a different profession/trade. He would have to do that without the benefit of his family's experiences and connections.

Within this hierarchical social structure, each member of the community finds his/her social position according to the hereditary position of the family. Even if a child does not perform the traditional role of his/her parents, the child's status remains as theirs.

The Farming Community

The concept of land for the Egyptians (Ancient and *Baladi*) doesn't accept the premise that land is a property that can be owned. For them, people have the right to occupy a land, only if they work it, and they can only own the fruit of their labor. The Ancient Egyptians had no verb meaning *to possess*, *to have*, nor any verb meaning *to belong to*.

Farmers are allowed access to the land only if they cultivate it. This concept of land is found in many countries in the world—being called public land (or some other similar term). The idea is the land is "owned" by the government (meaning people) and access is provided to people to work it in a certain way (mining, grazing, etc).

The farmers' work was/is closely associated with local (and regional) water resource superintendents. In order for the farmers to focus on being productive, the elders facilitated the interaction with others for needs such as equipment, material storage, trades, etc. These elders were/are referred to as "nobles".

The term, *noble*, came from the Ancient Egyptian Neb/Nab/Naba, which is one of the titles of the leaders throughout Ancient Egypt. Neb means *gold* (traditionally the finished perfected end product—the goal of the alchemist). As such, a noble was not a rich aristocrat, but rather a *good* person.

The excellent and productive farming of the Egyptians both allowed and benefited the development of numerous cities. These centers attracted industries, such as textiles, ceramics, glass, metal, leather, etc.

13

The Manufacturing Industries

The Egyptian Knowledge of Metallurgy and Metalworking

At an early period, the Egyptians learned how to work metals, and all agree that 5,000 years ago the Ancient Egyptians had already developed the techniques of mining, refining, and metalworking.

Ancient Egypt did not have several kinds of mineral ores, such as silver, copper, tin, lead, etc, even though they produced large quantities of electrum (an alloy of gold and silver), copper, and bronze alloys. The Ancient Egyptians used their expertise to explore for mineral ores in Egypt and in other countries. Ancient Egypt had the means and knowledge to explore for the needed mineral ores, establish mining processes, and transport heavy loads for long distances, by land and sea.

Because of it being the largest and richest population in the ancient world, Egypt imported huge quantities of raw materials, and in return exported large quantities of finished goods. The Ancient Egyptians' finished metallic and non-metallic products are found in tombs throughout the Mediterranean Basin, European, Asiatic and African countries.

The Egyptians possessed considerable knowledge of chemistry and the use of metallic oxides, as manifested in their ability to produce glass and porcelain in a variety of natural colors. The Ancient Egyptians also produced beautiful colors from copper, which reflects their knowledge of the composition of various metals, and the knowledge of the effects produced on different substances by the earth's salts. This concurs with our "modern" definition of the subjects of chemistry and metallurgy.

• Chemistry is the science dealing with the composition and properties of substances, and with the reactions by which substances are produced from or converted into other substances; the application of this to a specified subject or field of activity; the chemical properties, composition, reactions, and uses of a substance.

• Metallurgy is the science of metal, especially the science of separating metals from their ores and preparing them for use, by smelting, refining, etc.

The methods of metalworking: melting, forging, soldering, and chasing of metal, were not only much practiced, but also most highly developed. The frequent references in Ancient Egyptian records of metalworking gives us a truer conception of the importance of this industry in Ancient Egypt.

The skill of the Egyptians in compounding metals is abundantly proven by the vases, mirrors, and implements of bronze, discovered at Ta-Apet (Thebes), and other parts of Egypt. They adopted numerous methods for varying the composition of bronze, by a judicious mixture of alloys. They also had the secret of giving a certain degree of elasticity to bronze, or brass blades, as evident in the dagger now housed in the Berlin Museum. This dagger is remarkable for the elasticity of its blade, its neatness and perfection of finish. Many Ancient Egyptian prod-ucts, now scattered in European museums, contain 10 to 20 parts tin, to 80 and 90 parts copper.

Their knowledge of metal ductibility is evident in their ability to manufacture metallic wires and threads. Wire-drawing was achieved with the most ductile met-als such as gold and silver, as well as brass and iron. Gold thread and wire were the result of wire-drawing, and there is no instance of them being flattened. Silver wires were found in the tomb of Twt Homosis (Tuthomosis) III, and gold wires were found attached to rings bearing the name of Osirtasen I, who lived 600 years before Twt Homosis III [1490–1436 BCE].

The Egyptians perfected the art of making the thread from metals. It was fine enough for weaving into cloth, and for ornamentation. There exists some Amasis deli-cate linen, with numerous figures of animals worked in with gold threads, which required a great degree of de-tail and finesse.

The science and technology to manufacture metallic products and goods were known and perfected in Ancient Egypt, which was able to produce numerous metallic al-loys in large quantities. Examples of the manifestation of their knowledge are shown next.

The Golden Silver (Electrum) Products

The Ancient Egyptians utilized gold, which was mined in Egypt. They also used silver, which was/is not found in Egypt, but was imported from the Iberian Pen-insula. They used silver individually or combined into the golden-silver alloy known as electrum. Ancient Egyptian records indicate that the **neteru** (gods/goddesses) are *made from electrum*—as the source of energy in the universe. In addition to making religious objects such as statues, amulets, etc, this amalgam was often used for personal adornment and for ornamental vases. The proportion of the gold to the silver was generally two to three. An Ancient Egyptian papyrus from the time of Twt Homosis III (1490-1436 BCE) indicates that an official received a "great heap" of electrum, which weighed 36,392 uten, i.e. 7,286 lbs. [3,311 kg. 672 g.].

Gold and silver were also cast to make small statues in the same manner as copper and bronze. The two metals are often found in the form of solid beads, which are at least 6,000 years old.

At the Middle Kingdom tombs of Beni Hassan, the scenes give a general indication of the goldsmith's trade. The process of washing the ore, smelting or fusing the metal with the help of the blow-pipe, and fashioning it for ornamental purposes, weighing it, recording of materials inventory, and other vocations of the goldsmith, are all represented in these tombs.

When the gold was not cast solid, it was flattened into a sheet of even thickness. Gold in sheet form was used to decorate wooden furniture. Thicker gold sheets were hammered directly on to the wood and fixed by small gold rivets. Thinner sheets were attached by an adhesive, probably glue, on a prepared base of plaster. Very fine sheets were used as a coating for statues, mummy masks, coffins, and other items. It was applied over a layer of plaster, but the nature of the adhesive used by the Egyptian craftsman has not been identified.

The ability to work large masses of the material is shown in the 300 lbs. [136 kg.] gold coffin of Twtankhamen, now displayed at the Cairo Museum.

The Copper and Bronze Products

Ancient Egypt lacked mineral ores to produce copper and bronze alloys—copper, arsenic, and tin—which were obtained abroad. The Ancient Egyptians manufactured large quantities of these alloys, more than 5,000 years ago.

Egyptian copper was hardened by the addition of arsenic. The content of arsenic in the copper alloy varied depending on the intended use. Variation in composition has been observed: for example, daggers and halberds had stronger cutting edges, and contained 4% arsenical copper, while axes and points contained 2% arsenical copper. Arsenical copper was used from the pre-dynastic times [c.5000 BCE] right up to and including the Middle Kingdom [2040–1783 BCE].

The Ancient Egyptian stone (known as the "Palermo Stone" and now housed in the Palermo Museum) records the making of a copper statue of Khasekhemwy of the 2nd Dynasty [c.2890–2649 BCE]. A copper statue of Pepi I [2289-2255 BCE], the earliest surviving example of metal sculpture, is presently housed in the Cairo Museum. It is undoubtedly the precious nature of all metals in Egypt that explains the rarity of early pieces, since much of the metal would eventually have been melted down and re-used several times.

In addition to manufacturing arsenic copper, the Ancient Egyptians also manufactured bronze products. The addition of a small proportion of tin to copper produces bronze, and results in a lower melting point, an increased hardness, and a greater ease in casting. The content of tin varies widely between 0.1% and 10% or more. Many bronze items of a very early period have been found. A cylinder bearing the name of Pepi I [2289–2255 BCE], showing clean-cut lines as well as other bronze articles of the same period, indicates that the molding of bronze items dates to earlier than 2200 BCE.

The bronze industry was very important for the country. Bronze was perfected and employed in Egypt for large vessels as well as for tools and weapons. There are numerous examples of perfected bronzes that come from all periods since the Old Kingdom [2575–2150 BCE], such as the Posno Collection, which is now housed at the Louvre in Paris.

Ancient Egyptian bells of various kinds were found carefully wrapped in cloth, before they were placed in tombs. A large number of these bells are now housed in the Cairo Museum.

Bells were made mainly of bronze, but were also occasionally made of gold or silver. They came in different forms. Some have the form of bells with a jagged mouth, which is to represents a flower calyx, among a whole line of other types. The large number of Ancient Egyptian bell molds [now in the Cairo Museum, cat. #32315a, b] provides good evidence of metal founding in Ancient Egypt. The influx hole for the liquid metal can be clearly seen in these molds. The chemical analysis of the typical Ancient Egyptian bell was found to be 82.4% copper, 16.4% tin, and 1.2% lead.

The Egyptians employed various kinds of bronze alloys, as we learn from the texts of the New Kingdom, where there is frequent mention of *"black bronze"*, and the *"bronze in the combination of six"*, i.e. a six-fold alloy. Such variations produced different colors. Yellow brass was a compound of zinc and copper. A white (and finer) kind of brass had a mixture of silver, which was used for mirrors, and is also known as "Corinthian brass". Adding copper to the compound produced a yellow, almost golden appearance.

Copper and bronze provided material for a wide range of domestic utensils, such as cauldrons, pitchers, basins, and ladles, in addition to a wide range of tools and weapons—daggers, swords, spears, and axes, as well as battle-axes. In the Old and Middle Kingdoms, rounded and semi-circular forms of battle-axes predominated.

Records from the Middle Kingdom Period [2040–1783 BCE]—such as those depicted in Beni Hassan tombs, show the variety of Ancient Egyptian weapons such as the various shields [depicted herein], with several variations of riveting.

During the New Kingdom [1550–1070 BCE], the Ancient Egyptians raised a large military in order to protect their borders. The Egyptians hired mercenaries for their military forces and the Egyptians manufactured their necessary fighting equipment.

A secure and prosperous Egypt was able to produce large quantities of metal goods in the 18th Dynasty [1575–1335 BCE]. This increase in number of goods corresponded to the increase in mining activities and the increase in number of Egyptian copper and bronze items in Iberian tombs of the same period, as is referenced at the end of the next chapter.

The Ancient Egyptian demand for large quantities of copper, arsenic, and tin developed more than 5,000 years ago. The three mineral ores were imported from the only source known in the ancient world—Iberia. Archeological records show the early utilization of the mineral wealth in southern Iberia of copper and arsenic. As for the tin, we are aware of the "Tin Route", which ran along the western coast of the Iberian Peninsula, where the tin came from Galicia and possibly Cornwall. Strabo, in Vol 3 of his *Geography*, tells us that,

> *Tin . . . is dug up; and it is produced both in the country of the barbarians who live beyond Lusitania, and in the Cassiterides Islands; and tin is brought to Massilia from the British Islands.*

Evidence of early contacts along the "Tin Route" that came from the eastern Mediterranean region—namely Ancient Egypt—is shown in our book, *Egyptian Romany: The Essence of Hispania*, by Moustafa Gadalla.

The Glazing (Glass and Glazing) Products

The Ancient Egyptians produced numerous types of glazed articles as early as the Pre-Dynastic Period [c. 5000 BCE]. Glazed objects from this early time were mostly beads, with solid quartz or steatite being used as a core. Steatite was used for carving small objects like amulets, pendants, and small figures of *neteru* (gods/goddesses), as well as a few larger articles, and it proved an ideal base for glazing. Glazed steatite objects are found throughout the Dynastic Period [3050–343 BCE], and it is by far the most common material for scarabs. The same glazing techniques were used to mass-produce funerary equipment (amulets, shabti-figures) and house decoration (tiles, inlays of floral patterns).

The variety and high quality of the Ancient Egyptian glazing articles are indicative of the Ancient Egyptian knowledge of metallurgy. The most common colors of the Egyptian glaze were blue, green, or bluish-green. The color is the result of adding a copper compound. More brilliant results were achieved by using a mixture of copper and silver.

The Ancient Egyptian glass was formed by strongly heating quartz sand and natron with a small mixture of coloring agents such as a copper compound or malachite, to produce both green and blue glass. Cobalt, which would have been imported, was also used. After the ingredients were fused into a molten mass, the heating ceased when the mass reached the desired properties. As the mass cooled, it was poured into molds, rolled out into thin rods or canes, or other desired forms.

Glass-blowing is shown at the tombs of Ti [2465–2323 BCE] at Saqqara, Beni Hassan (more than 4000 years ago), and other later tombs.

Since glaze contains the same ingredients fused in the same manner as glass; glass making may therefore be attributed to the Egyptians even at a much earlier date. The hard glossy glaze is of the same quality as glass. The technique that was applied to the making of glass vessels was a natural development in the technique of glazing.

Egyptian glass bottles are shown on monuments of the 4th Dynasty [2575–2465 BCE]. Egyptian glass bottles of various colors were exported into other countries such as Greece, Etruria, Italy, and beyond.

The Ancient Egyptians displayed their excellent knowledge of the various properties of materials in the art of staining glass with diverse colors, as evident from the numerous fragments found in the tombs at Ta-Apet (Thebes). Their skill in this complicated process enabled them to imitate the rich brilliance of precious stones. Some mock pearls have been so well counterfeited, that even now it is difficult with a strong lens to differentiate them from real pearls. Pliny confirmed that they succeeded so completely in the imitation as to render it,

difficult to distinguish false from real stones.

The spectrum of colors in these semi-precious stones is fascinating—it ranges from the limpid blue of lapis-lazuli to the turbulent blue of turquoise and the speckled gold of cornaline, these being the three stones that are most representative of the Egyptian jeweler's art. But there were also agate, amethyst, and haematite. In addition, we should note that Egyptian craftsmen worked wonders with enamel, large plaques of which were decorated with hieroglyphs or cartouches.

Glass mosaics were made of various parts, which were made separately, and then united with heat by applying a flux. The Ancient Egyptian glass mosaics have wonderful, brilliant colors.

Glass is frequently found in what is commonly called Egyptian cloisonné work, a term used to describe an inlay consisting of pieces of glass, faience, or stone set in metal cells and fixed with cement. The process consisted of putting powdered glass in the cloison and applying enough heat to melt the powder until it became a compact mass.

Glazed pottery, tiles, and other ceramics were major industries in Ancient Egypt. Some tiles had high glazes and designs in an intense blue. They also produced ceramics with an iridescent metallic sheen.

Some tiles were painted in pigments made by mixing metallic oxides (of copper, manganese, cobalt, etc.) and alkaline silicates with water. Glazed tiles of the highest

An elegant Egyptian faience bowl, now in the Berlin Museum, decorated with a painting of three fish with one head,and three lotus flowers.

quality are to be found in Saqqara from about 4,500 years ago. The "Southern Tomb", only 700ft [300m] from the Step Pyramid, was discovered unmolested at Saqqara by Lauer and Firth in 1924-26. It consists of several chambers lined with blue tiles exactly like the burial chambers of the Step Pyramid.

The Iron Products

Although the pyramids were built before the "bronze and iron ages", meteoritic iron was known to the Egyptians of the Pyramid Age. The Ancient Egyptian name for *iron* was bja. The word, bja, is mentioned repeatedly in the Unas Funerary (Pyramid) Texts—UFT—that are found in the Saqqara Complex (about 4,500 years ago) in connection with the 'bones' of the star kings,

I am pure, I take to myself my iron (bja) bones, I stretch out my imperishable limbs which are in the womb of Nut. . . [UFT 530]

My bones are iron (bja) and my limbs are the imperishable stars. [UFT 1454]

The King's bones are iron (bja) and his limbs are the
imperishable stars. . . [UFT 2051]

Iron was utilized in Ancient Egypt, and iron mines
can be found in the Egyptian desert. Herodotus mentions
iron tools being used by the builders of the pyramids.
Herodotus' account is confirmed by pieces of iron tools
embedded in old masonry, which were discovered by 19th
century Egyptologists, in various places. Also, the monuments of Ta-Apet (Thebes), and even the tombs around
Men-Nefer (Memphis), dating more than 4,000 years ago,
represent butchers sharpening their knives on a round
bar of metal attached to their apron, which from its blue
color can only be steel. The distinction between the bronze
and iron weapons in the tomb of Ramses III, one painted
red, the other blue, leaves no doubt of both having been
used at the same periods.

Homer distinctly mentioned the use of iron in *Iliad*
[xxiii, 261] and how the red hot metal hisses when it is
submerged in water.

Academia's arbitrary dating of "metal developments"
(copper, bronze, iron, etc) Ages is absolutely baseless.
Bronze articles of various kinds such as swords, daggers,
other weapons, and defensive armor were in continuous
use, by all nations, long after iron was known and used
by them. Western academia cavalierly deny Egyptian
knowledge and use of iron products, because the Ancient
Egyptians never abandoned the use of bronze items. Yet
the discovery of Greek and Roman arms and tools, made
of bronze, was never used by western academicians to
claim the Greek and Roman ignorance of iron. It is therefore that the knowledge and production of the Ancient
Egyptian iron products can't be arbitrarily ignored.

The Egyptian Mining Experience

In the orderly nature of the Ancient Egyptian civilization, they maintained written records showing the nature of their expeditions and the arrangements of their mining activities. The surviving Ancient Egyptian records show a tremendous organization of mining activities more than 5,000 years ago, in numerous sites throughout Egypt and beyond.

The turquoise mines at Serabit el Khadem in the Sinai Peninsula show a typical Ancient Egyptian mining quarry, consisting of a network of caverns and horizontal and vertical passages carefully cut with proper corners—as were the quarries of the Ancient Egyptians in all periods. The Ancient Egyptians were able to cut deep and long into the mountains with proper shoring and support of excavated shafts and tunnels. Underground water seepage into the tunnels and shafts was safely pumped out to ground level. These Egyptian pumps were famed worldwide, and were used in the mining activities in Iberia, as per the following testimony of Strabo, in his *Geography* [3. 2. 9]:

> So Poseidonius implies that the energy and industry of the Turdetanian miners is similar, since they cut their shafts aslant and deep, and, as regards **the streams that meet them in the shafts, oftentimes draw them off with the Egyptian screw**.

The very religious Egyptians have always built temples/shrines along with commemorative stelae near/at each mining site. The same exact practice was found in mining sites outside Egypt, such as in the Iberian Peninsula , where mines of silver, copper, etc. were extracted since time immemorial.

The Ancient Egyptian mining site at Serabit el Khadem in Sinai provides a typical mining site, with its small temple of Het-Heru (Hathor), called *"the Lady of the Turquoise"*, which stood on a high rocky terrace that dominates the valley, since the 4th Dynasty [2575–2465 BCE], or possibly much earlier. This temple was afterwards enlarged by the kings of the New Kingdom, especially by Twt Homosis III. In front of the temple, for at least a half mile, is a kind of avenue that was arranged through numerous massive stelae covered on four sides with inscriptions commemorating mining expeditions. Inscribed stelae are also found at other mines throughout Egypt describing the work at each mining site.

At the mines of Wadi Maghara, in Sinai, there still stand the stone huts of the workmen as well as a small fort, built to protect the Egyptians stationed there from the attacks of the Sinai bedouins. There was a water well not far from these mines, and sizeable cisterns in the fortress to hold water. The mines of Wadi Maghara were actively worked all throughout the dynastic era [3050–343 BCE].

Inscriptions of the 19th Dynasty in the desert temple of Redesieh relate that King Seti I [1333–1304 BCE] commissioned stonemasons to dig a water well to provide water for both the mining operations as well as the mining workers. When the well was finished, a station and *"a town with a temple"* were built. Ramses II [1304–1237 BCE], his successor, mediated plans to provide for boring additional water along the roads to mining sites, where it was also needed.

Each mining site was conceived and planned for, with actual plans drawn up. Two Ancient Egyptian papyri were found, which include site maps, related to mining for gold

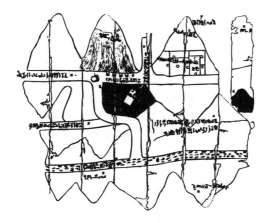

during the reigns of the Pharaohs Seti I and Ramses II. One papyrus, which is only partially preserved, represents the gold district of the mountain Bechen in the Eastern Desert, and belonging to the time of Ramses II. The site plan on the found papyrus [shown above] depicts two valleys running parallel to each other between the mountains. One of these valleys, like many of the larger valleys of the desert, is covered with underwood and blocks of stone to control the soil erosion as a result of surface water runoff. The prepared site plan shows the major details of the site, such as the road network within the mining site and its connection to the outer roadway system, and *"routes leading to the sea"*. The site plan also shows treatment areas of ore metals (such as washing, etc), small houses, storage areas, various buildings, a small temple, a water tank, etc. The area surrounding the mining site shows cultivated ground, to provide the food needed for the mining site colony.

The Ancient Egyptian records also show the various division and specialties of the manpower at mining sites.

The Ancient Egyptian records show the organizational structure of the mining operations. Ancient Egyptian surviving records show the names and titles of various officials who, during the Old and the Middle Kingdoms, directed the works at Hammamat, at Bechen mines in the Eastern Desert. They included engineers, miners, smiths, masons, architects, artists, security details, and ship captains—who maintain the integrity of the parts of the ships that will be put back together when the expedition reaches navigable waters. [More details on pages 242-3, regarding Egyptian ships.]

The ore metals were treated on site before transporting by land and water, under heavy security, to the populated areas of Egypt by the Nile Valley. [Details of transportation systems in chapter 14, *Transportation Infrastructure*.]

Egyptian mining activities were very organized with people traveling back and forth to check the site work, to ensure proper efficiency of operation, and to provide frequent rotation of the workforce at the mining sites, as well as to provide amenities to these fortified sites. Under the Ancient Egyptian King Pepi I [2289–2255 BCE], the records show the name of the director of the quarries and the names and titles of the higher officials who conducted inspection visits to the site. Inscriptions mention many titles, such as: *"the chief superintendent of all the works"*, and *"the chief architect"*. This great man paid two visits of inspection to Hammamat—once accompanied by his deputy, and once, when it was a question of the religious texts on the walls of a temple, with a superintendent of the commissions of the sacrificial estates.

A document that dates to the reign of Ramses IV [1163–1156 BCE] provides a report of an expedition to the mountain of Bechen in the Eastern Desert, under the direction of the *"superintendent of the works"*. Altogether the expedition consisted of 8,368 people. These men included more than 50 civil officials and ecclesiastics, as well as 200 officials from various departments. The field work was carried out by miners, stonemasons, and other related work forces, who worked under three superintendents, and the "chief superintendent". The labor work was carried out by 5000 miners, smiths, masons, etc, and 2,000 various types of labor. There were at least 110 officers supervising 800 men of the barbarian mercenaries for security details.The security forces were needed for the protection of the mining sites and transportation of people and material. The management of this large number of people is extraordinary—8,368 people is the size of a large community, even nowadays.

The Ancient Egyptians sought raw materials from other countries and used their home-grown expertise to explore, mine, and transport raw materials from all over the inhabited world. The Ancient Egyptian mining characteristics are found in many places—such as Iberia.

Fortification of Isolated Communities

Ancient Egyptian mining sites and other remote sites were provided with adequate protection to ensure the security needs of each individual settlement. Egyptians were experts in building new settlements. An example is found south of the Egyptian frontier, where there is archeological evidence of major public work projects in Kush, which were built in order to establish a permanent presence in the area during the Middle Kingdom. King Senwasert III [1878–1844 BCE] established (present-day) Semna as a natural strong point, with three fortresses, in order to provide security for the African trade caravans.

A system of regular fortification was adopted in the earliest times, and the form of the fortresses was quadrangular. The outer walls were typically formed of crude brick 15 ft [4.5m] thick, and often 50 ft [15.2m] high, with square towers at intervals along each face. The towers, like the rest of the walls, consisted of a rampart and parapet. The parapet was crowned by the usual round-headed battlements, in imitation of Egyptian shields, like those on their stone walls. Towers were placed at each side of every angle.

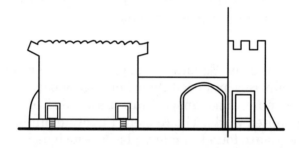

A fort from a Beni Hassan tomb. (Middle Kingdom)

Large fortresses were each typically provided with a long wall, on the side most exposed to attack, projecting from 70 to 100 ft [21 to 30m], at right angles from (and at the same height as) the main wall, upon which the besieged were able to run out and sweep the faces, or curtains, by what we call "flanking fire." In order to keep the enemy as far from the main wall as possible, the wall was raised on a broad terrace or basement, or was provided with an outer circuit, or low wall of circumvallation, parallel to the main wall, and distant from it, on every side, from 13 to 20 ft [4 to 6m]; and a tower stood at each side of the entrance, which was towards one corner of the least exposed face.

Whenever it was possible, the fortress was square, with one (or occasionally two) entrances, and a sally port (or a water gate, if near the river or canal). For an irregularly-shaped landscape, the fortress was made to conform to the contours of the ground.

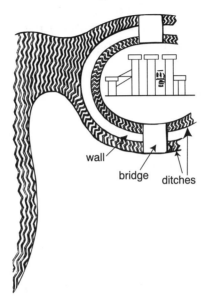

wall

bridge   ditches

Another more effective defense used with larger fortifications, was a huge ditch surrounding the fortress. A continuous stone wall was built along the center of the ditch. Over the ditch was a wooden bridge that was removed during a siege. The fortress stood on a platform on the scarp in the center [as depicted in the Ancient Egyptian wall painting shown above].

Diodorus of Sicily describes such a defensive arrangement, which was provided at the mouths of the seven branches of the Nile Delta, in his *Book I,* [33.5-8]:

> . . . *At each mouth is a walled city, which is divided into two parts by the river and provided on each side of the mouth with pontoon bridges and guard-houses at suitable points.*

Miscellaneous Products

In addition to the Ancient Egyptian metallic products mentioned earlier in this chapter, the Ancient Egyptians also excelled in the production of many non-metallic products, such as: wood, leather, linen, with skills including: dyers, tanners, carpenters, cabinet-makers, masons, etc.

Woodwork

Despite the lack of wood in the dry-weather climate of Egypt, the Egyptians were masters in the production of woodwork items. Egypt, which was one of the largest timber-consuming countries of antiquity, lacked timber that was essential for her buildings, her boats, her furniture and fuel, and especially her funerary equipment.

Phoenicia was Ancient Egyptian's main source of high quality lumber. Byblos became the center of a lumber trade, where vast quantities of cedar and pine trees were felled in the adjacent Lebanon hills, rolled or carted down to Byblos, and from there towed in rafts to Egypt. The destiny of the Phoenicians was thus tied to the demands of lumber by Egypt.

The technical skill of the Egyptian woodworker is evident in their boat-building and chariot-making. Both objects consist of small pieces built to withstand many internal and external stresses and strains in their use. As such, they must have been knowledgeable of the design properties of different woods, which led to the manufacture of durable and stable moving parts of the joinery.

More than 4,000 years ago, Egyptians had already invented and commonly used a form of pole to make chariots [see opposite page].

Egyptian boxes in form of geese,
now in the Leiden Museum.

Egyptian box
(now in the
Berlin Museum),
showing the lid
open.

Egyptian chair (now in the
British Museum).

Manufacturing the moving parts of a chariot. [Beni Hassan tomb]

The quality (and quantity) of the Ancient Egyptian ships are discussed in chapter 14.

The best line of furniture can be seen in the Hetepheres room, at the Cairo Musuem. In the long history of the world, there is very little to match this furniture that was manufactured in the Old Kingdom, 4,500 years ago. The contemporary feel of the Hetepheres furniture combines simplicity with sophistication.

Numerous pieces of furniture were depicted and/or recovered from Ancient Egyptian tombs that included stools, low seats, double and single chairs, ottomans, couches, tables, beds, boxes in all sizes and shapes (such as birds), etc. They were very well constructed and elegant with numerous design variations.

Practically the only modern carpenter's tool that the Ancient Egyptian did not possess was the plane, but he could do such fine work with the adze that the plane was not needed. Many examples of carpenter tools have been found in Egyptian tombs: squares, levels, chisels, drills, horns of oil, nails, mallets, and saws, all of which are very similar to their modern counterparts.

Glue was used in woodwork at a very early stage by the Ancient Egyptians. Several wooden boxes and coffins have been found in which glue was employed to fasten the joints.

A scribe wrote of a woodcarver:

Each artist who works with the chisel
Tires himself more than he who hoes [a field]
The wood is his field, of metal are his tools.
    In the night—is he free?
He works more than his arms are able,
In the night—he lights a light.

An elegant Egyptian wooden box with one part open, and one covered.

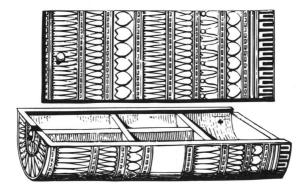

A semi-circular, fully decorated Egyptian wooden box with compartments. Notice how the lid slides into a groove.

A handsome Egyptian painted box, showing how the lid opened.

Fabrics

There are some interesting examples of Ancient Egyptian weaver's looms and shuttles in the British Museum which are basically the same design as those used today, except that they were manually operated.

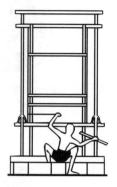

The Egyptians were always celebrated for their manufacture of linen and other cloths, and the produce of their looms was exported to (and eagerly purchased by) foreign nations.

Because of their knowledge in chemistry in the process for dyeing or staining cloth, they were able to bring about certain changes in the fabrics' hues, by the same means adopted nowadays. The Egyptians were even capable of dyeing their old clothes, to extend their use and beauty.

Pliny noted the Egyptians' use of the dye. He described the most characteristic of its properties, which was the emission of a beautiful purple vapor when exposed to heat.

The Egyptians had carpets from a very early time. Homer, who mentioned them, gave them the same name which they are still known by—Tapeta—hence *tapis* and *tapestry*.

The threads used for nets were remarkable for their fineness, and Pliny stated,

. . .some of them were so delicate that they would pass

through a man's ring, and a single person could carry a sufficient number of them to surround a whole [forest].

Flax was used for making ropes, string, and various kinds of twine. The Egyptians excelled in rope making. Specimens exist of rope made from palm fiber, five inches thick. These ropes are as strong and well made as any manufactured today.

Pottery

Deep rooted in the Ancient Egyptian religious beliefs is that mankind was made out of clay. A long time before the recorded history of dynastic Egypt, the **neter Khnum's** divine function was to fashion men on the potter's wheel. The scene of **Khnum** working at the wheel is shown in many places all over Ancient Egypt, thousands of years before the Greeks ever used it.

Various types of pottery had religious significance for the Egyptians, since time immemorial. Workmen making pottery on the wheel [as shown herein] are depicted throughout Ancient Egyptian tombs.

Leather

The tanning and preparation of leather was also a branch of art in which the Egyptians showed considerable skill.

The process of curing and dyeing the skins, as well as stretching and bending leather over a form, are frequently represented at Ta-Apet (Thebes). The semicircular knife, similar to that of our modern times, was commonly used by the Ancient Egyptians in this leather process.

Shoes, or low boots, were common in Egypt. Many of them have been found at Ta-Apet (Thebes).

Paper

Paper making of papyrus has survived the ages. The preserved papyri in the less arid climate of the Nile Delta still maintain their pliability; and as such they may be bent or twisted in any way, without breaking, or without being more injured than a piece of our common paper.

The Egyptian-made paper was exported to all the surrounding areas. Indeed, today the records found of the Greek and Roman eras were preserved on Egyptian made paper.

The Egyptian word was pa-pe-ra. The Greeks called it *papyrus*. One can easily see that the English word *paper* came from the Egyptian pa-pe-ra.

Your dictionary will also confirm that the word *Bible* is of Egyptian origin. The word, *Bible*, or book, was derived from *byblos*, which is the Egyptian hieratic word for papyrus.

Miscellaneous Technological Applications

Technology is by definition the technical method of achieving practical purposes. Most historians and scholars agree on the pragmatic and practical characteristics of the Ancient (and *Baladi*) Egyptian. Here are just glimpses of some technological achievements.

The Yale Lock: In 1848, Linus Yale supposedly invented the compact cylinder pin-tumbler lock and his name became a generic term for this kind of lock. Yale's invention was a reinvention of the Ancient Egyptian's pin-tumbler mechanism, commonly employed in the locks of their houses, thousands of years ago.

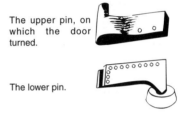

The upper pin, on which the door turned.

The lower pin.

The Egyptians utilized the **bellow**, one of which is represented in the tomb of Twt Homosis III. It consisted of a leather bag, secured and fitted into a frame, from which a long pipe extended for carrying the wind to the fire. Bellows were worked by the feet. From the painting, it was observed that when the man left the bellows unattended, they did not deflate; and, this would affirm the Ancient Egyptian knowledge of the **valve**.

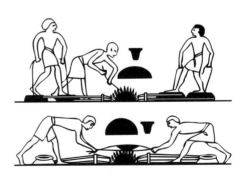

The **siphons** were also invented in Egypt, at least during the reign of Amunoph II [c. 1500 BCE].

In a tomb at Ta-Apet (Thebes), bearing the name of Amunoph, one observes a priest pouring a liquid into some vases, and another priest drawing it off, by applying the siphon to his mouth, and then to a large vase. Similar scenes are also shown in the paintings in Ramses III's tomb.

Heron of Alexandria, a notable early writer from the time of Ptolemy Euergetes II, reported that the Egyptians employed siphons as hydraulic machines on a grand scale, for draining lands, or conveying water over a hill from one valley to another.

They also invented **syringes**, used for injecting liquids into the head and body of mummies, during the embalming process. They were also famed for their **pumps** worldwide. This pump was simply called the *Egyptian screw* by Strabo and others of his time.

Dikes were followed by, or accompanied by, the invention of **sluices, and all their operating mechanisms**. Sluices were essential in the regulation of the supply of water to the fields. Much scientific skill was required to operate the sluice so as to release the prescribed quantity of water to the designated land.

Egyptians were knowledgeable of the **pulley** as evident by the one found, and now displayed in the Leiden Museum.

14

Transportation Infrastructure

General

Transferring people, minerals, and goods between Ancient Egypt and other faraway places was much more extensive and common than is generally imagined. The seas were not barriers, but high roads for active international commerce. Traveling by water has been (and continues to be) the most effective, economical, and safest way to travel for both people and goods. Travel by land complements travel by water for major/large goods.

The Ancient Egyptians had the means to travel the high seas—with a large number of high quality ships. They also had the geographic knowledge to travel the open seas. The evidence shows that their means and knowledge enabled them to reach the farthest countries of the earth. The following pages will detail the wealth of high quality ships and the Ancient Egyptian knowledge of high seas travel.

Previously in chapter 11, *Total Science*, we showed the Ancient Egyptian knowledge of the stars as well as the surface of the earth (including water).

The Egyptian Ships

Ancient Egypt had the means, knowledge, material, and experience to transport people and goods by sea and land. The quality of the Ancient Egyptian ships were truly recognized and appreciated when the Khufu (Cheops) boat (4500 years old) was found next to the Great Pyramid in Giza, during the 1970s. That boat, now housed in a museum next to the Great Pyramid, is superior

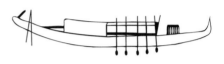

Khufu's Boat

and much more seaworthy than Columbus' Santa Maria, the Mayflower, or the Vikings' ships. The physical evidence is clear that the Egyptians had the means to travel on the high seas. Sizes of even larger ships than Khufu's will be detailed later.

Khufu's boat is one of the largest ancient ships found to date. The longest of Viking boats found in Europe was about 98.5 ft [30m], while Khufu's boat is 142.5 ft [43.4m] long. It is about 19.4 ft [5.9m] wide and 5.75 ft [1.75m] deep and has a displacement of over 40 tons. The prow, formed in the shape of a papyrus-bundle, is about 20 ft [6m] tall. Its stern rises to 23 ft [7m]. Its rudder consists of two massive oars. The boat has several cabins on its deck. There is some evidence that Khufu's boat was actually used in water. Marks caused by abrasion between the ropes and the wood of the vessel are still clearly visible in many places.

The boat consists of several pieces of wood that are held together with ropes. The ropes shrink when wet, while the wood expands when wet. Such shrinkage and expansion provided tight, secure seals, and eliminated any need for metal nails. This method of boat construction allowed the Ancient Egyptians to disassemble the boat and carry the pieces, while traveling on land, until they reached a safe and navigable waterway. This ingenious construction technique allowed the Ancient Egyptians to travel deeper inland. Numerous Ancient Egyptian papyri from all ages testify to this method of land-water travel.

The Ancient Egyptians were famed for their shipbuilding throughout the Mediterranean Basin, even though the timber necessary for large-scale carpentry and for boat building was unavailable in Egypt. The Ancient Egyptians had a large fleet, as evident from the huge quantities of timber that they had imported from Phoenicia. The need for timber supplies explains, at least in part, the importance of the permanent settlement—a kind of protectorate—which the Egyptians had with the Phoenicians, from the earliest days of the Old Kingdom [c. 2575 BCE].

The Egyptians built a whole range of practical boats, well adapted to different uses and to the geography and climate

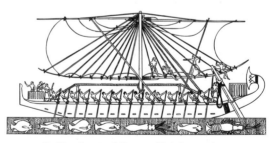

Sailing boat of Queen Hatshepsut on the voyage to Punt.

for the transportation of both passengers and freight. The Egyptian ships traveled the waters of the Nile and the high seas, since the most ancient times. Ships varied enormously in size. Some of them were huge. Diodorus mentions one, made of cedar, built during Sesostris' reign, which measured about 450 ft [140m].

All types of commercial and military vessels were known, more than 5,000 years ago, transferring goods to the northern shores of Britain, Ireland, and Europe. This was long before the Phoenicians became seafarers in the 1ˢᵗ millennium BCE.

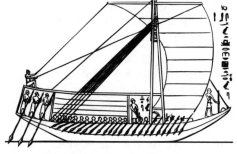

In very early times, boat building was carried on extensively. Even under the Old Kingdom [2575–2150 BCE], boats were built of large dimensions, thus we hear of a **broad ship of acacia wood, 60 cubits long and 30 cubits broad. . .**

Large boat with sail, a double mast, and many rowers. In a tomb at Kom Ahmar, above Minya.

i.e. nearly 100 ft [30.5m] long and 50 ft [15.25m] across, and a boat of this immense size **was put together in 17 days. . .**

The pictures under the Old Kingdom represent several types of boats, such as square boats, stern boats, towboats, etc. Each type is fit for certain functions/situations. Several types of boats were utilized at harbors such as Canopus (pre-Alexandria), to suit harbor operations. Besides the freight vessels, there were special small boats that were used for carrying smaller loads.

There were some very large freighters, used for transporting grain, stone, bricks and even the gigantic obelisks, which were hewn out of a single block in the quarries of **Sunt** (Aswan), and then carried on the river to the site of the temple in **Ta-Apet** (Thebes/Luxor), and elsewhere.

Nearly all the boats were made to be adaptable for sailing as well as for rowing. When sailing was impossible—owing to contrary

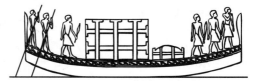

Towboat [c. 2400 BCE], The lath-crate stores breakable items during transport.

winds, or if going through calm navigation canals, the sailors utilized towing techniques of towlines and smaller boats. Also, vessels that were intended to carry large freight were towed either by men or by other vessels, because they were too heavy for independent movement. Therefore, even during the Old Kingdom, most vessels were provided with a strong post on which to tie a towing rope. Many towboats were provided with short perpendicular posts at both ends for the towline. They were steered, like all vessels of the Old Kingdom, by means of long oars. This kind of vessel was employed in the transport of blocks (i.e. can carry tremendous weights) from the quarries.

The rudders of most Ancient Egyptian ships, since the Old Kingdom era, consisted of two massive steering oars.

Throughout the Egyptian history, most boats were decorated and were adorned in the fore part with large paintings. The stern resembled a gigantic lotus flower; the blade of the rudder-oar resembled a bouquet of flowers, and the knob at the top was fashioned into the head of a *neter* (deity).

The Ancient Egyptians also had a naval fleet, the size of which varied according to defensive needs on the high seas, during the different eras of the Ancient Egyptian history. Special boats were built purposely for war. Herodotus and Diodorus both mention the fleet of long vessels, or ships of war, fitted out by Sesostris on the Arabian Gulf. They

Egyptian Boat from the Middle Kingdom

were 400 in number and there is every reason to believe that the trade, and the means of protecting it with ships of war, existed there at least as early as the 12th Dynasty, about 4,000 years ago.

The galleys (ships of war) employed to protect the traveling commercial fleet from sea piracy outside of Egypt differed from those of the Nile. They were lower at the head and stern. On each side was a high wooden bulwark along the entire length of the ship. It protected the rowers from the missiles of the enemy. The handles of the oars passed through an aperture on the lower part.

Major Egyptian Coastal Harbors

The commercial and naval ships were served by several ports, guiding landmarks, water markers, loading and unloading facilities, freshwater supplies, comfort stations and amenities/necessities. Several roads, along with supply stations, were provided between the seaports and the populated centers along the Nile.

The strategic location of Egypt's waterways facilitated commerce between the then three active continents of Europe, Africa, and Asia. Man-made navigation channels allowed access between the Mediterranean Sea at Canopus (Alexandria) and the navigable River Nile channel. Another navigable channel connected the Nile to the northern tip of the Suez Gulf, which allowed access to the Red Sea, Africa, India, and the Far East.

In addition to the frequent harbors along the navigable River Nile, there were/are significant harbors along the Egyptian coasts of both the Red Sea and the Mediterranean Sea. Such harbors allowed transportation of goods and people to and from all continents.

All this transportation infrastructure (by water and land) was in existence prior to the Greeks and Romans. Western academia loves to give "Greek-sounding" names to these Ancient Egyptian facilities/harbors—in order to lay (false) claim to European *ingenuity*—in the name of Greek and Romans.

We will overview the Ancient Egyptian major harbors along the Egyptian coasts of both the Mediterranean and Red Seas.

The Greater Canopus Harbor (Alexandria before Alexander) was Maiden of the Seas.

The present-day metropolitan city of Alexandria was called Canopus in ancient times, even long after Alexander's death in 323 BCE. The Canopus region is very extensive and old, and extended for about 18 mi [30 km] from the Canopus mouth at its eastern end, to the Pharos harbors at its western end. It was an already established multi-harbor region with several fabulous temples, long before Alexander's arrival. Numerous ancient texts speak of the importance of the region and its constituent quarters/towns, even prior to the Greek historian Herodotus.

The huge Ancient Egyptian site of the Greater Canopus region included several quarters (towns), several deepwater harbors, navigable canals to bypass the rough seas and the Nile siltation at the mouth of the Canopic Delta branch, freshwater supply from the Nile's canals, as well as numerous temples for Ancient Egyptian neteru (gods), such as Herakles, Apis, Auset (Isis), etc.

The magnificent harbors of the Canopus region accommodated an immense volume of maritime trade with the Mediterranean world and also made Canopus an important center of the shipbuilding industry. Throughout the history of the ancient world, Canopus (ancient Alexandria) remained the most important commercial city of the Mediterranean world. The strategic location of Canopus allowed access, not only to the Mediterranean Basin, but also to the Nile Valley, which was also connected to commerce in the east via the Red Sea. The significance of Canopus is well described in the tribute of Dio of Prusa (Dio Chrysostom),

> *Not only have you a **monopoly of the shipping of the entire Mediterranean because of the beauty of your harbours**, the magnitude of your fleet, and the abundance and marketing of the products of every land, but also the outer waters that lie beyond are in your grasp, both the Red Sea and the Indian Ocean... The result is that the trade, not merely of islands, ports, a few straits and isthmuses, but of practically the whole world is yours. **For Canopus is situated, as it were, at the crossroads of the whole world**...*

The most westerly Delta branch—the Canopic branch (one of seven branches of the Nile Delta)—was historically the most important branch. Herodotus entered Egypt through this gate in 450 BCE, but Strabo entered Egypt in 24 BCE, via the Pharos harbor, at the western end of the Greater Canopus region.

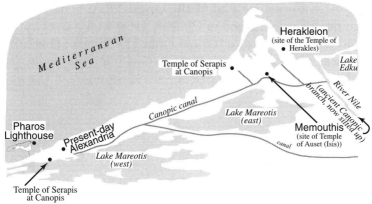

Layout of the Greater Canopus Region During the Pharaonic Era

The Ancient Egyptian religious monuments of the Greater Canopus region were ravaged by the early Christians, and the Arab nomads finished the ugly job in the 7th century. A lack of maintenance of the shorelines allowed the sea waves to destroy the ancient sites. The ruins of the great monuments are now being revealed through underwater archeology, in these two areas:

The city of Herakleion, which got its name from its magnificent temple of Herakles, was a very important economic center. Herodotus described this magnificent temple. In the water near the Herakleion area, archeologists found huge buildings and heads of Pharaonic statues of kings about 13 ft [4m] high, as well as the remains of hundreds of granite pillars from temples.

The City of Menouthis is located about 2.5 miles [4 km] from Herakleion. An area of about 550 x 765 yds [500m x 700m] was found of the city of Menouthis underwater, which shows destroyed pillars, sphinxes and statues, heads of kings and **neteru**. Some of the statues are up to 13 ft [4m] high, and the sphinx statues represent kings of several pharaonic periods.

At the western end of the Greater Canopus area is the deepwater harbor of Pharos, created by a rocky island, less than a mile [1.6 km] long. The fame of this harbor was mentioned in Homer's *Iliad*, along with its renowned lighthouse—one of the seven wonders of the ancient world.

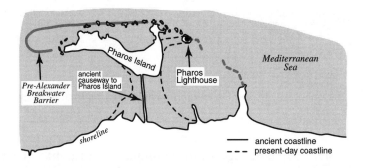

In 1915, underwater excavations adjacent to Pharos Island revealed the remains of huge quays, a breakwater, and a harbor extending from the north to the west of the island. The stones used in the harbor were huge, weighing several tons. The huge size of the quay indicates the magnitude of maritime trade at Pharos Island.

This most westerly harbor served as the last port of call before entering Egypt through the Canopic mouth of the Nile about 18 miles [30 km] from Pharos. According to Herodotus, all vessels had to enter Egypt through the Canopic branch, where customs dues were collected.

There is no historical evidence to support the notion that during Alexander's era, a causeway connecting the island of Pharos with the coast near Rhakotis was established. All indications are that the causeway existed *before* the arrival of Alexander, and that it was regularly maintained and widened. This tongue of land divided the water body south of Pharos Island into two capacious water bodies.

The Ancient Egyptians used their expertise in harbor building and management throughout the world. For example, ancient Cádiz, at the southern tip of the Iberian Peninsula, was similar in many ways to the deepwater multi-harbors of Canopus in Egypt. Cádiz was also located at a major crossroad, providing access to Africa, northern Europe, and beyond. Cádiz carries an Egyptian name (meaning *sacred/holy*), and has been occupied since time immemorial by the tan-skinned Romany—the descendants of the Ancient Egyptians. The foundation of Cádiz is arbitrarily attributed—contrary to archeological evidence—to the Phoenicians. Maríe Cruz Fernández Castro, in *Iberia in Prehistory* [1995, page 179], shows how "Phoenician" biases are in conflict with archeological evidence,

> **Traditionally, therefore, the foundation of Gades is considered to have taken place at around 1100 BC.** *This date accords well with the **mythical affinity** between Gades and Tartessus, **but so far it has defied archaeological investigation. . . . "Phoenician" Gades does not make any impact on Spanish archaeology before the eighth century BC.***

The facts actually point to Ancient Egypt. The design and layout of these two deepwater harbors at Cádiz and Pharos (Alexandria before Alexander) are very much alike—each has a protective island barrier, is near a freshwater supply, has several significant temples, and has a famed lighthouse. Strabo, in his *Geography* [3. I. 9-2, I], tells us about the look-alike Egyptian and Spanish lighthouses,

> *. . .and the (barrier) island that is enclosed by the two mouths has a coastal boundary of one hundred stadia, or, as some say, still more than that. **Hereabouts is . . .** also **the tower of Caepio, which is situated upon a rock that is washed on all sides by the waves, and, like the Pharos tower is a marvelous structure**. . . . .*

The Red Sea Coast [location map pg 255]—has had several harbors that are recognized by "Greek" names, even though they were in existence long before the Greco-Roman era. Several roads—with rest stations—connected these harbors to the Nile Valley. The following are the major harbors along the Red Sea coast:

1. Suez (Arsinoe), located at the northern end of the Red Sea. It was connected to the Nile Delta via a series of natural lakes and manmade navigation canals.

2. Hurghada (Myos Hormos) is a spacious harbor. It has/d an adequate supply of fresh water (wells) to meet the water demands of the town and ships. In addition to serving ship travelers to and from the Far East, this port connected mining sites in Sinai to Sharm el-Sheikh—a short sail from its port. Several roads united at the gates of the town, from Berenice and Port Safaga (Philoteras) on the south, from Suez (Arsinoe) on the north, and from Coptos on the west, and stations suplied those who passed to and from the Nile with water and other necessaries.

3. Safaga (Philoteras) is a main port and town, 32 mi [53 km] south of Hurghada.

4. Qusier (Leukos Limen) is 52 mi [85 km] south of Safaga and 98 mi [160 km] east of Coptos (Qift) on the Nile. It was a thriving center of trade and export.

5. Berenice is 177 mi [290 km] south of Qusier. It is an excellent harbor with an extensive town, and had a small but elegant temple of Sarapis. It was connected by several roads to the Nile Valley.

6. Between Quseir and Berenice are many other ports (the "Portus multi" of Pliny), along the coast. They all have landmarks to guide boats approaching their rocky entrances.

Land Transportation

Transferring heavy loads by sea and land is documented in Ancient Egypt since time immemorial. As such, there was an excellent network of roads—local, regional, national, and international—provided with water, food, comfort, and aid stations. Both water and land transportation systems were integrated and coordinated for maximum productivity/efficiency. The combination of transportation by land and water in place was facilitated by the Ancient Egyptian ships, which could be disassembled in order to be carried on land [see pages 242-3 re. Khufu boat].

Transportation of all mannerer of goods was carried out. In Ancient Egyptian mining records, details were recorded as to how the ore metals were treated on site before transporting by land and water, under heavy security, from mining sites in Sinai and the Eastern and Western Deserts to the populated areas of Egypt by the Nile Valley.

The capability of the Ancient Egyptians to transport tremendous loads by land and water is evident in the case of granite. The quarries of Sunt (Aswan) were the only sources in Ancient Egypt to obtain granite. This granite was worked even during the Old Kingdom [2575–2465 BCE]. Some of the granite blocks in the temple of King Khafra [2520–2494 BCE] not far from the great Sphinx, measure 14 ft [4.26m] in length, and those under the architraves in the sanctuary of Sebek in the Fayoum, built by Amenemhet III [1844–1797 BCE], are even more than 26 ft [7.9m] long. Huge blocks were carved and transported by heavy-duty means on land, water, and land again, for several hundred miles, from Aswan to the Nile Delta and Canopus (Old Alexandria). In other words, Ancient Egypt had a strong road system and impressive navigable canals throughout the country.

Among the Theban obelisks there is one more than 107 ft [32.6m] high, while a papyrus speaks of an obelisk of some kind from the quarries of Aswan, which measured 120 cubits, i.e. nearly 200 ft [61m]. These again are surpassed in bulk by the colossal seated statue of red granite, which lies shattered in the Ramesseum [1304–1237 BCE] at Ta-Apet (Thebes); this colossus was hewn out of a single block 55 ft [16.75m] high and correspondingly broad. The statue weighed, according to one reckoning, more than 1,000 tons.

From the above accounts, the reader will appreciate how the Egyptians were able to safely transport all types of cargos and loads.

Ancient Egyptian records since the Old Kingdom (2575–2150 BCE) show that good roads were built and provided with frequent intermediate aid stations. As shown on pages 226-7, roadway construction plans were prepared with proper grading and stormwater management. The map on the opposite page shows some of the most recognized roads in Ancient Egypt that were connected to the populated Nile Valley. Also see other roads on the map on page 20.

The Ancient Egyptians used their expertise to facilitate the planning and construction of networks of roads throughout the known world. They also provided for the safety and security of traveling caravans as well as aid stations. As a result, many trading posts were established along strategic points of the network. The Ancient Egyptian influence at such trading centers throughout the inhabited world is evident in the Ancient Egyptian ruins of small temples, stelae, etc, at these locations. When Ancient Egypt went through hardships and foreign invasions, these trading centers suffered. Eventually they died when the Romans and then the Arabs occupied Egypt, as will be discussed at the end of this chapter.

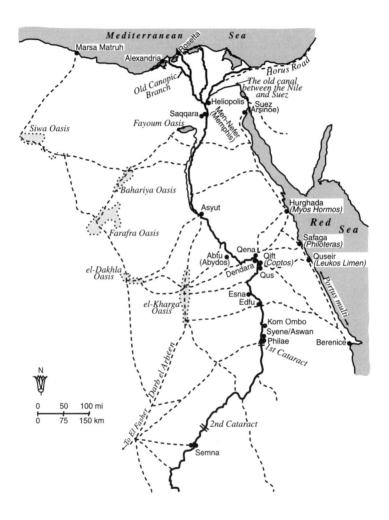

A map showing the main Ancient Egyptian coastal harbors and the main Ancient Egyptian roadways in the Eastern and Western Deserts.

Patrons and Shrines of Travel

The Ancient Egyptians (as per Herodotus' testimony) were the most religious people of all nations of the world. The Ancient Egyptians believed in One God who was represented through the functions and attributes of "His" domain. These attributes were called the **neteru** (pronounced *net-er-u*; masculine singular: **neter**; feminine singular: **netert**). The religious beliefs and practices that relate to the traveling activities by land and/or sea were:

1. Deities with special attributes important to the well-being of the travelers;

2. Land and shoreline sanctuaries and temples with special associations for travelers;

3. Religious ceremonies or acts performed by the travelers regarding the safety of the voyage.

The Ancient Egyptians, since time immemorial, had established numerous temples and shrines dedicated to their patron deities, along the shores of their navigable waterways, as well as their roads. All travelers, like their classical and modern counterparts, were making distinct offerings to their patron deities at these shrines. The seaside and roadway shrines gave a link to their divine protectors while away from homeport, as well as serving as landmarks that aided navigation and marked freshwater sources.

The following are the most recognized deities who are related to travel in Ancient Egypt, and which were later adopted by the Phoenicians and others. [Regarding the "different" pronunciation of "names", read about the phenomenon of sound shifts on page 77 of this book.]

Reshpu (Reshef/Resheph)— represents wilderness and travel. As such, **Reshpu** (Reshef) appears unshaven, as per the Ancient Egyptian custom of not shaving while traveling. The tradition of the unshaven Egyptian traveler was well recognized by classical Greek and Roman writers, such as Diodorus, who wrote in his *Book I,* [2]:

*And when all his [travel] preparations had been completed Osiris made a vow to the gods that he would let his hair grow until his return to Egypt and then made his way through Ethiopia; and this is the reason why this custom with regard to their hair was observed among the **Egyptians until recent times, and why those who journeyed abroad let their hair grow until their return home**.*

This is the reason that some male deities are shown in beards and long hair—not because they are "Syrians", but because they are Egyptians during travel. Such unshaven representation of male deities will be naturally found in shrines and temples outside Egypt proper, because that is where the travel occurs.

Anat — represents the motherhood aspect of guardianship. The symbol of a mother protecting her offspring is the most powerful representation. A good guard is always ready to deter any outside threat. Therefore, **Anat** is represented as a woman holding a shield and an axe. **Anat** is associated with **Sekhmet**—the lion-headed **netert** (goddess)—the Fearless One.

Anat is one of the 10,000 aspects/attributes of the Great Mother **netert Auset** (Isis).

Het-Heru (Hathor)/Astarte— like
other Egyptian deities, is also commonly
known as Asera / Serah / Sarah, which
means *a noble lady*. To leave no doubt of
her Egyptian origin, Aserah is always
portrayed in her Egyptian form with a
crescent-and-disk on her headdress. Het-
Heru (Hathor) represents the matrix of
the metaphysical spiritual principle, providing spiritual nourishment, healing,
joy, lovemaking, music, and cheerfulness.

Het-Heru (Hathor), as the symbol of
spiritual nourishment, also plays an important role in the transformational

Het-Heru/Astarte
(Hathor)

(funerary) texts, furnishing the spiritual nourishment/
guidance required by the soul of the deceased, as it trav-
els across the cosmic sea. Consequently, Het-Heru
(Hathor)/Aserah is the Egyptian travel and sailing patroness, and as a result she appears in this role more
often outside Egypt. An Egyptian coffin text [coffin text no.
61] from the Middle Kingdom [2040–1783 BCE] describes
her as <u>Het-Heru the Lady who is said to 'hold the steering
oars of . . . barks'.</u> Het-Heru's head is therefore always
depicted right above the stern of ships, where the twin
rudders (which expert pilots used to guide the vessel)
were mounted.

In her role as a guardian of travelers, Het-Heru is
called Astarte. Her temples were found at border cities—
being a traveler patroness. Her temple at Cádiz was one
of the major monuments at this holy city. The role of
Astarte in Ancient Egypt is well documented. From small
fragments of the time of Ramses II [1304–1237 BCE],
the role of Astarte as patroness of overseas travel is evident. In one fragment, the role of Astarte as seafarer patroness is clearly stated:

. . . Behold, <u>Astarte dwelleth in the region of the sea.</u> . .

In another fragment, Renenutet addresses Astarte:

Behold, if thou bringest him tribute, he will be gracious unto thee. . .Therefore give him his <u>tribute in silver, gold, lapis lazuli, and. . . wood.</u>

And she said unto the Ennead of neteru(gods/goddesses):
    . . . the <u>tribute of the sea; may he hearken unto us.</u> . .   .

Hercules was the Egyptian Lord of Travel.

One finds several ways to spell the name, *Herakles / Hercules / Horakles*, who is considered in some regards as a god/ god-like man. In either/both case(s), he is purely Ancient Egyptian (not Greek), as acknowledged by classical Greek writers, such as the testimony of the Greek historian Herodotus, in his *Book 2* [102], where he states emphatically,

__It was not the Egyptians who took the name Heracles from the Greeks. The opposite is true: it was the Greeks who took it from the Egyptians__ – those Greeks, I mean, who gave the name to the son of Amphitryon. There is plenty of evidence to prove the truth of this, in particular the fact that __both parents of Heracles – Amphitryon and Alcmene – were of Egyptian origin__.

Herodotus, once again in *Book 2* [102], states,

> . . . **the Egyptians have had a god named Heracles from time immemorial.** *They say that 17,000 years before the reign of Amasis the 12 gods were produced from the 8; and of the 12 they hold Heracles to be one.*

Diodorus, *I,* [23-24, 1-8], also confirms how Herakles is Egyptian, and that it was he who set up the pillars [23,8—24,1-8],

> **The Greeks appropriate to themselves the most renowned of both Egyptian heroes and gods, and so also the colonies sent out by them.** *[Diodorus I. 23. 8]*
>
> 24. **Heracles, for instance, was by birth an Egyptian,** *who by virtue of his manly vigour* **visited a large part of the inhabited world and set up his pillars at the end of Libya** *(meaning the African continent); [The Pillars of Heracles are described in Book 4. 18. 4-7.]* . . . . .

Herakles, through the tales of his adventurous twelve tasks, became the paradigm of the intrepid traveler, and is prominently found at travel stations, promontories, islands, and ports. Pausanias stated clearly that the statue of Herakles, which was found *in the god's temple in Erytheia at Cádiz came from Egypt on a wooden raft.*

15

The Market Economy

The Market Economy

The principles and practices of modern-day "free market economy", "capital economy", etc, were found in Ancient Egypt, without the need for a "flashy name"—as in our times. The whole society was aware of the interdependence of all groups within the society. An active exchange of goods and services took place between the different individuals and groups, either directly or via intermediate brokers and traders who were also able to expand activities between various communities. Moreover, the excellent and productive farming of the Egyptians both allowed and benefited the development of numerous cities. These centers attracted industries, such as textiles, ceramics, glass, metals, wood, and leather, the manufacturers of linen, dyers, tanners, carpenters, cabinet-makers, handicraft, leather-cutters, etc. These industrial centers were very active.

Goods and services were exchanged at various locations. Public marketplaces provided the means to exchange and buy goods. There were weekly/seasonal marketplaces that were held locally and/or regionally to purchase non-local products.

The Ancient Egyptian tombs at Saqqara show us the scenes of daily life in a market of the time of the Old Kingdom. A fish dealer is busy cleaning a great sheath-fish, while negotiating the price with his customer. The latter carries her objects for bar-  ter in a box, while negotiating the price with the salesman. Nearby, another tradesman is offering ointments for sale. Another is selling some objects that look like white cakes. Brisk business is being carried on around the greengrocer. There is another dealer squatting before his basket of red and blue ornaments, bargaining with a potential buyer. During the New Kingdom era— such as in the tomb of the oft-named Cha'emhet, the superintendent of the granaries under Amenhotep III, there is a picture of marketing shown in the same style. It shows great ships that have brought provisions, disembarking in the harbor of Ta-Apet (Thebes). The sailors are busy discharging the freight, while other sailors and travelers are purchasing various products from local traders.

The home trade in Egypt flourished, as with commerce with foreign countries, which was carried on with brisk activity.

Exports and imports were traded at wholesale prices, at points of entry to the populated Nile Valley. An example is the island of Elephantine, where the Ancient Egyptians exchanged the produce of their own country, and the goods that they had obtained from communities further to the south. [Other examples are shown under *Land Transportation and Major Egyptian Coastal Harbors*, in the previous chapter.]

Business Transactions

A few years ago, a Nobel Prize was awarded to a U.S. economist who endorsed a "cashless society" as the most effective mode of business transactions. It is ironic that in Ancient Egypt, goods and services were being exchanged on the same cashless premise—by barter—trading goods and services without exchanging money. Barter (cashless exchange) requires that a medium object of an agreeable value be used as a measuring device of the exchanged goods/services. This medium can be anything acceptable to the parties of the transaction. Thus, the buyer and seller reckon the present market value of their goods against a third commodity of common use. In international trade nowadays, the medium commodity is gold, U.S. dollars, etc. No exchange of gold or dollars takes place between the parties, except maybe a small amount to adjust some slight difference between the values of the exchanged goods.

Several Ancient Egyptian contracts have been recoverd that show the terms and details of barter agreements between parties involved in exchanging goods and services. A good example are the contracts of Hepd'efae, that were recovered from Asyut, dating to the Middle Kingdom [2040–1783 BCE]. These contracts show that it was possible to carry on complicated commercial transactions with these conditions of payment. [Details in Erman's *Life in Ancient Egypt*, pgs. 494-8].

For those business transactions that could not be achieved with barter, the Ancient Egyptians utilized coins. In Ancient Egypt, coins were used on a limited basis, mostly to pay off foreign mercenaries—who could send the money to their home country or take it to their home country with them—where it could then be exchanged for goods and services.

The Ancient Egyptian terms used for monies were also used for weights. Likewise, in present-day Britain, the term *pound* means both a unit of weight as well as a unit of currency. We also find the Hebrew word for money is *shekel/sheqel*, which is a slight soundshift of the Egyptian (and Arabic) word of *theqel*—meaning *weight/money*.

Coins in Ancient Egypt were made in the form of rings of gold, silver and copper, with specific weights, which were certified by specialists. The word for seal/stamp and ring is the same, in the Egyptian language. All weights were measured and certified. Gold coins are found on the paintings from tombs during the reign of Twt Homosis III [1490–1436 BCE]. Documents were recovered from the times of Amenhotep II [1436–1413 BCE], showing that values of different articles were expressed in terms of pieces of metal—gold, silver, and copper, of fixed weight and value—which were used as means of exchange. Similar examples were recovered from the Ramesside times.

The concept of weighing was an important and common theme for the Ancient (and *Baladi*) Egyptian—that extends to every aspect of life. Scales are found everywhere—from buying vegetables to representations of musical harmony, to poetry forms, to the scale of justice that was depicted in the Judgment Day scene [see page 75].

Likewise, in our present time, the English word, *scale*, is used for weighing goods as well as in music— *musical scale*.

Depictions in Ancient Egyptian tombs show public weighers and notaries ascertaining the exact weight of everything they were called upon to measure, in the public street or market, where they temporarily erected their scales. They were employed as governmental officials, with the strictest regard to justice, without favoring either the buyer or seller.

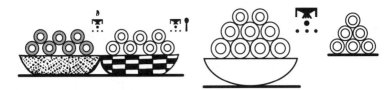

Rings of gold and silver from tombs at Ta-Apet (Thebes).

Official certification of weights in the marketplace.

A scribe or notary is shown marking down the amount of the weight, whatever the commodity might be; and this document, being given or shown to the parties, completely sanctioned the bargain, and served as an official certification of the transaction.

The same custom is still retained by the *Baladi* Egyptians—the scales of the public *kabbaneh* who measure and certify the accuracy of the weights—which are returned in writing on the application of the parties.

Egyptian Exports (Goods and Services)

The eminence of Egypt in the ancient world made it the source of expertise in all aspects of life, as discussed throughout this book. Additionally, Egyptian agricultural and manufactured goods of all kinds were sought worldwide. The quality of all types of Egyptian goods and products, most notably glass, textiles, luxury goods and papyrus, found ready markets in the east and the west and the latter, at least, continued to do so for centuries after the Arab invasion of Egypt in 639 CE.

Bottles of various kinds—glass, porcelain, alabaster, and other materials—many containing numerous colors, were frequently exported from Egypt to other countries. The Greeks, the Etruscans, and the Romans received them as articles of luxury—prized as ornaments for the table because of their remarkable quality. When Egypt became a Roman province, part of the tribute annually paid to the Roman conquerors consisted of Egyptian-made glass vases. It is careless and wrong to consider items possessed by the Romans (as a result of "spoils of war" and tribute), as "Roman made"!!

The Egyptian glassware, in particular, was of the finest quality, as noted by Strabo. Glass bottles of various colors were eagerly bought from Egypt, and exported into other countries; and the manufacture, as well as the patterns of many of those found in Greece, Etruria, and Rome, show that they were of Egyptian work.

Other high quality exports included stained glass of various hues, artificial emeralds, amethysts, and other precious stones.

The exported Ancient Egyptian vases were very numerous, and varied in shape, size, and materials (hard stone, alabaster, glass, ivory, bone, porcelain, bronze, brass, silver, gold, glazed pottery, or common earthenware), which had beautiful shapes, ornamental designs, and superior quality of the material. The design patterns of their vases and painted pottery had different styles: floral decoration, figurative, harmonically geometric, or combinations of two or all three types, as shown below.

Gold vases of the time of Twt Homosis III. Ta-Apet (Thebes).

Vase decorated with two heads. Ta-Apet (Thebes).

Gold and silver cups were often beautifully engraved, and studded with precious stones. Among these we can identify the green emerald, the purple amethyst, and other gems. When an animal's head adorned their handles, the eyes were frequently composed of these gems, except when enamel, or some colored composition, was employed as a substitute. Many of their ornamental vases, as well as those in ordinary use, were very elegant shape. They bear a strong resemblance to the productions of the best epochs of ancient Greece, both in their shape and in the fancy devices upon them, that some might even suppose them borrowed from Greek patterns. But they were purely Egyptian, and had been universally adopted in the Nile Valley, long before they were known in Greece— a fact invariably acknowledged by those who are acquainted with the remote age of Egyptian monuments, and of the paintings that represent them.

Egyptian Imports

In return for the Egyptian exports of high quality goods and services, Ancient Egypt imported items and materials not available in Egypt. The needs of a civilized society, such as the Ancient Egyptians, are not fully satisfied with the produce of its homeland.

The Nile provided access deep into Africa. Aswan was a major trading point for African trade.

The cast of the scene from the temple of Ramses II at Beit el-Wali in Kush, shows clearly what items the Egyptians were accustomed to importing from interior Africa. They brought leopards, leopard-skins, giraffes, monkeys, selected cattle, antelopes, gazelles, lions, ebony, ivory, ostrich feathers and eggs, etc.

Other African products that Egypt imported included: wood, gum, incense, carnelian (a stone prized both as jewelry and for arrowheads), haematite (red ochre), amazon stone, perfumes, oils, and dogs.

[For more information re. trading routes and goods, see _Exiled Egyptians: The Heart of Africa_, by M. Gadalla]

The Mediterranean Sea gave the Ancient Egyptians access to countries in the eastern Mediterranean Basin, Europe, and even northern Europe and the Americas.

Timber suitable for large scale carpentry and for boat building was imported from Phoenicia (Lebanon).

Ancient Egyptians consumed large amounts of mineral ore, which was unavailable in the eastern Mediterranean region, and was only available in Iberia. Copper, silver, tin, etc. were imported from Iberia (Spain and Portugal) and/or Britain.

An Ancient Egyptian papyrus, from the Middle Kingdom—identified as a St. Petersburg papyrus—shows that for a long time the Egyptian people traveled the open waters of the high seas to obtain raw material and mineral ores. Portions of the papyrus read:

I was traveling to the mines of <u>faraway places,</u> and I had put to sea in a ship which was 150 cubits [258 ft/ 79 m] long and 40 cubits [69 ft/21 m] broad, and was manned by 150 of the choicest Egyptian sailors, <u>who knew both the sky and the earth,</u> . . .

. . . when we were on the sea there arose a gale, and the waves became 8 cubits [14 ft/4.2 m] high. . .

The Red Sea gave access to Africa and the Far East. Egypt had reached the shores of western Africa (such as Punt), the Arabian Sea, the Indian Ocean and India. The principal imports from Arabia and India were spices and various oriental productions. A number of precious stones, lapis lazuli, and other items brought from those countries, are frequently discovered in the tombs of Ta-Apet (Thebes).

Among the many bottles found in the tombs of Ta-Apet, and other places, there were a considerable number of Chinese manufactured bottles bearing inscriptions in the Chinese script.

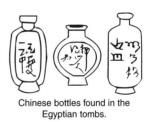

Chinese bottles found in the Egyptian tombs.

It is also worth noting that the older statues of Buddha bear a striking resemblance to those of Amon's.

Since they had the knowledge and vessels to travel that distance, why do some dismiss the possibility that they went further?!

The Rise and Fall of International Commerce

Egypt was the economical engine of the ancient world, in addition to its immense influence on all aspects of life throughout the world—as referred to in this and other books by Gadalla .

There were thriving trade activities throughout the ancient world. The Ancient Egyptians were responsible for the establishment of trading routes and trading centers throughout the world.

Archeological evidence shows us that many thriving cities/communities around the world have vanished. This evidence indicates that the disappearance of such thriving centers were caused by loss of economical significance. There is a direct correlation between the rise and fall of events in Egypt and corresponding rise and fall of such "vanished" economical centers throughout the world. These trading centers and ancient prosperous regions— which some call "lost civilazations"—were vacated/shut down, when Ancient Egypt fell prey to foreign invaders.

Classical writers such as Plutarch, Herodotus, and Diodorus told how Ancient Egypt had peaceful colonies [see page 54] throughout the world. Diodorus of Sicily, *Book I,* [29, 5], states:

> *In general, the Egyptians say that their ancestors* **sent forth numerous colonies to many parts of the inhabited world, by reason of the pre-eminence of their former kings and their excessive population;**

The following are three examples of such areas that lost their economical significance due to the demise in Ancient Egypt.

A. Diodorus, *Book I,* [28, 1-4], tells of an Egyptian colony at present-day **Moab** [location map on page 16],

> *... that the nation of the Colchi in Pontus and **that of the Jews, which lies between Arabia and Syria, were founded as colonies by certain emigrants from their country [Egypt]; and this is the reason why it is a long-established institution among these two peoples [Arabs and Jews] to circumcise their male children, the custom having been brought over from Egypt.***

Recovered archeological evidence, from the above-mentioned region, shows that this was a major trading center that was established and protected by the Ancient Egyptians. The famed Ancient Egyptian "Road of Horus" connected Egypt to Moab and beyond. The Ancient Egyptian influence extended to all aspects of life there. When this prosperous center (as well as Egypt itself) was attacked by the Assyrians, Persians, and then the nomadic Arabs, it ceased to exist and turned into a "ghost" center.

The people of this Ancient Egyptian colony (Moabi) spoke and wrote the Egyptian language. Scripts found in the Moabi region look exactly like the Ancient Egyptian demotic style of writing. [Also see page 143, showing the Egyptian origin of the "Moabite" script.]

The Moabi region was also the source of the Arabic, Hebrew, and Aramaic/Syriac dialects, which were off-shoots of the Ancient Egypt language. Ibn Hazm (d. 1064), the medieval Arabic scholar of Córdoba, Spain, recognized that Aramaic/Syriac, Hebrew, and Arabic were kindred dialects, derived from the **Mudar**, the dialect in which the Koran had been disclosed. The name **Mudar** is an abbreviated form of the Ancient Egyptian term, **Medu-Neter**, meaning the *words/language of angels/gods*. It is no accident that Moslems say that Arabic is the *"language of angels"*.

B. Present-day **Yemen** and the **United Arab Emir-ates** held a strategic location at the entrance of the Red Sea to the Indian Ocean. The archeological evidence shows abandoned temples and ancient script—that are identical to Egyptian shrines and script.

It was from this region that the Ancient Egyptians imported a large quantity of incense and myrrh, which were necessary for all religious services. When the Ancient Egyptian temples were closed by the foreign invaders, Yemen and their neighboring communities lost its main source of export and thus the thriving communities became "ghost towns".

C. The **Iberian Peninsula** was the main source of several mineral ores for Ancient Egypt. The Portuguese coast was dotted with thriving ports to serve the heavy traffic along the "Tin Route", named after the tin mines in Galicia, Ireland, and Britain—that were mined extensively to transport this material to the most populous and richest country in the ancient world—Egypt. All these thriving communities vanished and turned into "ghost towns", when Egypt became the victim of foreign invasion.

We will show next how the rise and fall of events in Ancient Egypt correlated directly to events in the Iberian Peninsula.

The archeological findings indicate that in southern Spain and central Portugal, the prelude to metallurgy seems to have emerged quite suddenly, before the end of the 4th millennium BCE. The evidence shows that certain so-called Early Bronze Age sites in the Iberian Peninsula are actually colonies established by people coming from the eastern Mediterranean. The Copper Age settlements such as Los Millares, Vila Nova de Sao Pedro and Zambujal are known to have been constructed around 2700 BCE—2,000 years before the arrival of Phoenician traders. These settlements have been described as solitary, heavily-defended settlements situated in a culturally foreign environment, i.e. for the purpose of mining—similar to Ancient Egyptian mining sites.

The fluctuation in the rate of mining activities and sizes of settlements correlate exactly with events and use of ore materials in Ancient Egypt. Such parallels can be drawn between the metallurgical production in Ancient Egypt [as noted in chapter 13] and the following archeological evidence, during the same periods in the Iberian Peninsula.

- Copper was in use in Egypt in pre-dynastic times (c. 6,000 years ago), and the early settlements of prehistoric Iberia were located in those regions in which copper and silver were either available or accessible: the provinces of Almeria, Granada and Murcia in the southeast, and the areas of Huelva, Algarve, Baixo Alentejo and Estremadura in the southwest.

- The walled and bastioned forts, as well as the mining activities and the abundance of metal objects of Almeria and the Lower Tagus, dropped sharply around 2200 BCE, which coincided with the collapse of the Old Kingdom in Ancient Egypt. As a consequence, the Iberian Millaran culture met a similar fate.

- The low frequency of tin-bronzes and their variation in composition, during the Iberian Argaric Period, has been attributed to the occurrence of tin in small pockets in one area—La Union, near Cartagena, in southern Murcia. Likewise, there was a limited production of tin-bronze in pre-dynastic and early dynastic eras of Ancient Egypt.

- More mining of copper and tin resources of north-west Iberia began in earnest at the end of the 2nd millennium BCE. Judging by the number of known necropoles of the early Bronze Age in the southwest, it can be concluded that there was a considerable increase in the population by the second half of the 2nd millennium BCE, which coincides with the very active Egyptian economy during the Middle Kingdom Era (2040–1783 BCE).

- At the end of the Iberian Argaric culture, and after the initial phase of the Later Bronze Age, there is a marked break in metal types and frequencies. In Almeria and Granada there is a dramatic fall in the number of metal objects. This corresponds to the turmoil in Egypt during and after Akhenaton's rule [1367–1361 BCE].

A large group of people, who still live in those same archeological sites of these mentioned Iberian locations, look, act, and declare themselves to be descendants of the Land of the Pharaohs. It is these people that connect Egypt and Hispania—archeologically, historically, ethnologically, linguistically, etc. [For more info, see *Egyptian Romany: The Essence of Hispania*, by M. Gadalla.]

Appendices

The Universal Egyptian Allegory

In chapter 3, under subchapter, *Egyptian Cosmology and Allegories*, the brilliant Egyptian mode of conveying complex knowledge into allegorical form was explained. Here, we will show how the famous Ancient Egyptian allegory of **Auset** (Isis) and **Ausar** (Osiris) explained several facets of knowledge.

The following is a shortened version of the story of the **Auset/Ausar** Egyptian allegory, to highlight the Egyptian source of Christianity, as well as the matrilineal principles, conflict resolution by jury trial, etc. This narrative is compiled from Ancient Egyptian temples, tombs, and papyri, dated 3,000 years before Christianity, and goes as follows:

The self-created **Atum** begat the twins **Shu** and **Tefnut**, who in turn gave birth to **Nut** (the sky/spirit) and **Geb** (the earth/matter). [More details about the creation of the universe and man in chapter 3 of this book, and other related books by M. Gadalla.]

The union of **Nut** (spirit) and **Geb** (matter) produced four offspring: **Ausar** (Osiris), **Auset**

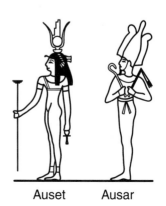

Auset   Ausar

(Isis), Set (Seth), and Nebt-Het (Nepthys).

✦ Like the biblical Jesus, Ausar (Osiris) symbolizes
   the divine in a mortal form—combining both spirit
   (Nut) and matter (Geb).

The Egyptian allegory goes that Ausar married
Auset, and Set married Nebt-Het. Ausar became King of
the land (Egypt) after marrying Auset.

• The story sets the basis for the matrilineal/matri-
  archal society. Auset is the legal heiress. [Details of
  matriarchal society in chapter 4.]

Ausar brought civilization and spirituality to the
people, enabling them to achieve prosperity. He gave
them a body of laws to regulate their conduct, settled
their disputes justly, and instructed them in the science
of spiritual development.
   Having civilized Egypt, he traveled around the world
to spread the same instructions. Wherever Ausar (Osiris)
went he brought peace and learning to the people.

✦ **Between the two evangelists (Ausar and
   Jesus), there are vivid similarities. The divine
   son comes down from heaven. God came down
   to earth to guide the world. Both had traveled
   to spread the word.**

When Ausar returned from his mission, he was
greeted with a royal feast. Ausar was tricked by Set
(Seth)—the evil one—and his accomplices into lying
down inside a makeshift coffin. The evil group quickly
closed and sealed the chest, and threw it into the Nile.

Set became the new pharaoh—as the coffin containing the lifeless body of Ausar flowed into the Mediterranean Sea.

✦ **Both Jesus and Ausar/Osiris were betrayed by dinner guests (Jesus by Judas, and Ausar/ Osiris by Set (Seth/Typhon) at their own privately-held banquets.**

The story continues that the coffin of Ausar was taken by the waves to the shoreline of a foreign land. A tree sprang up and grew around it, enclosing the body of Ausar in its trunk. The tree grew large, beautiful, and fragrant. [See an Ancient Egyptian temple depiction below.] News of this magnificent tree came to the king of this alien land, who ordered that the tree be cut down, and its trunk brought to him. He utilized the trunk as a pillar in his house without knowing the great secret it contained within.

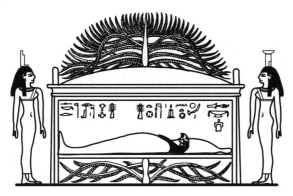

✦ **This is reference to the Tree of Life, and with all that that implies. It is also a reference to the Tet (Djed) pillar of Ausar (Osiris).**

In Christianity, this became the Christmas tree.

Auset had a revelation in her dreams that Ausar's body was in this alien land, so she immediately traveled there. When she arrived she dressed as a commoner and befriended the queen's handmaidens and was able to get a job in the palace as a nurse of the baby prince.

Later on, Auset confessed her identity to the queen, and the purpose of her mission. Auset (Isis) then asked the king that the pillar be given to her. The king granted her request, and she cut deep into the trunk and took out the chest.

Auset returned back to Egypt with the chest containing Ausar's lifeless body. She hid the body in the marshes of the Nile Delta. Auset used her magical powers [according to Pyramid Texts number 632, 1636, and murals at Abtu (Abydos) and Philae] to transform herself into a dove. Drawing Ausar's essence from him, she conceived a child—Heru (Horus). In other words, Auset was impregnated by the holy ghost of Ausar.

✦ **This action symbolizes reincarnation and spiritual rebirth—a key to understanding the Egyptian belief in life after death.**

✦ Auset's (Isis') role in the Egyptian Model Story and the story of the Virgin Mary are strikingly similar, for both were able to conceive without male impregnation. Heru (Horus) was conceived and born after the death of Auset's husband, and, as such, Auset was revered as the *Virgin Mother.*

The Virgin (Auset) and Child (Heru)

When Set heard about the new child (Heru), Set went to kill the newborn. Hearing that Set was coming, Auset was told to take him to a secluded spot in the marshes of the Nile Delta.

✦ **This is the source of the story in which Herod, upon hearing about the birth of the biblical Jesus, set out to destroy all the newborn males. In the New Testament the angel of the Lord says to Joseph, "Arise and take the young child and his mother and flee into Egypt."**

The story continues that one night (while Auset was giving birth to Heru in hiding), and when the moon was full, the evil Set and his accomplices found the chest containing the dead body of Ausar and cut him into 14 pieces (the 14 symbolizes the number of days required to shape a full moon). Ausar represents the lunar principle in the universe and is known as Ausar *the Moon*.

When Auset (Isis) heard about how Set and his accomplices cut Ausar into different pieces and scattered them throughout the land, she searched near and far, to find and collect the broken pieces and put them back together.

✦ *To bind or tie together* **is the meaning of the Latin word** *religio*, **which is the root of the word** *religion*.

As soon as Heru (Horus) had grown to manhood, he challenged Set (Seth) for the right to the throne in what was called the Great Quarrel/Struggle in the Wilderness.

Finally, both Heru and Set went to the council of neteru (gods/goddesses) to determine who should rule.

Both presented their cases. The council of **neteru** decided that **Heru** should rule over the habitable/populated areas, and **Set** should rule over the deserts/wastelands.

Auset, with the help of others, collected all the pieces... all except the phallus (indicative of physical reproduction), which had been swallowed by a fish in the Nile. She then reunited the dismembered body of **Ausar** and, with the help of others, wrapped it in linen bandages, and mummified it.

Tehuti (Thoth/Hermes/Mercury), **Auset**, and **Heru** performed the *Ceremony of Opening The Mouth* upon the mummy, and **Ausar** was brought back to life as the Judge and King of the Dead (the past), while **Heru** (Horus) was to take his place as king of the living (the present). **Set** remained the *Lord of Wilderness*.

Easter is the happiest day in the Christian calendar. Easter is and has been celebrated since time immemorial, and was initiated to celebrate the death, burial, and disappearance of **Ausar** (Osiris), and to celebrate his resurrection the following third day (Sunday). The Christian Easter is a mirror image of the Ancient Egyptian Easter in timing, details, theme, and objectives.

[For more information about the Ancient Egyptian roots of Christianity, both historically and spiritually, see *The Ancient Egyptian Roots of Christianity*, by M. Gadalla.]

The Ancient Egyptian allegory of **Auset** and **Ausar** serves to convey other meanings. On the symbolism and significance of the **neteru** (gods/goddesses) and the human being, Diodorus of Sicily states in his *Book I*, [11. 5-6],

> *These two neteru (gods)-Auset (Isis) and Ausar (Osiris)- they hold, regulate the entire universe, giving both nourishment and increase to all things . . . .*
> *Moreover, practically all the physical matter which is essential to the generation of all things is furnished by these two neteru (gods), Auset (Isis) and Ausar (Osiris), symbolized as the sun and the moon. The sun contributing the fiery element and the spirit, the moon the wet and the dry, and both together the air; and it is through these elements that all things are engendered and nourished. And so it is out of the sun and moon that the whole physical body of the universe is made complete; and as for the five parts just named of these bodies-the spirit, the fire, the dry, as well as the wet, and, lastly, the air-just as in the case of a man we enumerate head and hands and feet and the other parts, so in the same way the body of the universe is composed in its entirety of these parts.*

Diodorus' statements highlight:

- The Egyptian concept that the **neteru** (gods/goddesses) are the forces of nature and not actual characters.

- The significance of the sun and moon on the human existence. [Also see pages 184-6.]

- The importance of the four elements of creation.

- The human body is a miniature universe.

The four elements of the world (water, fire, earth, and air) were described using four personified concepts: Ausar (Osiris), Auset (Isis), Heru (Horus), and Set (Seth), by Plutarch in his *Moralia, Vol. V*:

Ausar (Water)   Auset (Earth)   Set (Fire)   Heru (Air)

The Egyptians simply give the name of Osiris [Ausar] to the whole source and faculty creative of moisture, believing this to be the cause of generation and the substance of life-producing seed; and the name of Set [Typhon in Greek] they give to all that is dry, fiery, and arid, in general, and antagonistic to moisture.

As the Egyptians regard the Nile as the effusion of Ausar, so they hold and believe the earth to be the body of Auset [Isis], not all of it, but so much of it as the Nile covers, fertilizing it and uniting with it. From this union they make Heru [Horus] to be born. The all-conserving and fostering Hora, that is the seasonable tempering of the surrounding air, is Heru [Horus].

The insidious scheming and usurpation of Set [Typhon], then, is the power of drought, which gains control and dissipates the moisture which is the source of the Nile and of its rising.

We find the same characters/energies/powers of Ausar (Osiris), Auset (Isis), and their son Heru (Horus)—the relationship between the father, mother, and son are analogous to the right-angle triangle 3:4:5.

The 3:4:5 triangle, where the height is to the base as 3 is to 4, was called the "Osiris" Triangle by Plutarch. Plutarch wrote about the 3:4:5 right-angle triangle of Ancient Egypt in *Moralia, Vol V*:

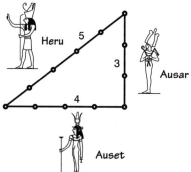

The Egyptians hold in high honor the most beautiful of the triangles, since they liken the nature of the Universe most closely to it, as Plato in the Republic *seems to have made use of it in formulating his figure of marriage. This triangle has its upright of three units, its base of four, and its hypotenuse of five, whose power is equal to that of the other two sides. The upright, therefore, may be likened to the male, the base to the female, and the hypotenuse to the child of both, and so Osiris may be regarded as the origin, Isis as the recipient, and Horus as perfected result. Three is the first perfect odd number: four is a square whose side is the even number two; but five is in some ways like to its father, and in some ways like to its mother, being made up of three and two. And panta (all) is a derivative of pente (five), and they speak of counting as "numbering by fives". Five makes a square of itself.*

This triangle was set out with the Egyptian rope (consisting of 12 equal segments), wound about three pegs so that it formed three sides measuring three, four, and five units, which provides a 90° angle between its 3 and 4 sides. It is very clear from Plutarch's testimony above, that the Ancient Egyptians knew that 3:4:5 is a right-angle triangle, since 3 is called *upright* and 4 is the *base*, forming a 90° angle. This type of triangle was used in Ancient Egypt for thousands of years before Pythagoras ever walked this earth.

Glossary

Animism – The concept that all things in the universe are animated (energized) by life forces. This concurs, scientifically, with the kinetic theory, where each minute particle of any matter is in constant motion, i.e. energized with life forces.

attributes – the Divine qualities and meanings that are the real causative factors of the manifested creations.

Baladi – local, a term used to describe those who settled in Iberia before the coming of the Syrians in 741. The same term—Baladi—applies to the present native silent majority in Egypt, which adheres to the Ancient Egyptian traditions, under a thin layer of Islam.

BCE – **B**efore **C**ommon **E**ra. Also noted in other references as BC.

Book of Coming Forth By Light (Per-em-hru) – consists of over 100 chapters of varying lengths, which are closely related to the *Unas Transformational/Funerary* (so-called *Pyramid*) *Texts* at Saqqara. This book is only found, in its complete form, on papyrus scrolls that were wrapped in the mummy swathings of the deceased and buried with him.

Book of the Dead – see *Book of Coming Forth By Light*.

CE – **C**ommon **E**ra. Also noted in other references as AD.

chord – the string of a musical instrument. A combination of three or more tones sounded together in harmony.

chromatic – chroma = color. A scale in which the intervals between the notes are all semitones.

Circle Index – designates the ratio of the circumference of a circle to its diameter, and is equal to $^{22}/_7$, or 3.1415927.

cosmology – The study of the origin, creation, structure, and orderly operation of the universe, as a whole and of its related parts.

cubit – The Ancient Egyptian unit of linear measurement, which is symbolized by the distance between the elbow and the tip of the middle finger of the extended hand. one cubit = 1.72 ft [0.5236m].

diatonic – A scale consisting of 5 whole tones and 2 semitones (from the 3rd to the 4th, and from the 7th to the octave).

enharmonic – designating a ¼ step/note or less.

Fifth, Perfect – can mean either: 1) the natural sound of the fifth tone of an ascending diatonic scale, or a natural tone four degrees above or below any given natural sounding tone in such a scale—dominant. 2) the interval between two such natural sounding tones, or a combination of them.

fret – narrow, lateral ridges fixed across the finger board of a stringed instrument, such as a guitar, etc., to guide the fingering.

halftone – *see* semitone.

interval – can mean either: 1) the ratio of the number of vibrations between two different tones. 2) The distance separating two consecutive musical notes. [Also see *tone* and *semitone*.]

Kush (Nubia) – the land of the Nile cataracts. The land from the First to Second Cataract is called Lower Kush (Nubia). The land beyond the Second Cataract is called Upper Kush (Nubia).

matriarchy – a society/state/organization, whose descent, inheritance, and governance are traced through the females. It is the woman who transmits political rights, and the husband she chooses then acts as her executive agent.

matrilineal – a society whose descent, inheritance, and governance are based on descent through the maternal line.

Neb (Golden) Proportion – is the *"key to the structure of the cosmos"*. If an approximation must be made, its value is 1.6180339-----.

neter/netert – a divine principle/function/attribute of the One Great God. Incorrectly translated as *god/goddess*.

notes – in Western musical terms, the letters *A* (*La*) to *G* (*Sol*) are used to designate notes.

nutation – a periodic variation in the inclination from the vertical of the rotation axis of a spinning body.

papyrus – could mean either: 1) A plant that is used to make a writing surface. 2) *Paper*, as a writing medium. 3) The text written on it, such as *"Leiden Papyrus"*.

pentatonic – a scale consisting of five tones—three of which are wholetones, and two semitones—like that of the black keys on a keyboard.

perfect – the name given to certain intervals—the Fourth, Fifth, and Octave. The term is applied to these intervals in their natural sounds (not "tempered").

"Pyramid" Texts – a collection of transformational (funerary) literature that was found in the tombs of the 5th and 6th Dynasties (2465-2150 BCE).

sacred geometry – The process by which all figures are to be drawn or created by using only a straight line (not even a ruler) and a compass, i.e. without measurement (dependent on proportion only).

scales – any series of eight tones to the octave—arranged in a step-by-step rising or falling of pitch, which consists of a given pattern of intervals (the differences of pitch between notes). Conventional music relies on the use of scales, which consist of a given pattern of intervals (the differences of pitch between notes). These intervals are described in terms of tones, semitones, and smaller measurements.

The most common scales are: diatonic, chromatic, and enharmonic.

semitone – the intervals between *B* (*Si*) and *C* (*Do*), and between *E* (*Mi*) and *F* (*Fa*). [Also see *tone*].

stanza – a group of lines of verse forming one of the divisions of a poem or song. It typically has a regular pattern in the number of lines and the arrangement of meter and rhyme.

stele (plural: *stelae*) – stone or wooden slab or column inscribed with commemorative texts.

step – interval of sound.

tone – the combination of pitch, intensity (loudness) and quality (timbre). The interval between each of the notes is a tone, except between *B* (*Si*) and *C* (*Do*), and between *E* (*Mi*) and *F* (*Fa*), where the interval is a semitone in each case.

tonality – the relationship between musical sounds or tones, taking into account their vibratory relationships and their appreciation by the ear. A systematic musical structure.

zodiac – An imaginary belt in the heavens extending for about eight degrees on either side of the apparent path of the sun and including the paths of the moon and the principal planets: it is divided into 12 equal parts, or signs, each named for a different constellation.

Selected Bibliography

Badawy, Alexander. *Ancient Egyptian Architectural Design*. Los Angeles, CA, USA, 1965.

Baines, John and Jaromir Málek. *Atlas of Ancient Egypt*. New York, 1994.

Blackman, Aylward M. *Gods, Priests and Men: Studies in the Religion of Pharaonic Egypt*. London and New York, 1998.

Blackman, Winifred S. *The Fellahin of Upper Egypt*. London, 1968.

Bleeker, C.J. *Egyptian Festivals: Enactments of Religious Renewal*. Leiden, 1967.

Brecher, K. and Feirtag, M. *Astronomy of the Ancients*. Mass., 1979 ed.

Budge, Sir E.A. Wallis. *Egyptian Language, Easy Lessons in Egyptian Hieroglyphics*. New York, 1983.
The Gods of the Egyptians, 2 volumes. New York, Dover, 1969.
Osiris & The Egyptian Resurrection (2 vols.). New York, 1973.

Chace, Arnold Buffum. *The Rhind Mathematical Papyrus*. Ohio, USA, 1929.

Choisy, Auguste. *Historie de L'Architecture, I*. Paris, France, 1899.

Daniels, Peter T & Bright, William. *The World's Writing Systems*. Oxford, 1996.

De Cenival, Jean-Louis. *Living Architecture*. Tr. by K.M. Leake. New York, 1964.

Diodorus of Sicily. *Books I, II, & IV*, tr. By C.H. Oldfather. London, 1964.

Egyptian Book of the Dead (The Book of Going Forth by Day), *The Papyrus of Ani*. USA, 1991.

Engel, Carl. *The Music of The Most Ancient Nations*. London, 1929.

Erman, Adolf. *Life in Ancient Egypt*. New York, 1971.

Erman, Adolf. *The Literature of the Ancient Egyptians*. Tr. By A.M. Blackman. London, 1927.

Firth, C. M., Quibell, J. E. and Lauer, J.-P. *The Step Pyramid*. 2 vols. Cairo, 1935-36.

Gadalla, Moustafa.

The Ancient Egyptian Roots of Christianity. USA, 2007.

Egyptian Cosmology: The Animated Universe - 2nd edition. USA, 2001.

Egypt: A Practical Guide. USA, 1998.

Egyptian Divinities: The All Who Are THE ONE. USA, 2001.

Egyptian Harmony: The Visual Music. USA, 2000.

Egyptian Mystics: Seekers of the Way. USA, 2003.

Egyptian Rhythm: The Heavenly Melodies. USA, 2002.

Egyptian Romany: The Essence of Hispania. USA, 2004.

Exiled Egyptians: The Heart of Africa. USA, 1999.

Historical Deception: The Untold Story of Ancient Egypt. USA, 1999.

Pyramid Handbook – 2nd Edition. USA, 2000.

Tut-Ankh-Amen: The Living Image of the Lord. USA, 1997.

Gardiner, Sir Alan. *Egyptian Grammar: Being an Introduction to the Study of Hieroglyphs, 3rd ed*. Oxford, 1994.

H.M.N. *The Egyptian Prescription*. Cairo, 1988.

Herodotus. *The Histories*, tr. A. de Selincourt. New York and Harmondsworth, 1954.

Hickmann, Hans. *Musikgeschichte in Bildern: Ägypten.* Leipzig, Germany, 1961.
45 Siecles de Musique Dans L'Egypte Ancienne. Paris, France, 1956.

Iversen, Erik. *The Myth of Egypt & Its Hieroglyphs.* Copenhagen, 1961.

James, T.G.H. *An Introduction to Ancient Egypt.* London, 1979.

Kastor, Joseph. *Wings of the Falcon, Life and Thought of Ancient Egypt.* USA, 1968.
Kepler, Johannes. *The Harmony of the World.* Tr. by E. J. Aiton. USA, 1997.

Lambelet, Edouard. *Gods and Goddesses in Ancient Egypt.* Cairo, 1986.
Lane, E.W. *The Manners and Customs of the Modern Egyptians.* London, 1836.

McPherson, J.W. *The Moulids of Egypt (Egyptian Saints-Days).* Cairo, 1941.

Parkinson, R.B. *Voices From Ancient Egypt, An Anthology of Middle Kingdom Writings.* London, 1991.
Peet, T. Eric. *The Rhind Mathematical Papyrus.* London, 1923.
Pennick, Nigel. *Sacred Geometry.* New York, 1982.
Petrie, W. M. F. *The Formation of the Alphabet.* London, 1912.
Piankoff, Alexandre. *The Litany of Re.* New York, 1964.
The Pyramid of Unas Texts. Princeton, NJ, USA, 1968.
Mythological Papyri. New York, 1957.
The Shrines of Tut-Ankh-Amon Texts. New York, 1955.
Plato. *The Collected Dialogues of Plato including the Letters.* Edited by E. Hamilton & H. Cairns. New York, USA, 1961.

Plotinus. *The Enneads, in 6 Volumes*, Tr. by A.H. Armstrong. London, 1978.

Plutarch. *Plutarch's Moralia, Volume V.* Tr. by Frank Cole Babbitt. London, 1927.

Polin, Claire C. J. *Music of the Ancient Near East.* NY, 1954.

Reeves, Carole. *Egyptian Medicine.* Great Britain, 1992.

Romant, Bernard. *Life in Egypt in Ancient Times.* Tr. by J. Smith. Italy, 1986.

Sachs, Curt. *The History of Musical Instruments.* New York, 1940.

The Rise of Music in the Ancient World. New York, 1943.

The Wellsprings of Music. The Hague, Holland, 1962.

Siculus, Diodorus. *Vol 1.* Tr. by C.H. Oldfather. London, 1964.

Strabo, *The Geography of Strabo*, Tr. By Jones, Horace Leonard. London, 1917.

Taylor, Isaac. *The History of the Alphabet*, 2 Vols. New York, 1899.

Touma, H.H. *The Music of the Arabs.* Portland, Oregon, USA, 1996.

Wilkinson, J. Gardner. *The Ancient Egyptians: Their Life and Customs.* London, 1988.

Several Internet sources.

Numerous references in Arabic language.

Sources and Notes

The author is extremely knowledgeable in several languages, such as the Egyptian and Arabic tongues. He is also very knowledgeable in Islam, being born-Moslem in Egypt and subjected to Islamic studies all his life.

References to sources in the previous section, *Selected Bibliography* are only referred to for the facts, events, and dates—not for their interpretations of such information.

Part I. The Peoples of Egypt

1. The Beginning
The Rising Valley – Wilkinson, Herodotus, Gadalla (*Historical Deception*), Baines.
The Point of Beginning – Herodotus, Gadalla (*Historical Deception, Egyptian Cosmology*), Plato.
The Age of Leo and the Sphinx – Herodotus, Gadalla (*Historical Deception, Pyramid Handbook, Egyptian Cosmology*).
The Egyptian Calendar – Strabo, Gadalla (*Egyptian Cosmology, Egyptian Mystics*), Plato.

2. The Egyptian Populous
The Unchanging Egyptians – Herodotus, Gadalla (*Egyptian Cosmology, Egyptian Mystics*), Lane, Ibn

Khaldun, Plato, Gadalla (being a native Egyptian), W. Blackman, and numerous "Arabic" references.

The "Racial Religions" – Budge (*Gods I & II*), Gadalla (*Exiled Egyptians, Egyptian Rhythm, Egyptian Cosmology, Egyptian Mystics*), numerous "Arabic references, Gadalla (being a native Egyptian).

The Mortal Mentality – Wilkinson, Diodorus, Erman (*Life in Ancient Egypt*), James, Budge (*Osiris*), Gadalla (being a native Egyptian), W. Blackman, Lane.

The Two Lands – Gadalla (*Egyptian Cosmology*), Gadalla (being a native Egyptian).

Housing and Gardens – Wilkinson, Erman (*Life in Ancient Egypt*),Romant.

Egyptians: The Most Populous – Diodorus, Herodotus, Gadalla (*Exiled Egyptians, Egyptian Rhythm*).

Foreign Visitors and Mercenaries – Diodorus, Herodotus, Gadalla (*Exiled Egyptians, Egyptian Rhythm*).

3. The Most Religious

Egyptian Cosmology and Allegories – Gadalla (*Egyptian Mystics*), Budge (*Gods*), A.M. Blackman, Kastor, Plutarch, Diodorus.

Monotheism and Polytheism – Budge (*The Gods of the Egyptians*), Wilkinson, Gadalla (*Egyptian Cosmology, Egyptian Divinities, Historical Deception*), Lambelet.

Animal Symbolism – Gadalla (*Egyptian Cosmology, Egyptian Divinities, Historical Deception*).

Creation of the Universe – Gadalla (*Egyptian Cosmology, Egyptian Mystics, Egyptian Divinities, Historical Deception*), Budge (Gods (I & II).

The Image of God – Gadalla (*Egyptian Cosmology, Egyptian Mystics, Egyptian Divinities, Historical Deception)*

Go Your Own Way (Ma-at) – Gadalla (*Egyptian Cosmology, Egyptian Mystics*), practically all references.

Judgment Day – Gadalla (*Egyptian Cosmology, Histori-cal Deception*), practically all references.

The Spread of the Egyptian Religion – Budge (Osiris & Gods), Gadalla (*Egyptian Romany, Exiled Egyptians, Egyptian Mystics*), Herodotus, Plutarch.

4. The Social/Political Order

Matrilineal/Matriarchal Society – Gadalla (*Egyptian Cosmology*), Herodotus, Diodorus.

The Matrilocal Communities – Gadalla (*Egyptian Cosmology, Exiled Egyptians*), Erman (*Life in Ancient Egypt*), several "Arabic" references.

The Grassroots Republic System – Wilkinson, Plato, Gadalla (*Exiled Egyptians*).

The Dual Overseeing/Adminstration System – Erman (*Life in Ancient Egypt*).

Lady Justice and Harmony – Diodorus, Gadalla (*Histori-cal Deception*), Plutarch, Erman (*Life in Ancient Egypt*), Wilkinson.

The Documentation Order – Erman (*Life in Ancient Egypt*), Wilkinson.

Part II. The Cosmic Correlations

5. As Above, So Below

Cosmic Consciousness – Gadalla (*Historical Deception, Egyptian Cosmology, Egyptian Mystics, Egyptian Rhythm*), Wilkinson, Erman (*Life in Ancient Egypt*), Romant.

Energizing the Diatonic Week – Gadalla (*Egyptian Rhythm*).

The Cyclical Renewal Festivals – Bleeker, Wilkinson, Herodotus, Gadalla (*Egyptian Mystics*), Plutarch, W.

Blackman, McPherson, Lane.

In Rhythm With the Zodiac Ages – Gadalla (*Egyptian Cosmology*).

6. The Pharaoh, The Cosmic Link

The Master Servant – Gadalla (*Egyptian Cosmology, Historical Deception*), Wilkinson.

"Women Pharaohs" – Gadalla (*Historical Deception*).

The Divine (Virgin) Birth – Gadalla (*Egyptian Cosmology*).

The People Rule – Diodorus, Wilkinson, Gadalla (*Egyptian Cosmology, Exiled Egyptians*).

The Heb-Sed Festival (Time of Renewal) – Gadalla (*Egyptian Cosmology*), practically all references.

The Victorious King – Gadalla (*Historical Deception, Egyptian Mystics, Egyptian Cosmology*).

7. Egyptian Temples

The Function/Objective of the Temple – DeCenival, Badaway, Gadalla (*Egyptian Harmony, Egyptian Mystics*), Choisy.

The Building Code – Badawy, DeCenival, Gadalla (*Egyptian Harmony*), Plato.

The Harmonic Design Parameters – Badawy, DeCenival, Gadalla (*Egyptian Harmony*).

Part III. The Learned Egyptians

8. The Divine Language

The Divine Mother Language – Plato, Iverson, Gadalla (*Egyptian Harmony*).

The Alphabetical Form of Writing – Daniels, Erman (*Literature*), Plato, Petrie, Taylor, Gadalla (*Egyptian Harmony, Historical Deception, Egyptian Romany*).

The Imagery and Alphabetical Writing Modes – Budge (*Egyptian Language*), Gardiner, Gadalla (*Historical Deception, Egyptian Romany*).

The Pictorial Metaphysical Symbols/Script – Budge (*Egyptian Language*), Diodorus, Gardiner, Iverson, Petrie, Plato, Plotinus, Plutarch, Gadalla (*Egyptian Cosmology, Egyptian Harmony, Historical Deception*).

The Cultured Language – Erman (both books), Gardiner, James, Parkinson, Gadalla (*Historical Deception, Egyptian Romany*).

9. The Egyptian Musical Heritage

The Egyptian Harmonic Musical Laws – Gadalla (*Egyptian Rhythm*), Plato, Sachs (all books).

The Musical Heritage – Gadalla (*Egyptian Rhythm*), Wilkinson, Engel, Hickmann (both books), Polin, Sachs (all books), Touma.

The Musical Orchestras – Gadalla (*Egyptian Rhythm*), Wilkinson, Engel, Hickmann (both books), Polin, Sachs (all books), Touma.

The Vocal Music (Singing & Poetry) – Gadalla (*Egyptian Rhythm, Egyptian Romany*), Erman (both books), Wilkinson.

Dancing & Ballet – Gadalla (*Egyptian Rhythm*), Wilkinson, Plato, Erman (*Life in Ancient Egypt*).

10. Health and Medicine

General – Gadalla (*Historical Deception, Egyptian Cosmology*).

International Reputations – Gadalla (*Historical Deception, Egyptian Cosmology*).

The Harmonic Sound Man – Gadalla (*Historical Deception, Egyptian Cosmology*), Herodotus.

Healthy Body – Gadalla (*Egyptian Mystics*), Romant, Wilkinson, Erman (*Life in Ancient Egypt*), Diodorus, H.M.N., Reeves.

Medical Profession – Gadalla (*Historical Deception*), H.M.N., Reeves, Wilkinson, Erman (*Life in Ancient Egypt*).

The Medical Library – Gadalla (*Historical Deception*), H.M.N., Reeves, Wilkinson, Erman (*Life in Ancient Egypt*).

Cures & Prescriptions – Gadalla (*Historical Deception*), H.M.N., Reeves, Wilkinson, Erman (*Life in Ancient Egypt*).

11. Total Science

Scattered vs. Total Science – Gadalla (*Historical Deception, Egyptian Cosmology*).

Astronomy – Gadalla (*Historical Deception, Egyptian Rhythm, Egyptian Harmony, Egyptian Cosmology*), Erman (*Life in Ancient Egypt*), Kepler, Diodorus, Strabo, Brecher, Gadalla being a civil engineer.

Geodesy – Gadalla (*Historical Deception, Egyptian Harmony*), Wilkinson, Herodotus, Gadalla being a civil engineer.

Sacred Geometry and Natural Science – Gadalla (*Egyptian Harmony, Historical Deception, Pyramid Handbook*), Wilkinson, Pennick, Badawy, Petrie.

Mathematics & Numerology – Gadalla (*Egyptian Harmony, Historical Deception*), Wilkinson, Badawy, Chace, Peet.

The Sacred "Ratios" – Gadalla (*Egyptian Harmony*).

Part IIII. The Vibrant Economy

12. The Cultivating Culture

Dry-weather Farming – Herodotus, Diodorus, Wilkinson, Strabo.

Division of Labor – Gadalla (*Egyptian Cosmology, Exiled Egyptians*), Herodotus, Diodorus, Wilkinson.

Inborn Destiny (Genetic History) – Gadalla (*Egyptian Cosmology, Exiled Egyptians*), Diodorus, Wilkinson.

The Farming Community – Gadalla (*Egyptian Cosmology, Exiled Egyptians*), Diodorus, Herodotus, Wilkinson.

13. The Manufacturing Industries

The Egyptian Knowledge of Metallurgy and Metalworking – James, Erman (Life in Ancient Egypt), Wilkinson, Gadalla (*Historical Deception, Egyptian Romany*).

The Golden Silver (Electrum) Products – James, Erman (*Life in Ancient Egypt*), Wilkinson, Gadalla (*Historical Deception, Egyptian Romany*).

The Copper and Bronze Products – James, Erman (*Life in Ancient Egypt*), Wilkinson, Gadalla (*Historical Deception, Egyptian Romany, Egyptian Rhythm*), Strabo.

The Glazing (Glass and Glazing) Products – James, Wilkinson, Gadalla (*Historical Deception, Egyptian Romany*), Erman (*Life in Ancient Egypt*), Firth.

Iron Products – Wilkinson, Gadalla (*Historical Deception*).

The Egyptian Mining Experience – Erman (*Life in Ancient Egypt*), James, Gadalla (*Egyptian Romany*), Strabo.

Fortification of Isolated Communities – Erman (*Life in Ancient Egypt*), Wilkinson, Gadalla (*Egyptian Romany*), Diodorus.

Miscellaneous Products – Wilkinson, James, Erman (*Life*

in Ancient Egypt), Gadalla (*Historical Deception*).

Miscellaneous Technological Applications – Wilkinson, Erman (*Life in Ancient Egypt*), Gadalla (*Historical Deception*).

14. Transportation Infrastructure

General – Wilkinson, Erman (*Life in Ancient Egypt*), Gadalla (*Historical Deception, Exiled Egyptians, Egyptian Romany*).

The Egyptian Ships – Erman (*Life in Ancient Egypt*), Wilkinson, Gadalla (*Historical Deception, Egyptian Romany*), Diodorus, Herodotus.

Major Egyptian Coastal Harbors – Erman (*Life in Ancient Egypt*), Wilkinson, Gadalla (*Egyptian Romany*), Herodotus, Strabo, Baines.

Land Transportation – Wilkinson, Erman (*Life in Ancient Egypt*), Gadalla (*Historical Deception, Exiled Egyptians*), Baines.

Patrons and Shrines of the Travel – Erman (*Life in Ancient Egypt*), Wilkinson, Gadalla (*Egyptian Divinities, Egyptian Romany*)

15. The Market Economy

The Market Economy – Erman (*Life in Ancient Egypt*), Wilkinson, Gadalla (*Historical Deception, Egyptian Romany*).

Business Transactions – Erman (*Life in Ancient Egypt*), Wilkinson, Romant, Gardiner.

Egyptian Exports (Goods and Services) – Wilkinson, Erman (*Life in Ancient Egypt*), Romant, James, Gadalla (*Historical Deception, Exiled Egyptians, Egyptian Romany*).

Egyptian Imports – Erman (*Life in Ancient Egypt*), Wilkinson, James, Gadalla (*Historical Deception,*

Egyptian Romany, Exiled Egyptians).

The Rise and Fall of International Commerce – Gadalla (*Egyptian Romany, Exiled Egyptians*), Diodorus, Herodotus, practically all references lead to the same conclusion, but never admitted to, due to false European pride.

Appendix

The Universal Egyptian Allegory – Budge (*Gods I & II, Egyptian Religion, Egyptian Resurrection*), Diodorus, Plutarch, Gadalla (*Ancient Egyptian Roots of Christianity, Egyptian Harmony, Egyptian Cosmology, Historical Deception, Egyptian Divinities, Egyptian Mystics*).

Index

About TRF Books

Tehuti Research Foundation (T.R.F.) is a non-profit, international organization, dedicated to Ancient Egyptian studies. Our books are engaging, factual, well researched, practical, interesting, and appealing to the general public. Visit our website at:

http://www.egypt-tehuti.org
E-mail address: info@egypt-tehuti.org
eBooks can be ordered at:
http://www.egypt-tehuti.org/gadalla-books.html

The books listed below are authored by T.R.F. chairman, Moustafa Gadalla.

Egyptian Mystics: Seekers of the Way
ISBN-10: 1-931446-05-9 (pbk.), 192 pages, US$ 11.95
eBook: 1-931446-15-6, 192 pages, US$ 7.95

This book explains how Ancient Egypt is the origin of alchemy and present-day Sufism, and how the mystics of Egypt camouflage their practices with a thin layer of Islam. The book also explains the progression of the mystical Way towards enlightenment, with a coherent explanation of its fundamentals and practices. It shows the correspondence between the Ancient Egyptian calendar of events and the cosmic cycles of the universe.

Egyptian Cosmology: The Animated Universe, 2nd ed.
ISBN-10: 0-9652509-3-8 (pbk.), 192 pages, US$ 11.95
eBook: 1-931446-03-2, 192 pages, US$ 7.95

This book surveys the applicability of Egyptian cosmological concepts to our modern understanding of the nature of the universe, creation, science, and philosophy. The Egyptian cosmology is humanistic, coherent, comprehensive, consistent, logical, analytical, and rational. Discover the Egyptian concept of the universal energy matrix, how the social and political structures were a reflection of the universe, and the interactions between the nine universal realms, ...etc.

Egyptian Rhythm: The Heavenly Melodies
ISBN-10: 1-931446-02-4 (pbk.), 240 pages, US$ 14.95
eBook: 1-931446-14-8, 240 pages, US$ 9.95

Discover the cosmic roots of Egyptian musical, vocal, and dancing rhythmic forms. Learn the fundamentals (theory and practice) of music in the typical Egyptian way: simple, coherent, and comprehensive. Detailed descriptions of the major Egyptian musical instruments, playing techniques, functions, etc. are reviewed. Discover the Egyptian rhythmic practices in all aspects of their lives. This book will make your heart sing.

Egyptian Harmony: The Visual Music
ISBN-10: 0-9652509-8-9 (pbk.), 192 pages, US$ 11.95
eBook: 1-931446-08-3, 192 pages, US$ 7.95

This book reveals the Ancient Egyptian knowledge of harmonic proportion, sacred geometry, and number mysticism, as manifested in their texts, temples, tombs, art, hieroglyphs, ...etc., throughout their known history. It shows how the Egyptians designed their buildings to generate cosmic energy, and the mystical application of numbers in Egyptian works. The book explains in detail the harmonic proportion of about 20 Ancient Egyptian buildings throughout their recorded history.

Egyptian Divinities: The All Who Are THE ONE
ISBN-10: 1-931446-04-0 (pbk.), 128 pages, US$ 8.95
eBook: 1-931446-07-5, 128 pages, US$ 5.95

The Egyptian concept of God is based on recognizing the multiple attributes of the Divine. The book details more than 80 divinities (gods/goddesses), how they act and interact to maintain the universe, and how they operate in the human being—*As Above so Below, and As Below so Above.*

Tut-Ankh-Amen: The Living Image of the Lord
ISBN-10: 978-0-9652509-9-7 (pbk.), 144 pages, US$ 9.50
eBook: 978-1-931446- 12-1 ,144 pages, US$ 6.50

This book is out of print and has been substituted by the book, *The Ancient Egyptian Roots of Christianity.*

The Ancient Egyptian Roots of Christianity
ISBN-10: 978-1-931446-29-7 (pbk.), 192 pages, US$ 12.95
eBook: 978-1-931446- 30-3 , 192 pages, US$ 8.50

This book reveals the Ancient Egyptian roots of Christianity, both historically and spiritually. This book consists of three parts to coincide with the terms of trinity. The first part demonstrates that the major biblical ancestors of the biblical Jesus are all Ancient Egyptian prominent characters. The second part demonstrates that the accounts of the "historical Jesus" are based entirely on the life and death of the Egyptian Pharaoh, Twt/Tut-Ankh-Amen. The third part demonstrates that the "Jesus of Faith" and the Christian tenets are all Egyptian in origin—such as the essence of the teachings/message, the creation of the universe and man (according to the Book of Genesis), as well as the religious holidays.

Exiled Egyptians: The Heart of Africa
ISBN-10: 0-9652509-6-2 (pbk.), 352 pages, US$ 19.95
eBook: 1-931446-10-5, 352 pages, US$ 13.95

Read a concise and comprehensive historical account of Egypt and sub-Sahara Africa for the last 3,000 years. Read about the forgotten Ancient Egyptians, who fled the foreign invasions and religious oppressors. Read how they rebuilt the Ancient Egyptians model system in Africa, when Egypt itself became an Arab colony. Read about the Ancient Egyptians' social, economical, and political systems, and their extended application into sub-Sahara Africa. Find out how the Islamic jihads fragmented and dispersed the African continent into endless misery and chaos. Discover the true causes and dynamics of African slavery.

Pyramid Handbook - Second Edition
ISBN-10: 0-9652509-4-6 (pbk.), 192 pages, US$ 11.95
eBook: 1-931446-11-3, 192 pages, US$ 7.95

A complete handbook about the pyramids of Ancient Egypt during the Pyramid Age. It contains: the locations and dimensions of interiors and exteriors of the pyramids; the history and builders of the pyramids; theories of construction; theories on their purpose and function; the sacred geometry that was incorporated into the design of the pyramids; and much, much more.

Egyptian Romany: The Essence of Hispania
ISBN-10: 1-931446-19-9 (pbk.), 272 pages, US$ 16.50
eBook: 1-931446-20-2, 272 pages, US$ 10.95

This book reveals the Ancient Egyptian roots of the Romany (Gypsies) and how they brought about the civilization and orientalization of Hispania, over the past 6,000 years. The book also shows the intimate relationship between Egypt and Hispania-archeologically, historically, culturally, ethnologically, linguistically, etc., as a result of the immigration of the Egyptian Romany (Gypsies) to Iberia.

Egypt: A Practical Guide
ISBN-10: 0-9652509-3-0 (pbk.), 256 pages, US$ 8.50
eBook: 1-931446-13-X, 256 pages, US$ 5.95

Quick, easy, and comprehensive reference to sites of antiquities. Detailed plans and descriptions of all major temples and tombs in Ancient Egypt. Tips are included to help understand both the modern and ancient Egyptian cultures. This pocket-sized book is informative, detailed, and contains an illustrated glossary. A no-nonsense, no-clutter, practical guide to Egypt, written by an Egyptian-American Egyptologist.

Historical Deception: The Untold Story of Ancient Egypt
ISBN-10: 978-0-9652509-2-X (pbk.), 352 pages, US$ 19.95
eBook: 978-1-931446- 09-1 ,352 pages, US$ 13.95

This book is out of print and has been substituted by the book, *The Ancient Egyptian Culture Revealed.*

For out of print and most recent publications in paper and electronic formats, visit

http://www.egypt-tehuti.org/gadalla-books.html

or contact the publisher.

Tehuti Research Foundation
Ordering Information (Paperback Books)

Name _____

Address _____

City _____

State/Province _____

Country _____ Tel. (____) _____

_____ books @ $19.95 (*AE Culture Revealed*)　　= $

_____ books @ $16.50 (*Egyptian Romany*)　　= $

_____ books @ $11.95 (*Egyptian Mystics*)　　= $

_____ books @ $11.95 (*Egyptian Cosmology*)　　= $

_____ books @ $ 8.95 (*Egyptian Divinities*)　　= $

_____ books @ $11.95 (*Egyptian Harmony*)　　= $

_____ books @ $12.95 (*AE Roots of Christianity*)　= $

_____ books @ $19.95 (*Exiled Egyptians*)　　= $

_____ books @ $11.95 (*Pyramid Handbook*)　　= $

_____ books @ $ 8.50 (*Egypt: Pract. Guide*)　　= $

_____ books @ $14.95 (*Egyptian Rhythm*)　　= $_____

　　　　　　　　　　　　　Subtotal　　= $

North Carolina residents, add 7% Sales Tax　　= $

Shipping: (U.S.A. only) $1.00 each book　　= $

　Outside U.S.A. (per weight/destination)　　= $_____

　　　　　　　　　　　　　Total　　= $

Payment: [ ] Money Order or Check
　　　　　[ ] Visa [ ] MasterCard [ ] Discover

Card Number: _____

Name on Card: _____ Exp. Date: ___/___

Tehuti Research Foundation
P.O. Box 39406
Greensboro, NC   27438-9406   U.S.A.

Call TOLL FREE (within USA) and order now   888-826-7021
Call to order (outside USA): 336-855-8111
Fax (within USA): 888-202-7818
e-mail: info@egypt-tehuti.org